Women an
Erotic Ficti

Women and Erotic Fiction

Critical Essays on Genres, Markets and Readers

Edited by
KRISTEN PHILLIPS

McFarland & Company, Inc., Publishers
Jefferson, North Carolina

"Refiguring Penetration in Women's Erotic Fiction" is abridged and reprinted with permission from *Explicit Utopias: Rewriting the Sexual in Women's Pornography* by Amalia Ziv, the State University of New York Press © 2015, State University of New York. All rights reserved.

LIBRARY OF CONGRESS CATALOGUING-IN-PUBLICATION DATA

Women and erotic fiction : critical essays on genres, markets and readers / edited by Kristen Phillips.
     p.   cm.
Includes bibliographical references and index.

ISBN 978-0-7864-9584-9 (softcover : acid free paper) ∞
ISBN 978-1-4766-2260-6 (ebook)

1. Erotic stories—History and criticism. 2. Fiction—Women authors—History and criticism. 3. Feminist literature—History and criticism. 4. Women and literature. I. Phillips, Kristen, 1981– editor.

PN3448.E76W66 2015
809.3'93538082—dc23   2015025780

BRITISH LIBRARY CATALOGUING DATA ARE AVAILABLE

© 2015 Kristen Phillips. All rights reserved

No part of this book may be reproduced or transmitted in any form or by any means, electronic or mechanical, including photocopying or recording, or by any information storage and retrieval system, without permission in writing from the publisher.

Front cover images © Thinkstock

Printed in the United States of America

McFarland & Company, Inc., Publishers
 Box 611, Jefferson, North Carolina 28640
 www.mcfarlandpub.com

Table of Contents

Acknowledgments   vii

Introduction: Shattering Releases
    Kristen Phillips   1

Part 1: Originating the Erotic

From Black Lace to Shades of Grey: The Interpellation of the "Female Subject" into Erotic Discourse
    Simon Hardy   25

Steamy, Spicy, Sensual: Tracing the Cycles of Erotic Romance
    Katherine E. Morrissey   42

Refiguring Penetration in Women's Erotic Fiction
    Amalia Ziv   59

Erotic Pleasure and Postsocialist Female Sexuality: Contemporary Female "Body Writing" in China
    Eva Chen   79

Part 2: Interrogating the Erotic

Good Vibrations: Shaken Subjects and the Disintegrative Romance Heroine
    Naomi Booth   99

On Not Reading *Fifty Shades*: Feminism and the Fantasy of Romantic Immunity
    Tanya Serisier   117

Selling Gay Sex to Women: The Romance of M/M and
M/M/F Romantica
    CAROLE VELDMAN-GENZ   133

Permissible Transgressions: Feminized Same-Sex Practice
as Middle-Class Fantasy
    JUDE ELUND   150

Part 3: Uses of the Erotic

The Politics of Slash on the High Seas: Colonial Romance
and Revolutionary Solidarity in *Pirates* Fan Fiction
    ANNE KUSTRITZ   169

Male Homoerotic Fiction and Women's Sexual Subjectivities:
Yaoi and BL Fans in Indonesia and the Philippines
    TRICIA ABIGAIL SANTOS FERMIN   187

Selling Authentic Sex: Working Through Identity in Belle
de Jour's *The Intimate Adventures of a London Call Girl*
    VICTORIA ONG   204

Sexing Education: Erotica in the Urban Classroom
    ALYSSA D. NICCOLINI   225

Bibliography   241

About the Contributors   259

Index   261

Acknowledgments

I want to thank the twelve contributors to this volume for their intellectual engagement with this topic and for their patience with delays and rounds of edits. This project would probably have remained unfinished if it wasn't for the fact that I really wanted to see their important research published and read by other scholars. You all have inspired and developed my thinking and teaching on this topic—it has been a privilege and a pleasure to work with you.

Thank you to Claire Trevenen, my friend and colleague, with whom I originally began this project. If it wasn't for her enthusiasm and considerable work in the early stages, this book would never have happened. She has inspired me with her intellectual rigor, good sense of humor, and avid and diverse reading practices, and also loaned me countless books and introduced me to many forms of erotic fiction. I thank the fantastic colleagues who gave me advice on how to put an edited collection together, read proposals and drafts, and were consistently supportive and encouraging; in particular Christina Lee, Kara-Jane Lombard, Robert Briggs and Janice Baker; and a very talented proofreader, Alzena MacDonald. More generally, I would like to acknowledge the support of the School of Media, Culture and Creative Arts in the Faculty of Humanities at Curtin University. I thank our head of school, Steve Mickler, and heads of department, Ron Blaber and Rachel Robertson, for fostering a strong research culture and supporting staff through difficult times.

Finally, thanks to my amazingly special Darcy Phillips-Hill and Cassidy Hill, who always ask clever and useful questions and who put up with a mum and girlfriend who usually has too many things going on.

Introduction

Shattering Releases

KRISTEN PHILLIPS

> Her release was shattering, shocking her as her body seemed to fragment and dissolve, as the earth moved and colors burst all around her, through her, in her ... [Feehan, 2000, p. 75].

This description of one of Savannah's many orgasms in Christine Feehan's erotic vampire novel *Dark Magic* is a useful starting point for this collection. The author's use of a familiar idiom, "shattering releases," evokes a number of the central themes herein. This project generates a critically-informed discussion about what erotic fiction means for women in the early twenty-first century, across multiple cultural spaces, genres and modes of expression. The collection takes seriously that which is apparently trivial, clichéd and "trashy" and explores its political significance. The contributors critically analyze the ideas and themes explored in popular erotic fiction and the ways it is categorized and consumed in the societies that produce and circulate it.

Firstly, this quote from Feehan's pulpy paperback highlights the collection's concern with the cultural significance of genre in relation to women's popular erotic fiction. It draws attention to the ways that knowledge about genre structures the meanings we make from texts. The intensely dramatic and excessively descriptive language of that sentence fragment lets the reader know that this is an example of "trashy" genre fiction of the paranormal romance variety. According to common-sense ways of speaking about texts, this is the kind of fiction that, compared to literary fiction, provides familiar, easy, "cheap" pleasures, has many generic replicas, and makes little claim to originality or artistic merit. It is also assumed to be basically conservative and to do ideological work in support of traditional gender relations. In this collection the contributors challenge common-sense ways of categorizing popular erotic fiction to identify the routine ways women's texts tend to be talked about (and dismissed or devalued), to avoid debates that have become banal, and to think about these texts in more creative and interesting ways.

Secondly, we are interested in how various genres and modes of erotic writing construct female sexualities, pleasures and desires. This book explores questions such as: Why are orgasms in women's popular erotic fiction so often represented as "shattering," shocking and world-changing? What other ways are there to talk about sexual pleasure and how does the language of "women's" popular erotic fiction compare to the construction of sexual pleasure in "men's" visual pornography or other textual forms? The contributors consider the critical and ideological potential of women's erotic expression, examining its exploration of concepts such as shattering, penetration, love, romance, heterosexuality, homosexuality and liberation.

From another angle, the collection critically engages with the emergence of a "shattering release" trope in popular journalism about women's erotic fiction. It is useful to bring critical attention to the repeated references to a sudden "explosion" of popular women's erotic fiction, stimulated by the development of e-readers and digital publishing, which has broken publishing records and, we are often told, set women (especially "mommies") free from sexual repression. We need to explore the cultural work done by this common-place speech about erotic fiction and women's sexual liberation, and its role in stabilizing a myth of post-feminist, liberated Western culture. This speech focuses on the supposed sexual liberation of some women (white, Western, straight, middle-class, secular and able-bodied) and is silent about the sexual experiences of other women.

Accordingly, this collection shakes up and shatters routine, discipline-bound ways of thinking and writing about categories such as romance, erotica, pornography, autobiography, fiction, fans, authors, readers, women, and heterosexuals. It offers a wide interpretation of the concept of erotic fiction, putting sex-worker autobiographies alongside slash fiction, "romantic" and erotic short stories. It also explores the ways that different forms of erotic writing by and for women force us to rethink common-sense distinctions between producers and consumers of erotica, or between gay and straight readers and writers. We begin with an exploration and interrogate the apparent explosion in the publication of erotic fiction.

New Waves of Pleasure?

By what criteria can we catalog a shift toward the erotic in the consumption of popular fiction? While we might begin with anecdotal and empirical evidence, such as the clusters of BDSM (Bondage, Dominance, Sadism and Masochism) and paranormal erotic romance books on the shelves, or the titles on bestseller lists, or the numbers of books sold via digital publishing, a more scholarly analysis requires critical attention to the ways the very criteria for determining this shift have come to seem natural and self-evident. Such an analysis begins with questions like: What constitutes the erotic and erotic fiction anyway? How is it that certain elements on certain book covers now automatically convey to readers that their content is "erotic"? How do we define the popular: is it simply a question of the number of items consumed, or something more intangible, a "zeitgeist" feeling? The claim that women's romance fiction has recently become more sexually explicit requires interrogation and, in particular, consideration of unexamined assumptions about the primacy of the Western cultural sphere. As discussed in the essays by Eva Chen and Tricia Abigail Santos Fermin, there are also other emerging (or established) trends in women's popular erotic fiction outside the West. To understand the apparent cultural shift in Western culture, it is useful to think of it as a shift that occurs at the level of discourse. Such an approach can make sense of the proliferation of speech about women's erotic fiction, highlighting the ways objects described as "women's erotica" or "filthy novels" or "books women read when no one can see the cover" started to appear with increasing frequency in intersecting popular discourses at a certain point, often as objects of concern. In early 2012, popular journalism in the West started to catalog the sudden popularity of something it chose to call erotic fiction aimed at a female market (see, for example, English, 2012; Bosman, 2012; Grose, 2012; Rosman, 2012; Happe, 2012; Costanza, 2012). While this was probably not the first use of the term "erotic fiction" in publishing discourse, the phrase started to take on a particular meaning at this time, referring to popular erotic romance novels aimed primarily at heterosexual women. It was reported that women's erotic fiction was appearing "week after week" on the *New York Times* bestseller list and that E L James' *Fifty Shades of Grey* had outsold *Harry Potter* (English,

2012). This publishing sensation began to routinely be attributed to the rise of independent electronic publishing and e-readers.

A series of similar statements began to be repeated about this sudden popularity and what it meant for American and British culture, for example, repeated invocations of the phrase "mommy porn" and statements such as "Screw what their husbands think—women are buying these titles in droves" (English, 2012). This does not mean, however, that similar material was not being consumed prior to this moment. Explicit depictions of sex have played a part in some popular romance fiction since at least the 1970s (Thurston, 1987; Frantz, 2012; McAlister, 2013). More broadly, it is arguable that women's popular romance fiction has always been a form of erotica as long as it has existed as a mass culture genre—after all, we might say that romance fiction is fundamentally concerned with sexuality and is consumed primarily for pleasure. However, at this particular cultural moment, texts that would previously have been categorized in some other way started to be described as erotic fiction, and the sale and consumption of erotic fiction became a "problem" in publishing discourse: an event that needed to be spoken about, accounted for, explained, and judged.

One way to understand this discursive shift is that it entails a collapsing of the categories of erotic fiction and romance fiction into one another, a blurring of the boundaries between the two, and the mainstreaming of subgenres that would previously have been classified as alternatives to romance, including most obviously BDSM fiction. For example, writing before the release of E L James' bestseller, in their 2009 book *Beyond Heaving Bosoms: The Smart Bitches Guide to Romance Novels*, authors Sarah Wendell and Candy Tan list erotic fiction as one of the many categories of romance fiction, alongside historical romance, paranormal romance, urban crime romance, and chick lit romance. Despite the fact that many of these other categories do contain erotic elements, Wendell and Tan set aside erotic romance fiction as a separate category which, they suggest, differs in that it contains sexual practices like BDSM and anal sex (2009, pp. 161–62). This is not to say that Wendell and Tan have made a category error here; rather, it indicates the ways the categorization of texts by genre and subgenre is always a matter of discourse and will change along with discursive shifts.

Earlier scholarly discussions about women's erotic fiction are an indication of the rather different ways in which this material was framed prior to 2011. Esther Sonnet (1999) and Simon Hardy (2001) have written in the journal *Sexualities* about Virgin Books' Black Lace series of erotic fiction for women sold in the 1990s which, along with a few other publishing imprints, appears to be a significant precursor to the mainstreaming of erotic fiction post–2011. Whereas Sonnet describes the Black Lace paperbacks as "ow[ing] much to the fictional formats and marketing of mass romance fiction" (1999, p. 168), Hardy highlights the connections to the generic narratives of popular visual pornography aimed at men as well as earlier erotic fiction not specifically aimed at women such as the work of Anaïs Nin. Both Sonnet and Hardy interrogate the ways the marketing of Black Lace invokes ideas of liberation: both women's liberation from patriarchal oppression and sexual liberation from moral conservatism. Through a discussion of Michel Foucault's insight that the compulsion to speak about sex, which is always constructed as a liberation, in fact serves to bring sex into discourse such that it can be subjected to surveillance and control, Sonnet contests the too-easy assumption that creating a "pornography for women" challenges the social order. Hardy and Sonnet's research provides a perspective from which to critically interrogate the more recent instances of repeated speech about women's sudden and dramatic liberation via their engagement with erotic fiction.

Preceding Hardy and Sonnet's research, Carol Thurston's *The Romance Revolution: Erotic Novels for Women and the Quest for a New Sexual Identity* (1987) is a study of 1970s and '80s texts she categorizes as erotic romances. She argues that "the popular romance genre since 1972 has been divided into two basic types—the sweet romance and the erotic romance—with the fundamental difference between them being the presence or absence of specific sexual behavioral norms and explicit sexual activities" (1987, p. 7). She includes statistics that indicate the erotic romance constituted more than half of the romance novel market at the time of her research (1987, p. 11), and she comments that these stories "were allowed to evolve as erotica without much notice and under the guise of a different label—romance" (1987, p. 9). The research of Thurston, Hardy and Sonnet indicates that popular erotic fiction has a significant twentieth-century history as an element of Western culture's popular romance fiction genre. Contextualizing books like *Fifty Shades of Grey* within this history does more than encourage us to be cynical about the recent characterization of women's popular erotic fiction as a sudden, new sensation. Rather, it allows us to subject this discursive event to scrutiny: to begin asking why and how women's popular erotic fiction suddenly entered discourse as a "problem" and an object of scrutiny at this particular cultural moment. It also allows us to notice the *routine* ways the problem of (straight, Western, white, middle-class) women's sexual experience erupts into public discourse periodically throughout history and is then made sense of and neutralized.

Perhaps one of the most significant aspects of the recent mainstreaming of women's erotic fiction is the potential it has for disrupting common-sense ways of speaking about genres, texts and their political effects. The sudden visibility of "women's erotic fiction" re-engages and reconfigures earlier debates about women, feminism and pornography (see Gibson, ed., 2004; Chancer, 2000). Recent theoretical work on pornography gives attention to the sexualization or "pornographication" of Western culture (see, for example, McNair, 2013; 2002; Attwood, ed., 2009; Paasonen et al., eds., 2007; Levy, 2005), exploring if this has democratic potential to open space for speech about sex or allows for new modes of controlling and exerting power over people, especially women. The mainstreaming of women's erotic fiction is part of this sexualization of Western culture: women (especially white, middle-class, heterosexual women) are now increasingly addressed as sexual subjects and sexual consumers (see Smith, 2007 and 2009; Juffer, 1998). This shift disrupts old debates about the harmfulness of pornography for women, because women are now addressed as the subjects of erotic material rather than its objects, and because erotic fiction often blurs the lines between supposed male modes of the erotic (assumed to be the "pornographic" and the visual form) and supposed female modes of the erotic (assumed to be the "romantic" and narrative and prose form).

The new visibility of women's erotic fiction also invokes broader debates about how we should define pornography and erotica. Popular journalistic discourse (see, for example, ABC Radio National, 2012) draws on a common-sense distinction between the two by regularly repeating questions about whether women's popular erotic fiction is "merely" porn for women or something more genuinely literary and less shameful we could call erotica. In her 2007 analysis of porn magazines aimed at women, Clarissa Smith gives an overview of the theoretical debates about the definition of pornography and the limitations of many of the attempts to define pornography. Following the work of scholars such as Walter Kendrick (1987) and Linda Williams (1986 and 2004), Smith notes that the object called pornography exists as an effect of the social regimes that seek to regulate it. That is, the pornographic has no essential characteristics but, rather is defined either as that which a society seeks to censor or regulate lest it corrupt, or as the opposite of "real art." Women's popular erotic fiction disrupts common-sense ways of speaking about pornography as that which needs to be managed in case it corrupts. It is true that in one sense women's erotic fiction is treated like "pornography": it is understood to be embarrassing and shameful, and there are certainly ideas in circulation about how some kinds of women's erotic fiction are harmful to women readers (specifically BDSM fiction, as Tanya Serisier discusses in this volume). However, anxieties about the harm caused by women's erotic fiction are complicated by two competing ideas: firstly, that women's sexual enjoyment is not to be taken seriously (it is often seen as something embarrassing, silly or humorous rather than a pernicious social harm), and secondly, that women's erotic fiction is empowering for women and represents an authentic expression of female sexual desire.

The proliferation of women's erotic texts is also part of the significant shift identified by porn theorists whereby digitization allows for new modes and genres of erotic material and new ways of circulating and engaging with the erotic. As Hardy (2009) notes, the digitization of culture is changing the nature of visual pornography dramatically as porn is now primarily accessed through the Internet. Pornographic forms like magazines, pin-ups and feature-length video recordings are being replaced by shorter clips and new genres or forms such as the gif. There is also more amateur and independent content, a diversity of types of content and more "extreme" types. Recent erotic fiction displays some aspects of this shift, most notably in an arguably greater diversity of content and more amateur producers (evident, for example, in the blurred lines between fan fiction and amateur authors). The most obvious shift is the rise of independent publishing: as English (2012) notes, many of the recent erotic fiction bestsellers began life as "indies." The dominance of the market by big romance publishing corporations, and the associated reading practice of choosing one's reading material on the basis of the brand instead of author, may be disappearing; Katherine E. Morrissey discusses this shift to digital publishing in her essay. The extent to which the rise of "indie" authors really means that the content of books is any more diverse remains to be discussed. It is evident that these shifts in the erotic are driven by technological change, yet also shaped by consumers' uses of texts.

Genre Boundaries and "Low" Cultural Forms

In making sense of the mainstreaming of women's mass market erotic fiction across Western culture since approximately 2011, it is important to notice that even as this material is being characterized in the popular media as "dirty," subversive and threatening to cultural morality (see, for example, Rosman, 2012), the kinds of texts that are most visible are often, in fact, quite socially conservative in their presentation of the relationship between romance and sex. That is, the privileging of certain kinds of texts (Rosman uses the term "romantica") tends to reinforce the idea that women prefer their erotic content blended with romance and that women "naturally" experience the most erotic pleasure when it is framed by romance. In "Breaking the Hard Limits: Romance, Pornography and Genre in the *Fifty Shades* Trilogy," Jodi McAlister (2013) makes the point that the sort of women's erotic fiction currently most popular and visible consists of a mixture of the narrative conventions of pornography and romance:

> The structure of *Fifty Shades* is simultaneously finite and infinite, locating the multiple climaxes of pornography within the overarching emotional climax of romance. The defining characteristic of romance is that it ends (happily): pornography, on the other hand, is cyclical and repetitive. The two generic frameworks that *Fifty Shades* fuses together allows it to create both instant and delayed gratification, creating a double erotic pleasure [2013, p. 1].

McAlister's analysis is also useful in that she identifies one of the common-sense definitions that underpins the categorization of certain texts as pornographic or erotic fiction (texts in which the explicit cataloging of a series of sex acts drives the narrative). This definition of pornography, and the resulting distinction between pornography and romance, seems to have been firmly established by the modes of discourse used by the popular media in characterizing the "*Fifty Shades* phenomenon." These modes of discourse are in keeping with earlier feminist debates about women, pornography and romance fiction, in which feminist theorists such as Ann Barr Snitow (1979) argued that romance fiction *is* women's erotic content, that "pornography for women is different" because women require their erotic content to be framed by romance and because women are more turned on by the written word than visual erotic forms.

As this idea that women prefer erotic content when blended with romance has started to be re-established in recent popular journalism, women's erotic content that does not fit this model, including erotic fiction which avoids the conventions of romance, tends to be sidelined. The earlier-mentioned Black Lace series, at least some of which seems to have been more closely modeled on the generic conventions of "men's" visual pornography in that it represented sex separate from romance, now seems like an anomaly. For example, the Black Lace novel *Dance of Obsession* focuses on a woman who is an exotic dancer in 1930s Paris at a very exclusive club where women pay a lot of money to go and choose male sexual partners and who has a sexual relationship with her stepson: this seems rather radical and confronting in the recent context where "erotic fiction" tends to be conflated with "erotic romance fiction" and applied to authors such as E L James, Sylvia Day, Kresley Cole and Joey Hill who take for granted a connection between sex and romance. Within this framework, in which we assume that women require their erotic content to be blended with romance, there is also little space to account for markets in "women's erotica" that include novels and anthologies of erotic short stories depicting sexual interactions not necessarily framed by romance. Some examples of this are the erotica generated by the feminist pro-porn movement, as discussed by Amalia Ziv in her essay, as well as the "urban erotica" by authors such as Zane which is loosely aimed at an African American market and depicts women having random or anonymous sexual encounters with multiple men or other women—see Alyssa D. Niccolini's discussion in this volume. For that matter, the sex versus romance analytical framework requires a little expansion to account for the sudden prevalence of novels, mostly sold through digital publishers, aimed at straight women but using a romantic framework to depict ménage relationships (usually involving one woman and two or more men) as well as gay male relationships, using both realist and paranormal fantasy modes (see Carole Veldman-Genz's essay in this volume). Similarly, it is difficult within this framework to account for women's enjoyment of other forms of writing such as slash fiction and autobiographical sex confessionals in which romance is not necessarily essential to the pleasure the text provides, or other traditions of erotic content, and ways of conceptualizing both the erotic and the romantic, which might be evolving in non–Western cultures. The essays in this volume by Eva Chen, Anne Kustritz, Tricia Abigail Santos Fermin and Victoria Ong make important contributions to expanding the concept of erotic fiction.

It is, therefore, important to examine the most visible genres and modes of popular erotic fiction with a critical eye on the discursive effects of genre; that is, treating genres not as fixed or self-evident categories but considering the ways they have emerged to categorize and make sense of texts. Why have certain genres and types of erotic material become visible at this moment at the expense of others? As critical theorists of genre suggest, genre studies needs to go further than analyzing how formulaic texts perform ideological work, or how landmark texts blend the conventions of different genres or make use of genre in new ways. More than this, critical attention to genre involves noticing that genre tells us *how* to read: it performs ideological work by regulating speech about texts, framing for us the ways we should interpret them and thus closing down other ways of reading (see Briggs 2003 and 2007, pp. 122–23). For example, while it is important to notice that much of the erotic fiction which has gained visibility involves a blending of the genre conventions of the pornographic and the romantic, we also need to ask how it is that the distinction between these two categories seems so natural in the first place and to critically consider the apparently self-evident meaning of both the pornographic and the romantic.

Constructing the Erotic: Pleasure, Politics, Identity and Transgression

The question of how women's erotic fictions, and the discussions around them, construct the erotic is necessarily a political question. For example, how does popular BDSM fiction construct the erotic, and what does this mean for the politics of gender, sexuality and other social categories? How can we critically scrutinize this "mainstreaming of kink" (Weiss, 2006)? On the one hand, a set of sexual practices previously socially marginalized as deviant or queer gain a certain kind of social legitimacy and visibility. On the other hand, in the process of this mainstreaming of BDSM via conservative romance plots, the otherness of these sexual practices is reinscribed as a form of kink or deviance, something for "normal" people to try, or a pathological effect of past trauma. Conversely, while some lesser-known BDSM authors such as Joey Hill and Cherise Sinclair present BDSM as a unique sexual identity akin to being gay or straight, they also reproduce an idea of sexuality as a fixed, essential element of a person's identity: it is assumed that you are born a submissive or a dominant (see Frantz, 2012). Authors who employ a more fluid notion of sexuality are less visible. There are many further questions about the subgenres of erotic fiction and the modes through which female readers explore the erotic across different cultures. In this final section of the introduction I raise some broad issues and questions about how the erotic is constructed in the kinds of texts that have recently become visible as "women's erotic fiction."

One significant sense in which erotic fiction departs from romance fiction is its apparent intention to transgress—or at least, this is the way in which it is discursively framed. Recently visible women's popular erotic fiction and the discourses surrounding it reproduce an understanding of the erotic deeply embedded in Western culture: that the erotic is concerned with transgression of social taboos, including a taboo on speaking about sex. As explored by porn theorists such as Attwood (2006 and 2009), Hardy (2001) and Smith (2007 and 2009), and by Sonnet (1999) in relation to erotic fiction, following the influential work of sexuality theorists such as Michel Foucault and Georges Bataille, "transgression" needs to be treated with caution. While it may offer genuinely critical and subversive possibilities, it can also conceal the exercise of social power behind a veneer of liberation. This is a recurring theme across the essays in this volume: see in particular the essays by Eva Chen, Jude Elund and Carole Veldman-Genz. We need to critically consider the ways transgression is offered in women's popular erotic fiction in genres and modes such as BDSM (as mentioned above), ménage, male/male, slash, lesbian erotica and sex confessionals. Furthermore, one effect of the recent eruption of speech about women's erotic fiction has been the centralization of the heterosexual woman as the imagined consumer and addressee of erotic fiction. Correspondingly, lesbian and bisexual readers and writers of erotic fiction have been largely rendered invisible, as Elund discusses in her essay.

Theorizations of the erotic in literature have often fallen back on a high art/low art hierarchy which has its origins in Frankfurt School critiques of popular culture. For example, in conceptualizing "the erotic" as something transgressive and challenging, scholars have traditionally looked for the erotic in literary, "avant garde" or experimental texts rather than those popular "genre" texts thought of as providing mundane, formulaic pleasures. This is evident in Roland Barthes' (1964) discussion of Bataille's short story "The Story of the Eye" and in Barthes' famous distinction between "readerly" and "writerly" texts: the former assumed to provide mere *plaisir*, the latter allowing the reader to experience the traumatic, ego-shattering pleasure he terms *jouissance* (1975). Susan Sontag (1967) interrogates this "pornography versus literature" distinction in her discussion of pornography, yet also reproduces it to some extent by focusing her analysis on "literary" erotic fiction. Recent public discussions about the mainstreaming of erotic fiction often invoke this high/low art distinction, assuming that "genre fiction" is worthless, always "simple" and its readers always ideologically duped, and that one should turn to "literary" erotic fiction such as the work of Anaïs Nin and Pauline Reage for true erotic edification (see for example the discussion of *Fifty Shades of Grey* on ABC Radio National [2012]). This routine and unreflexive dismissal of popular reading practices (especially women's reading practices) as trivial and ideologically bound has been significantly critiqued in theoretical work on popular romance fiction (see Regis, 2007; Wendell and Tan, 2009;

Selinger and Frantz, 2012; Radway, 1984 and 1986; Ang, 1987). The essays in this volume build on this work to take seriously readers' use of erotic fiction texts, noticing how they speak back to and reinterpret these texts to create their own forms of speech about the erotic. More broadly, the essays explore questions such as: What kind of idea of the erotic underpins women's popular romance fiction produced in the West and elsewhere? To what extent does it say something new about the erotic or represent a uniquely female expression of the erotic?

To explore this, it may be helpful to situate popular erotic fiction not just in relation to media and literary theory (seemingly the obvious place to start), but also philosophical and critical work on the nature of the erotic. For example, what if we consider women's popular erotic fiction in relation to the work of Georges Bataille, the much-cited philosopher of the erotic? Bataille's work has been taken up as an idea that the erotic is primarily concerned with transgression of boundaries and taboos and the privileging of the primal and the body over the rational mind. In the introduction to his book *Erotism*, Bataille characterizes the erotic as those experiences—physical, emotional or religious—that are about moving from discontinuity (the separate, complete individual) to continuity with another being or with the rest of the world. He gives an interesting explanation of this in gendered terms:

> The whole business of eroticism is to strike to the inmost core of the living being, so that the heart stands still. The transition from the normal state to that of erotic desire presupposes a partial dissolution of the person as he exists in the realm of discontinuity. Dissolution—this expression corresponds with dissolute life, the familiar phrase linked with erotic activity. In the process of dissolution, the male partner has generally an active role, while the female partner is passive. The passive, female side is essentially the one that is dissolved as a separate entity. But for the male partner the dissolution of the passive partner means one thing only: it is paving the way for a fusion where both are mingled, attaining at length the same degree of dissolution. The whole business of eroticism is to destroy the self-contained character of the participators as they are in their normal lives [1986, p. 17].

This notion that eroticism is about the transgression or obliteration of boundaries between the separate, self-contained individual and the other is, in an oblique sense, similar to Janice Radway's theorization of romance fiction. This may seem an odd comparison, as Bataille and Radway undertake very different scholarly projects in different theoretical traditions. However, there is a resonance that bears considering.

In her 1984 study *Reading the Romance: Women, Patriarchy and Popular Literature*, Radway argues that romance fiction tends to construct sexual pleasure as a radical loss of the self in the other. We can identify this as a continuing theme in contemporary erotic romance fiction, especially paranormal and BDSM—as evidenced in our epigraph from the paranormal romance novel *Dark Magic*, chosen for its generic typicality: sex and orgasm are constructed as a shattering of the ego, a blurring of the self with the world. Where Radway differs from Bataille is her claims of feminist psychoanalysis, that because women experience the Oedipal drama differently, they do not fully separate psychologically from their mothers and develop an adult identity as a "self-in-relation." Thus, Radway argues that the central pleasure romance fiction provides for women is its construction of love and sex as a radical interconnectedness with the other, a symbolic return to a state of symbiotic wholeness and total nurturing. For Radway, this central characteristic of romance fiction is ambivalent in political terms. It perpetuates the ideology that it is only in heterosexual, monogamous, patriarchal marriage that a woman can hope to experience this pleasurable and transcendent state of continuity. Her identity as a self-in-relation can only be completed by the true love of a man; and the apparently proud, cruel hero of 1970s and '80s erotic romance fiction, with his somewhat violent tendencies toward the heroine, ultimately offers her an experience of total nurturing. At the same time, Radway suggests that romance fiction provides an outlet for women in patriarchal marriages to explore their feelings about the inadequacies of marriage and motherhood to meet their emotional needs for nurturing and interconnectedness. Radway and Bataille would not, at first, seem to have much to say to each other. Yet both are concerned with exploring the nature of the erotic and the pleasures it provides, and indeed why it is often connected with violence.

In their aforementioned guide to romance fiction, Wendell and Tan make the case that there has been a distinct shift in romance fiction from the 1980s and '90s, whereby heroes are less cruel and violent, there is less of the "rape as seduction" trope, and the heroines are more likely to be self-actualizing and self-determining. They use the terms "old skool" and "new skool" to describe these different sorts of texts (2009, pp. 13–15). Thurston notes a similar shift whereby romance fiction in the 1980s seems to take into account some of the insights of feminism (1987, p. 11). However, some of the genres now proliferating and most visible in this apparent recent wave of erotic fiction, most obviously BDSM romance and paranormal romance, would seem rather like throwbacks to this previous era in their emphasis on excessive, "patriarchal" (or dominating) masculinity, the radical loss of the self and dissolution of ego boundaries, and the connections between sex and control or violence. What is the significance of this resurgence in a supposedly "postfeminist" era? Do these texts indicate a re-stabilizing of a "patriarchal" social structure? Or might this emphasis on the pleasures of ego-shattering and radical dissolution offer something subversive in a neoliberal context in which women are increasingly addressed as self-determining, separate, individualist subjects of capitalism? The popularity of such texts may offer a useful starting point for a more politicized, and gender conscious, exploration of Bataille's concept of the erotic as a violent shift from discontinuity to continuity. As noted, this is taken up by several of our contributors, especially Booth and Ziv.

Audre Lorde (1984) gives another, rather different, perspective on the erotic: she conceptualizes it as a life-giving, creative element of existence which has been suppressed and distorted in patriarchal Western culture, allowed only to exist in a stunted form in the sphere of sex. She argues for the need to see the erotic in all aspects of our lives rather than confining it to what she terms "pornography": "pornography is a direct denial of the power of the erotic, for it represents the suppression of true feeling. Pornography emphasizes sensation without feeling" (1984, p. 54). Lorde suggests that women have, historically, had a difficult relationship to the erotic:

> As women we have come to distrust that power which rises from our deepest and nonrational knowledge. We have been warned against it all our lives by the male world, which values this depth of feeling enough to keep women around in order to exercise it in the service of men, but which fears this same depth too much to examine the possibilities of it within themselves. So women are maintained at a distant/inferior position to be psychically milked, much the same way ants maintain colonies of aphids to provide a life-giving substance for their masters [1984, pp. 53–54].

Therefore, Lorde argues that women must stop fearing the erotic and embrace it as a source of power; not merely personal power but feminist power to challenge the social structure and bring about a world that is more just and more fully realized, wherein the erotic is no longer cut off from the rest of life. Lorde's conceptualization of the erotic may be read as essentialist, as implying that women are, by virtue of their sex, capable of producing a superior form of erotic material that goes beyond patriarchal ideology. Putting aside this essentialist flavor, Lorde's theorization of the erotic potentially has value in that it is an attempt to conceptualize the erotic beyond notions of transgression. An association between eroticism and transgression of taboos is so deeply embedded in Western culture, but in Lorde's description the erotic is instead associated with creativity, affirmation of life, criticality and political subversion. The diverse forms of women's erotic fiction available prompt us to consider whether we are able to imagine the erotic outside of an idea of transgression. As discussed by the contributors to this collection, popular erotic modes may offer pleasures other than transgression: for example, the creative imagining of alternative worlds, reworked characters and new relationship configurations, and the building of communities of readers. In various forms of women's erotic fiction, the production of sexual pleasure may have little to do with transgression and everything to do with the experience of a sexual scene from an opposite gender position, or from multiple positions of identification at the same time, or via something that feels like the disintegration of subjectivity.

The Essays

This book is divided into three parts. In "Part 1: Originating the Erotic," Simon Hardy, Katherine E. Morrissey, Amalia Ziv and Eva Chen explore different historical and generic trajectories of women's erotic fiction. While each gives an overview of the origins and development of an object that we might call women's erotica, the diversity of their accounts demonstrates how this object changes depending on one's discursive approach as well as the cultural and social context of the speaker.

Simon Hardy explores the changing role of a "female voice" in erotic writing in the West in the modern period. Hardy focuses his essay on E L James' *Fifty Shades* trilogy which, as naturalist fiction with a female narrative voice, is written as though it offers an "authentic" account of female sexual desire. This idea is also encouraged by the rhetoric in the popular media about the sexual liberation of the female, middle-aged readers of James' novels. Hardy puts this in context by providing a history of the mythology of "authentic" female sexuality in pornographic writing in the West since John Cleland's *Memoirs of a Woman of Pleasure*. Male-authored pornographic writing, Hardy notes, has historically often adopted a female narrative voice to give a sense of verisimilitude to its accounts of sex. Hardy traces a shift around the time of the Enlightenment whereby pornographic writing began to reflect an idea that female sexuality was inherently submissive and masochistic. Hardy then goes on to explore the use of a female narrative voice, as well as tropes of female submission and male dominance, in female-authored pornographic writing such as Virgin's Black Lace series, and recently popular works such as *Fifty Shades of Grey*.

Katherine E. Morrissey focuses on shifts in the romance publishing industry in the West, especially the United States. She critically analyzes claims that the development of digital publishing and e-readers prompted an explosion of women's erotic fiction, giving important context to these claims through a history of the publication of women's erotica by romance publishers. Drawing on Carol Thurston's research into the emergence of the "bodice ripper" and the "hot historical" in the 1970s and '80s, Morrissey traces the subsequent evolution of erotic romance fiction in the 1990s and 2000s via the emergence of niche erotic fiction publishers such as Red Sage, Ellora's Cave and Virgin Books' Black Lace series. She then explores how the shift to Internet-based marketing and distribution of books allows for a diversity of erotic content, more niche markets and more independent and niche publishers. This situation, Morrissey explains, was prompted by a "disequilibrium" in the market when big publishers were unwilling to publish boundary-pushing erotic content for fear of hurting their market image. It has played a key role in an expansion of forms of erotic fiction for women, albeit still within certain genre limitations.

While Morrissey and Hardy are both essentially prompted by the same aim (to give a history of women's erotic fiction), their accounts differ vastly due to the emphasis they place on a particular genre (pornography and romance, respectively). Amalia Ziv's approach is different again. Her focus is erotic fiction written by and for women inspired by "pro-sex feminism" and published in the United States from the 1980s onward—for example, the *Herotica* anthologies edited by Susie Bright. These deliberate attempts to create "feminist porn," often in the form of short stories that provide sexual stimulation and usually avoid the conventions of romance, do not fit within the histories of the romance and pornography industries but require their own account. Ziv explores how these stories interrogate prevailing Western cultural assumptions about penetration, whereby being penetrated is perceived as a loss of integrity of the subject, as disempowering. These stories, Ziv argues, offer a disruption of these assumptions and a resignification of sexual and bodily power relations.

Eva Chen explores another history of women's erotic writing: the recent trend termed "female body writing" which has emerged in postsocialist China in the form of novels and sex blogs. She focuses in particular on the work of two young Chinese women, both journalists: Weihui, who published a novel in 2000 called *Shanghai Baby*, and Muzimei, whose controversial sex blog emerged in 2003 and was released as a book in 2005. Chen situates this strand of erotic writing in the context of a cultural history of the erotic in China, which until recently, she argues, has provided little space for the exploration of what the erotic might mean for women. She explains the origins of Chinese ideas of the erotic in Confucianism, the subsequent influence of European concepts of personal sexual identity, the suppression of the erotic under state socialism and the emergence of new understandings of the erotic in the postsocialist era. Chen reflects on the role of neoliberalism in constructing an idea of the liberatory power of sexual expression. She interrogates the discourse of liberation surrounding "female body writing" which, she suggests, tends to conflate freedom of sexual expression with participation in consumer culture. In the process, she invites us to imagine a more critically-engaged idea of erotic desire that potentially disrupts rather than reinforces neoliberal discourse.

"Part 2: Interrogating the Erotic" contains essays by Naomi Booth, Tanya Serisier, Carole Veldman-Genz and Jude Elund, each offering a critical engagement with an aspect of erotic fiction. Firstly, Naomi Booth employs the critical concept of "shattering" borrowed from certain strands of queer, Marxist and post-humanist theory to identify some critical potential in the *Fifty Shades* trilogy. Booth opens with a provocative comparison between the recurring trope of the erotic romance heroine who shakes, quivers, shivers, faints, dissolves or (as in the epigraph) shatters, and arguments made by theorists such as Leo Bersani, Roland Barthes, Theodor Adorno and Jane Bennett about the radical potential of ego-shattering and self-dissolution. From different perspectives, these theorists develop the idea that dominant power structures associated with sexual normativity, capitalism and anthropocentrism can be challenged by ideas, experiences or texts which shake up the coherence of the ego or the stability of meaning. Such disintegrative tendencies, Booth argues, can appear in unexpected places such as apparently conservative erotic romance fiction. Booth invites us to read "against the grain" of James' trilogy to open new radical potential for women's popular erotic reading practices.

Tanya Serisier focuses on the popular speech surrounding the *Fifty Shades* phenomenon. She explores a discursive pattern whereby female reviewers employ a feminist rhetoric to dismiss James' trilogy as unworthy and harmful, assuming the right to worry about its effects on other women. Such speech becomes a ritualistic exercise which functions to confirm the speaker's status as middle-class, educated and sophisticated, thus affirming her feminist literary credentials. It constructs an imaginary reader who is vulnerable, impressionable, unsophisticated, a victim of ideology and (potentially) violence. Serisier is interested in the ways this speech about *Fifty Shades* forecloses the possibility of complex and contradictory readings of popular texts, in which pleasure and critical engagement might sit alongside one another. Serisier reminds us that any discussion of ideological power in relation to women's erotic writing, perhaps even before we turn to a consideration of textual content, needs to involve critical attention to the discursive framing of "women's fiction," its relegation to the margins of literature, and the enactment of social power via popular speech about women, reading and sexual expression.

Carole Veldman-Genz offers an interrogation of a different discourse of empowerment through a case study of a strand of popular erotic fiction from independent publisher Ellora's Cave. While Ellora's Cave publishes a range of different kinds of erotic romance fiction for increasingly niche markets, Veldman-Genz looks at m/m and m/m/f fiction (that is, male homosexual romantic pairings and threesomes involving two men and one woman) aimed at heterosexual female readers. She critically engages with assumptions that this fiction is empowering for its readers and is challenging to heteronormativity. She suggests that the development of this strand of fiction does represent a significant expansion of the category of the erotic by offering new subject positions for (straight) female readers. At the same time, she points out that these texts often apply a heteronormative logic to their depictions of gay male relationships. For example, they reinforce the idea that female readers only enjoy sexual content when it is framed by romance and perpetuate a heteronormative ideal of domesticity as the ultimate aspiration for non-heterosexual readers.

Jude Elund focuses her analysis on the representation of lesbianism in women's popular erotic fiction. Discussing popular speech about an apparent social phenomenon, whereby large numbers of women are suddenly buying and reading erotica, Elund exposes the ways this speech takes for granted that we are speaking about heterosexual women when we make claims about the liberation of female sexuality. Elund examines some lesbian fiction which appears to be aimed at straight women, arguing that it constructs lesbianism as little more than another fetish for straight women to try out in their newly-assigned role as sexual consumers. She argues that "[s]exual and gender diversity are marketable; they illustrate an apparent social consciousness while striving for an edginess that conservative hetero-culture cannot embody." Elund critically analyzes the ways in which an idea of transgression circulates in popular speech about women's erotica, and interrogates the assumption that transgression is always politically subversive, following critical work on the notion of transgression by authors such as Peter Stallybrass and Allon White. In particular, she draws attention to the ways in which women's popular erotic fiction often links "transgressive" sexual behavior (such as experimentation with non-heteronormativity) with extreme wealth and related forms of social privilege.

In "Part 3: Uses of the Erotic," Anne Kustritz, Tricia Abigail Santos Fermin, Victoria Ong and Alyssa D. Niccolini open the concept of women's erotic fiction by exploring erotic writing by and for women across a diversity of modes and genres, taking us beyond the erotic romance novel as the "primary" form (according to popular analysis and discussion). They give attention to what readers actually do with various forms of erotic writing as well as explore how these different modes function for writers.

Anne Kustritz focuses on *Pirates of the Caribbean* slash fiction (that is, fan fiction in which two ostensibly "straight" characters from a popular fiction text are rewritten in a homoerotic pairing as the basis for a new narrative) produced by authors in the West and circulated online. In particular she examines "Sparrington" slash, that is, narratives depicting the homoerotic pairing of Captain Jack Sparrow (the pirate played by Johnny Depp in the popular *Pirates of the Caribbean* film franchise) and British naval officer Commodore James Norrington. Kustritz gives an overview of key feminist and queer theory on slash fiction. She then goes on to use analyses of several different pieces of Sparrington slash to explore the multiple possibilities these fan-produced texts have for both critical and ideological work in relation to our modes of remembering and narrativizing histories of empire and colonialism. Her analysis provokes us to read the *Pirates of the Caribbean* franchise not simply as a mad-cap adventure story but, rather, as a politically significant narrative in which the conflict between Jack Sparrow and Commodore Norrington tends to distract from the more extensive and violent conflict between colonized peoples and the British Empire which is its setting. Kustritz asks, when slash writers queer the tension between Norrington and Sparrow, how do they engage with this other, marginalized tension between colonizer and colonized?

Tricia Abigail Santos Fermin's essay is a study of female fans of Japanese Yaoi and Boys' Love manga comics in the Philippines and Indonesia. Yaoi and Boys' Love are Japanese-produced manga which focus on homoerotic romantic and sexual relationships between young men, primarily created and consumed by heterosexual women, popular in Japan and partly disseminated in other Asian countries and the West. Some of this fiction includes fan-produced slash fiction using characters from other non-homoerotic manga and some develops original characters. Fermin examines the ways young female consumers of Yaoi and Boys' Love manga in Jakarta and Manila make sense of the homoerotic content in this fiction in relation to the dominant religious moralities of their respective societies, which treat homosexuality as a sin. She also explores the pleasure that reading male homoerotic content offers to these readers and its role in allowing them to reconceptualize sexuality beyond heteronormative understandings.

Victoria Ong's essay explores how autobiographical sex-work narratives allow their authors to make sense of and reconcile what they do in relation to dominant cultural assumptions about sex-work, labor, gender and sexuality. She focuses on Belle de Jour's *The Intimate Adventures of a London Call Girl*, analyzing Belle's use of humor and irony in her descriptions of sex. She argues that this "light" tone allows Belle to script her identity in positive terms, constructing herself as a new petite bourgeois subject offering experiences of "bounded authenticity." Ong explores the ambivalent positioning of popular sex-worker narratives in relation to critical theory on sex work, evidenced in criticisms that relatively class-privileged writers like Belle romanticize sex work. Ong's discussion provides a useful complement to Chen's analysis of sex blogs in China and Hardy's commentary on the important role of "authentic" female accounts in pornographic writing.

Finally, Alyssa D. Niccolini's essay is a study of female students at a New York urban public high school reading the erotic fiction of African American author Zane in the classroom. Zane is the most well-known and successful author in the genre known as "urban erotica," a significant departure from the more visible and notorious erotic romance novels that are usually the subject of popular discussion. Zane's work takes the form of short stories and novels and includes lesbian as well as straight erotica, and most of her protagonists are women of color. It often employs a grittier tone and downplays the importance of romance as a framework for sex. Niccolini explores how these reading practices offer resistive possibilities for readers in relation to the disciplinary apparatus of the education system, providing them with alternative forms of education about sex and relationships—what she calls an "affective pedagogy"—and engendering a community of readers.

These essays approach the topic of erotic fiction from a diverse range of disciplinary perspectives and concerns about genre. The resulting conversation is, of course, far from complete. Many genres, modes and communities of readers are not explored here. More work is needed on the consumption of erotic fiction in different cultural spaces, on the role of erotic fiction in reflecting and engaging with race, ethnicity and nation, its capacity to explore assumptions about bodies, age, ability and disability and reproduction, and its use of fantasy and science fiction modes as well as realism. Questions remain about the relationship of popular erotic fiction to "literary" erotica as well as visual pornography and about women's consumption of those forms. Indeed, there are productive questions about men's consumption of erotic writing. For that matter, a consideration of the readership or viewership of erotic material which interrogates this male/female dichotomy may also be incisive. We hope that these essays will prompt further critical work on the subject of erotic writing and its relationship to power, oppression, liberation and pleasure.

Part 1
Originating the Erotic

From Black Lace to Shades of Grey

The Interpellation of the "Female Subject" into Erotic Discourse

Simon Hardy

In the history of Western literature the production and consumption of texts mediating erotic discourse was once a masculine prerogative. Yet a notable feature of the male tradition of pornographic writing has been the common use of a female narrative voice. In this sense a "female subject" who creates and enjoys erotica has long been anticipated. Over the last twenty years there have been many works of erotic fiction and memoirs published that are genuinely written by women. This has rightly been seen as a sign of women's empowerment, but it raises the question of whether female authors are producing new forms of erotica or simply assimilating the patterns of erotic discourse established by the centuries-old tradition of male writers, often masquerading as female autobiographers. In theoretical terms we might ask whether female writers and readers are simply interpellated into the established erotic discourse or whether the new forms of erotic fiction provide space for the disruption and/or reworking of that discourse.

In practice this question can only be approached through a comparison of the continuities and divergences of selected texts drawn from the history of pornography and recent female-authored material, and it must be acknowledged right from the outset that the selection of other examples might well lead to different conclusions. After briefly setting out some relevant aspects of the tradition of male authored pornographic literature, this essay considers contemporary examples of erotic fiction by women that have achieved mass market circulation: ranging from the self-consciously pioneering Black Lace imprint to the "erotic romances" of such authors as E L James and Sylvia Day. A number of scholars (Downing, 2013; Harrison and Holm, 2013; Al-Mahadin, 2013; Nilson, 2013) have already highlighted the resonance of romantic fiction in E L James' *Fifty Shades* trilogy, yet its debt to written pornography has received less attention. In fact, E L James' work can be seen as perfecting the generic hybridization of romance with pornography, initiated by Black Lace, but doing so in a way that dissolves the radical potential of women's erotic writing, domesticating the play of erotic power dynamics in conformity with hetero-normative orthodoxy.

Pornography as a Masculine Literary Tradition

Since there is no universally accepted definition of "pornography" it is important to say that the term will be used here to refer to sexually explicit material that can be said to serve the primary purpose of sexual pleasure and arousal. Although the term was not widely used in this way until the late nineteenth century, the definition can be applied retrospectively to literary texts stretching back at least as far as John Cleland's germinal novel *Memoirs of a Woman of Pleasure*. No doubt when Cleland first published *Fanny Hill*, as it soon became known, in 1748 he had other motives for dissociating his name from a work he had written for cash and immediately wished "buried and forgot" (Foxon, 1965, p. 54). Yet, the serendipitous verisimilitude of implied female authorship must be seen alongside a series of quite deliberate stylistic devices that help to make *Fanny Hill* the first really influential "pornographic" prose work in the English language. These devices include the basic form of the epistolary novel and the use of first person, present tense narration, which give Fanny's account both immediacy and realism. But it is above all the coupling of these contemporaneous literary innovations to the skilful assumption of a female narrative voice that makes Cleland's novel function effectively as pornography.

Yet, for all its incipient modernism *Fanny Hill* also reflected an archaic view, which prevailed into the mid-eighteenth century, of the bodies and appetites of women as coterminous with those of men, although women were seen as less capable of exercising reason and self-control.

Thus Fanny is represented as becoming aroused by visual stimuli, readily masturbating, and as ejaculating in climaxes that synchronize perfectly with those of her male partners. Cleland's representation differed markedly from the dominant understanding of female sexuality that subsequently developed in the nineteenth century. In the Victorian age, medical and moral authorities conceived male and female sexual bodies as incommensurably opposite, and women as possessing a fundamentally different, obscure and limited sexuality (Laqueur, 1992). In this context the adoption of Cleland's descriptive formulas in the proliferation of anonymous, though certainly still male-authored, pornographic writing that occurred in the nineteenth century took on a new significance. For example, the pornographic trope of female sexual incontinence, in such works as *The Lustful Turk* (1828) and *The Pearl* (1879–80), expressed a conscious dissidence from bourgeois moral hegemony. Indeed, the fondly held belief in the passionless woman was a particular target of these subversive narratives, in which the virtue of chaste, upper-class female characters would rapidly dissolve into a torrent of incontinent desire and orgasmic ejaculation. Here then, the still common use of female narration took on the role of indicting the ideal of pure womanhood.

A further element that seems to have become conventional to pornographic writing in the nineteenth century is that the desire to which the female voice attests is often submissive, in the sense that chastity is overcome and pleasure attained through the agency of male sexual conquest or even rape. While the origins of the pornographic trope of female sexual submission are complex and may even pre-date the Marquis de Sade, we must recognize it as a historically specific construction rather than an expression of elemental truth. It is simply not present in *Fanny Hill*. Yet today female submission remains a common theme of erotic writing, which we will encounter repeatedly in this discussion of modern erotic literature. In short, Cleland's writing represented men and women as equally lascivious. Later, when "respectable" Victorian authorities established the notion of the passionless female, dissident pornographers opposed it by invoking the earlier tradition of female incontinence, but now with a new element: that this underlying female wantonness had to be brought forth as the submissive response to male sexual initiative.

Moreover, while it is impossible to trace adequately the development of the genre here, it is clear that by the turn of the twentieth century pornographic writing had acquired certain quite common features: it was written by men of the upper and middle classes, who often assumed a female voice in order to make what they said about women's sexuality—

namely, that women are essentially compliant and submissive—more convincing and therefore presumably more gratifying to their male readers. It was, of course, also at this very time that, in the rise of vernacular photography and especially in the moving image, pornography found its defining medium. As Linda Williams (1999) has argued, in the twentieth century visual documentation became the ultimate means of recording the "truth" of human sexuality. Yet, while the visual medium has largely diverted the attention of the male audience it has its own inherent limitations, especially its tendency to make the image occlude narrative and psychological complexity. Even after the coming of film, therefore, the written form has remained an important vehicle for erotic expression, and one that has increasingly been colonized by female readers and writers.

Even so, the legacy of male erotic writing would not prove easy to efface. As Anaïs Nin said of her "beginning efforts" in the 1940s:

> I realised that for centuries we had had only one model for this literary genre— the writing of men. I was really conscious of a difference between the masculine and feminine treatment of sexual experience ... I had a feeling that Pandora's box contained the mysteries of a woman's sensuality, so different from man's and for which man's language was inadequate [Nin, 1978, p. 14].

Concocting material from stories she had heard and her own inventions, Nin presented them as the diary of a woman and thus adopted the familiar realist techniques as well as a "style" derived from reading men's works. Moreover, while Nin felt that her own voice had not been "completely suppressed" and that she had often been intuitively using "a woman's language," there is something in the equivocation of this claim that itself seems to compound the sense that an "authentic" female sexuality was somehow inexpressible.

In Paris during the 1950s two avant-garde pornographic novels, *Histoire d'O* (Réage, 1954) and *L'Image* (de Berg, 1956), were published that featured women as sexually submissive and were written by women. The former was published under the pseudonym Pauline Réage, and the identity of the author remained a matter of controversy for the next forty years with many commentators refusing to believe it could have been created by a woman. Ironically, the true author, Dominique Aury, had written it precisely in response to the chauvinistic remark that a woman would be incapable of writing an erotic novel. *L'Image* was published under the masculine pseudonym Jean de Berg in accord with the male narrative voice, but actually written by Catherine Robbe-Grillet. What these examples seem to suggest is that while prevailing cultural attitudes continued to perceive women as essentially incapable of reproducing and manipulating the pornographic discourse of erotic power dynamics, they quite evidently could do so. Conversely, female writing did not automatically transform the content of eroticism in some intrinsically radical way, except perhaps in the sense that Angela Carter (1978) proposed: that by extending pornographic writing into the realms of Sadeian excess the implicit dynamics of heterosexuality are exposed to view. In any event, by this time it should have already been clear that the physiological sex of the author is irrelevant to the interpellation of the subject into the existing structures of meaning, and yet the idea that female authorship spontaneously produces a fundamentally distinctive "female" erotic language has stubbornly persisted.

Black Lace: Women Writing Sub/Dom Scenarios

When the Black Lace imprint first appeared in 1993 it could almost be regarded as putting into practice an experimental hypothesis arising from contemporary feminist debates over pornography and censorship. Critics of pornography (Dworkin, 1981; Griffin, 1981; Kappeler, 1986) had focused attention on a power dichotomy of male dominance and female submission that they perceived to be the essence of the genre in all its forms. However, other feminists (Assiter and Carol, 1993; Gibson and Gibson, 1993; Segal and McIntosh, 1992) vigorously disputed the claim that pornography was a singular entity that proselytized male supremacy or was necessarily antithetical to women's interests. From this point of view erotic representation was just another domain in which women needed to challenge male, as well as hetero-normative, prerogatives; while, insofar as much mainstream heterosexual pornography could justifiably be regarded as sexist, its content could be changed by female writers and film directors acquiring greater freedom of expression in this field. To many feminists this appeared a more positive alternative to the failed and divisive strategy of censorship that had been pursued by anti-porn campaigners.

In any event Black Lace, with its tag line of "erotic fiction by women and for women," seemed to realize the goal of empowering female erotic expression and exploration. Previous analyses of Black Lace have critically evaluated the claims of its editorial discourse to novelty and female empowerment, while highlighting the generic relation of its content to romantic fiction (Sonnet, 1999) and written pornography (Hardy, 2001). This discourse, as articulated by the editor Kerri Sharp (1999), rested on three main tenets: female authorship, entitlement to pleasure, and liberation through erotica. Implicit in all three is a notion of a sovereign female subject: one who, as an author, expresses an essential female eroticism, and who, in consuming explicit material, both fulfils her right to pleasure and liberates her native erotic psyche from the tiresome fetters of social repression.

In practice, the style and content of Black Lace fictions varied considerably. Some of the earlier novels drew heavily on the conventions of romantic fiction. For instance, Olivia Christie's *Dance of Obsession* (1996) offers an extended narrative of some two hundred and fifty pages of which only about 10 percent consists of sexual description. The story, set in 1930s Paris, concerns the erotic pursuit of the heroine Georgia by a younger man. The reader is clearly invited to identify with Georgia, while the external third-person narration facilitates a preoccupation with her appearance, as she gazes into mirrors or selects clothing for each occasion. The retro setting gives licence to the use of highly conventional gender codes. Much attention is also given to the "opulence" and "sumptuousness" of the material surroundings. In short, in texts such as this the explicit depiction of sexual scenes appeared to be only one, and not necessarily the primary, element of the mise en scène.

Other Black Lace fictions, especially as the imprint developed, were much more fully dedicated to sexual action. It is important to acknowledge the variations among these texts, both in terms of the often ambiguous ways in which the reader is invited to identify with characters, and the extent to which the power dynamics within the sexual scenes depicted conform to the model of male dominance and female submission. Yet many of them do seem to follow pornographic conventions, such as ithyphallic description: giving emphasis to the size of the penis, and connoting masculine power and virility. There is also the standard lexicon of obscene terminology ("fuck," "cock" and "cunt"), and frequent scenes of female submission to spanking, humiliation and verbal abuse ("slut," "bitch" and "whore"). A single short extract must here suffice for illustration. It is from Zoe le Verdier's short story *A Dangerous Addiction*, which despite the Sadeian allusion has a contemporary setting:

> The Marquis carried on where Johnny had left off. The whip screamed through the sticky air and landed across her shoulders. Her eyes and mouth jerked wide open; her expression a frozen moment of fear. "Fuck her, Johnny," the Marquis said. "She wants this. She deserves this." Again, the whip. Again, the jolt of every muscle in her body. Johnny fucked her faster, forcing deeper [le Verdier, 1999, p. 228].

This is but one example, yet by comparing a sufficient series of these texts a certain formula emerges: one that invokes a feminist narrative of empowerment while also having strong resonances with the male-authored pornography referred to previously. Black Lace fictions are stories of female sexual discovery, of women becoming active, pleasure seeking subjects. However, the goal of pleasure is usually attained only when the woman's social self finally yields to the natural lust residing in her body, as it responds to the agency of male sexual conquest. Female liberation is attained only in the act of submission.

The impression that much, if not most, Black Lace material presents submissive scenarios to its audience is reinforced, albeit in a rather circular way, by *The Black Lace Book of Women's Sexual Fantasies* (Sharp, 1999). This features one hundred and eighteen detailed fantasy scenarios sent in by female readers aged seventeen to sixty-six; of these, 49 percent cast the author herself, or some other woman with whom she clearly identified, in an explicitly submissive role and a further 25 percent in an implicitly or mildly submissive role, while 21 percent appeared to have no particular power dynamics, and just 5 percent cast the woman in what could be seen as a dominant role. It is interesting to note that the publisher has carelessly classified this text as non-fiction, thus implying that when women write down their sexual fantasies, rather than being recognized as the creative *fiction* of an authorial subject, the product is treated as a *non-fictional* object, offered up for precisely the kind of pseudo-scientific scrutiny with which pornography has always regarded that thing called "female sexuality."

By the turn of the millennium Black Lace had sold over three million books (Stoddart, 2000). This success, however, seemed to present something of a paradox. After the limited success of visual formats such as "couples films" and "beefcake" magazines, the traditional feminine forms of the novel and short story had provided a medium through which women now produced and consumed sexually explicit material on a newly increased scale. Yet, at the same time, the content of this material seemed far more obviously preoccupied with gendered power relations of domination and submission than is generally the case with the banal documentary stare of mainstream audio-visual pornography. Where previously women writing explicit scenarios of female submission had been confined to the Parisian avant-garde, it was now a commercially successful practice.

BDSM and the Genre of "Erotic Romance"

When we survey sexually explicit writing by and for women today the theme of female erotic submission, although by no means universal, still seems common and perhaps even prevalent. Much of the current material can be classed under the emerging and as yet ill-defined generic headings of "erotic romance," "adult romance" or "provocative romance" (James, 2013). Such fictions broadly follow the Black Lace formula of combining romance with sexually explicit content. This situation raises questions about the extent and significance of the trope of female submission as it is employed within this emergent genre.

Maria Nilson (2013) has suggested that until recently mainstream fiction for women had been dominated by the relatively "chaste" genre of chick lit, and that the current wave of mass-market explicit fiction was heralded by the recent vogue for women's erotic memoirs. Arguably such works as *The Sexual Life of Catherine M* (Millet, 2002), *One Hundred Strokes of the Brush Before Bed* (Melissa P., 2004) and Zoe Margolis' *Girl with a One Track Mind* (Lee, 2006) should be seen as an intermediate stage in the progress of a female erotic subjectivity. Like the *Black Lace Book of Women's Sexual Fantasies* (Sharpe, 1999) they tend to disavow the creative imagination of the female author, while claiming to place the authentic experience of a real woman before a general audience. In contrast it is clear that erotic romance is fictional writing by women and for women, so that we can surely say that a female subject producing and consuming explicit erotic material has arrived in mainstream cultural representation. Or can we? The term "erotic romance" seems to be applied by authors and publishers to a wide range of new work, some of which, though explicit within certain limits, also seems to hark back to older forms of romance.

At one end of the range is the prolific Cherise Sinclair, who caters to a niche BDSM market. Works such as *Make Me, Sir* (2011) contain fully explicit scenes narrated in the third person from an external perspective and depict a BDSM subculture in which men are seen in submissive roles, at least as a part of the backdrop if not at the centre of the action. These stories also offer a degree of psychological complexity in which the subjective motives of female submissives are explored as part of the narrative, rather than the identification with such desires being taken-for-granted as the intrinsic sexual preference of women *per se* (Frantz, 2012).

It is important to contrast the eroticization of heterosexual power dynamics in many contemporary, mass market erotic romance novels with the radical status of BDSM as a minority sexual identity, which is invoked in Sinclair's fiction. In Gayle Rubin's (1984) influential theory of the politics of sexual oppression, sadomasochism is one of a number of binary opposites that are excluded from the "charmed circle" of socially legitimated sexual practices and identities. Rubin's analysis has provided grounds for viewing the representation of BDSM as radically progressive. In regard to erotic representation, Stephanie Wardrop (1995) has argued that the ritualized roles of dominant and submissive are clearly two sides of the same imaginary play; therefore identification with one side necessarily implies a degree of identification with the other. While the roles may be mapped onto specific gender identities in any given scene, this is a contingent and inherently unstable arrangement. Indeed, it is clear that in interpersonal practice men often opt for the submissive role. In short, BDSM, both as an interpersonal practice and as mediated representation, is more likely to de-stabilize taken-for-granted cultural assumptions about male and female sexualities by rendering them explicit and necessitating a conscious process of inter-subjective reflection and negotiation than to further entrench their mystique. While Margot D. Weiss (2012) has cautioned that even consensual BDSM practices do not spring direcly from human nature but are a product of our social environment, we must also ask what happens when such a minority sexual identity is played out, or exploited, in mainstream representation. The applicability of the idea that BDSM play radically de-stabilizes traditional gender identity to any given instance of representation is empirically testable in terms of the extent to which the alignment of roles is indeed varied within the range of sexual scenarios presented. It is to the evidence of the contemporary scene of mass-market explicit sexual representation that we now turn.

Sinclair's fiction is obscure compared to the works of E L James, whose *Fifty Shades* trilogy has already sold over seventy million books (Child, 2013), and Sylvia Day, who has herself been cited as the *New York Times* number one bestseller. Although the latter's first novel of the *Crossfire* series, *Bared to You* (2012), has been cunningly packaged by Penguin in sepia tones as if a clone of *Fifty Shades*, it is in fact a rather different animal. Day's novel seems to be essentially a romance in which the sexually explicit content is subordinated to the narrative, rather than the latter merely serving as a thread connecting sexual scenarios, as one would expect in a pornographic text where the raison d'être is to provide sexual stimulation. Furthermore, the actual content of the scenes draw from a limited menu of activities: there is plenty of oral sex, both ways, but most of the scenarios end with Eva on her back in the missionary position. In fact, the one real "porno scene" toward the end of *Bared to You* is a foursome, involving Eva's bisexual flatmate, from which the heroine shrinks in disgust as if it were included specifically to emphasize the healthily possessive monogamy of the central couple. Moreover, unlike *Fifty Shades*, there is no explicit BDSM in any of the scenes. Rather the power dynamic resides in Gideon's overbearing nature and tendency to resolve arguments by forcing Eva into sexual acts and responses. This blurring of the line between rape and consent, coupled with the old trope of the treacherous female body that responds to the man's advances, is a cliché that recalls the hard-edged romantic fiction of the 1970s as well as much pornographic writing. In the era of second wave feminism, the apparently paradoxical popularity of so-called "bodice rippers" or "sweet savagery" that toyed with the theme of rape could be accounted for in terms of women's guilt about sex and need to have responsibility taken away (Faust, 1980). Since then, as women's sense of sexual entitlement has grown, Wardrop (1995) has argued that the appeal of the "rape" scenario lies more in the female reader's awareness of the power of the "masochist" within interpersonal dynamics. In female-authored romantic fiction, Wardrop (1995) claims, there is a play on the exchange of power in which the "raping hero" is ultimately defeated by his own emotional neediness, something which the female character does not fear. Day's novel *Bared to You* seems to follow this model closely; at one point, after a passionate scene, Gideon says to Eva:

> "I'm always hard for you, always hot for you. I'm always half-crazy with wanting you. If anything could change that, I would've done it before we got this far. Understand? ... Now show me that you still want *me* after that." His face was flushed and damp, his eyes dark and turbulent. "I need to know that losing control doesn't mean I've lost you" [Day, 2012, p. 186].

Later, when the tables are turning, Gideon pleads:

> "Are you going to punish me with pleasure?" he asked quietly. "Because you can. You can bring me to my knees Eva" [2012, p. 252].

In short, while Day's novel contains a dozen explicitly described sexual scenes, which often employ the pornographic hyperbole of copious female ejaculation and the big "steely erection"—and we are not *just* talking about Gideon's massive skyscraper here—the novel as a whole is really far more romantic than erotic. As such, one could argue that it represents the resurgence, albeit in ultra-modern guise, of an old sub-genre of hard-edged romance rather than anything really new. This, however, is not true of the E L James trilogy, which, for all that it avoids the cliché of the big cock, has the lineage of pornography much more strongly in its DNA. What makes *Fifty Shades*, to which we will now turn our attention, *remarkable* is not simply the scale of its sales but the fact that it seems to perfect, for the mass market, a hybridization of romance and pornography.

E L James' Fifty Shades

The formula used by E L James combines three elements: romantic narrative, pornographic scenes and a theme of conspicuous consumption and extreme material wealth. These elements work together to constitute an aspirational and idealized model of a heterosexual relationship for the twenty-first century that owes nothing to the feminist politics of the twentieth. The story's figurative female subject turns out to be a latent submissive whose sexuality is narratively actualized within a profoundly conservative and exclusionary hetero-normative fantasy of the perfect marriage, defined in opposition to outsiders who are sexual deviants and social inferiors.

The British author of *Fifty Shades* sets her story in the Pacific Northwest, and the narrative voice is that of the central character Anastasia Steele, a twenty-one-year-old American, whose tone is affected largely by the frequent repetition of such received colloquialisms as "jeez" and "holy crap." Ana's subjective, present-tense narration rolls along with little regard to style or grammar, although critics of the rudimentary writing miss the point: whether by accident or design, the style does not exceed the likely capacities of the undergraduate narrator, albeit a student of English literature. The stylistic limitations of the narrator are well illustrated at the very end of the first novel, when having walked out on her lover she uses this rather clunking metaphor:

> I head straight to my room, and there, hanging limply at the end of my bed, is a very sad, deflated helicopter balloon. Charlie Tango, looking and feeling exactly like me [James, 2012a, p. 356].

In short, Ana is a shallow and pointedly unliterary literature student. She is naïve and, as she frequently says, knows very little about anything, except cooking. What is more she is a virgin who has not yet experienced orgasm or masturbated; she has no sexual history and even finds wearing make-up intimidating. In other words, she is a blank space, easily available for identification by the intended reader, whom we may assume to be female. No doubt Ana is not the reader exactly as she is but as she might wish to be: an artlessly attractive, virginal body and an innocent, sympathetic personality, within whom the reader can enjoy the romantic and erotic journey to imaginary fulfilment. Of course, as Salam Al-Mahadin (2013) has pointed out, we should not assume these books directly "interpellate" readers into a pre-determined subject position. The text may be read in a variety of ways, and even when the reader *does* identify with Ana it is of course part of the function of fantasy to allow us to imaginatively inhabit positions that we would not otherwise entertain. The concept of interpellation, as originally formulated by Althusser (1971), does not appear to admit notions of agency or negotiation, which is one reason why it has been generally rejected within modern cultural studies. Nevertheless, it is an interesting exercise to apply it in this case, supposing that the very notion of agency is itself a delusion within a process of ideological recognition, whereby the subject perceives *herself* within the narrative discourse. After all, is it not often claimed in the more simplistic psychoanalytic and therapeutic commentaries on pornography precisely that by looking at it the individual "discovers" what they really want, their *own* repressed sexuality and, so to speak, inner "truth"?

In essence, the narrative arc of the *Fifty Shades* trilogy is an extended dialogue between Ana and her lover Christian Grey, the very tedium of which achieves a certain verisimilitude. Indeed, the real merit of E L James' fiction is perhaps the way that it captures something of the process of relationships in lived life that tend to develop as an overlapping and repeatedly circling series of conversations, which are broken off, half-forgotten, resumed in altered forms after events have intervened, and now of course extended remotely via email and other new media platforms. In our age of "reality" entertainment this unliterary naturalism is surely one of the keys to the series' mass appeal.

If Anastasia is the subject of this romantic narrative, the eponymous hero is the principle object. In many ways Christian is a classic romantic figure. At twenty-seven he is still young, though a little older than Ana and, unlike her, sexually skilled and experienced. In fact, Christian is prodigiously talented at all things, except cooking, of course, and especially in business, where his acumen has already made him rich. But above all, as Ana remarks at least once in every chapter, he is "beyond beautiful." He is, in short, an impossible combination of romantic masculine traits, both beautiful bad boy and powerful man of the world. There is an aesthetic objectification of Christian throughout Ana's discourse, but it does not position her as a subject in any radical way, or in the same way that pornography has positioned men to respond sexually to the sight of naked women. While there are countless references to Christian in white shirt and jeans, it is his face and clothed body, rather than really his naked body or sexual anatomy, which is the object of Ana's gaze. Beyond aesthetic portrayal, Christian is also the object of Ana's narrative in the sense of process, in that his highly desirable raw material is gradually transformed into a domesticated and marriageable form. It is the old fantasy of taming the bad boy, one who, in this version, is emotionally closed and who intends to use the heroine only as a contractual submissive. Confronted by a man who is both exciting and dangerous Ana must decide how much to risk and whether she is willing to be dominated. In sexual matters she accepts his tutelage and is entirely shaped by his script, at least until he beats her so severely that the experience takes her beyond her physical limits. Ana's rejection of him, at the end of the first novel, marks the turning point of the narrative and prepares the way for his transformation in the second novel.

Moreover, what drives the narrative is the gradual revelation of Christian's extensive sexual history. It is here that Ana will find clues to his proclivities and resolve the problems of their future. Mentally and physically scarred by his early experiences with a "whore" mother who did not protect him from abuse by her punters, Christian suffers from a fear of being touched intimately. Later, as a teenager, he had been seduced and initiated as a submissive into BDSM by an older woman called Elena, with whom he still maintains a friendship and who becomes the object of Ana's visceral loathing. Since then he has assumed the dominant role with a succession of submissive brunettes, but now his love for Ana has brought about a "Damascene conversion" so that he can be content with the more moderate power play for which he has already prepared her. From this point on, the central dynamic, or dialogue, gradually resolves itself in the direction of marriage, children and the promise of happiness ever after. In short, as others have noted (Harrison and Holm, 2013; Nilson 2013), Christian is the typical damaged alpha male of romantic fiction, who will be saved through the narrative arc of his relationship with the heroine. So, while it is clear that as a narrative *Fifty Shades* is firmly rooted in the existing "feminine" genre of romance, what part does pornography play in its genealogy?

Generic elements of pornography clearly influence the sexual scenarios that punctuate the narrative at regular intervals. To be sure certain elements that might prove rebarbative to a female audience are excluded, such as excessive verbal obscenity or ithyphallic description. At the same time, the promiscuous couplings so characteristic of pornography are also precluded by the contextual narrative of romance. Yet, while there are only ever the same two characters in each scenario, the dynamic between them is conventional. Christian is the initial and predominant subject of the action and Ana its object, both in the sense that things are done to her and in that her pleasure and bodily responses are the focus of attention, the *thing* that the reader is invited to scrutinize.

In setting the sexual agenda Christian tells her that they will "build up to various scenarios" (James, 2012a, p. 155), thus alluding directly to the underlying sequence of scenarios that forms a sort of parallel narrative infrastructure. He also introduces a pseudo contract, setting out the rules and obligations of their relationship and delineating its "hard limits" and "soft limits" (James, 2012a, pp. 122–24). In effect the "hard limits" define the boundaries that the text will not cross, and conveniently mark out for the reader those areas to be excluded as erotic themes, such as urination, defecation, piercing, blood, scarification, breath control, children and animals. In contrast, the "soft limits" that Ana is asked to sign up to effectively offer a menu of erotic acts that the reader may expect to see, including fellatio, cunnilingus, anal intercourse, vibrators, bondage, blindfolding, spanking, whipping and nipple clamps.

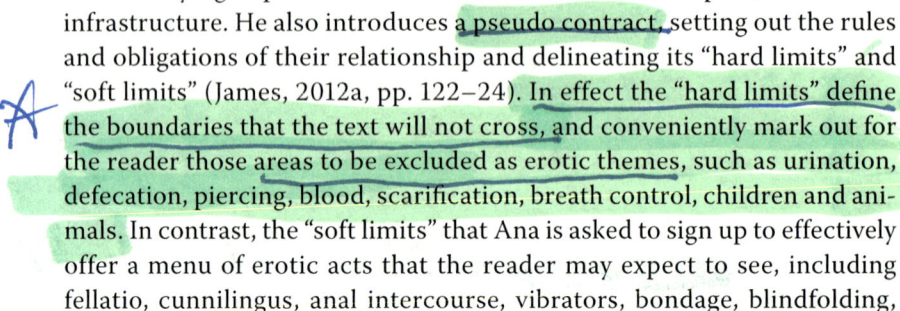

Since the contract is never signed there remains a degree of doubt as to Ana's consent to each of the latter activities. Yet, as in pornography, female consent is always already assured because the overwhelming force of masculine sexual agency has an ally in the "traitorous" female body. The trope of the feminine mind-body dualism is given a twenty-first century gloss when Ana researches Christian's proclivities by typing "submissive" into Wikipedia:

> Half an hour later, I feel slight [sic] queasy and frankly shocked to my core. Do I really want this stuff in my head? Jeez—is this what he gets up to in the Red Room of Pain? I sit staring at the screen, and part of me, a very moist and integral part of me—that I've only become acquainted with very recently, is seriously turned on. Oh my, some of this stuff is HOT. But is it for me? Holy shit … could I do this? [James, 2012a, p. 132].

Gradually Ana is drawn into the submissive role and her ultimate destination is that, frequently invoked yet never interrogated, "dark place" in her own psyche, where she finds that being tied and whipped is

> a sweet agony—bearable, just … pleasant—no, not immediately, but as my skin sings with each blow … I am dragged into a dark, dark part of my psyche that surrenders to this most erotic sensation. *Yes—I get this* [James, 2012a, p. 340].

The none-too-subtle play of light and dark, also noted by others (Harrison and Holm, 2013), hints at the central theme of the, by now marital, sex scenes of the final novel: the domestication of a mild form of BDSM eroticism within the imaginary safe haven of heterosexual monogamy, where the emotional bond between husband and wife makes Ana's submission safe and she has entirely identified with the role she has been given by her husband and sexual master.

In short, the course of the narrative establishes Ana's submissive sexual nature; the dark, ineffable truth, lurking beneath the surface of her characterization as a virginal yet thoroughly modern girl. While Christian's sexuality is elaborately accounted for, Ana's response to and identification with the submissive role is taken for granted; described in endless detail yet never explained, as if it were latent in her nature, or simply because she really is a blank slate to be inscribed by her lover. In contrast to the more nuanced treatment of female submission in the contemporary works of Sinclair and Day, it is above all in this fundamental essentialist silence that James' text most crucially bears the hallmark of the male tradition of pornographic writing referred to above. These borrowings from pornography are spliced into what is essentially a romantic narrative. In the process of doing this a generic hybridization is perfected: a genre in which *her* narrative reforms him for the love and marriage that she ultimately desires, while *his* erotic capital is fruitfully invested in her as the submissive sexual subject that fulfils his need.

But beyond these romantic and erotic themes there is a third notable dimension to *Fifty Shades* revealed in the obsequious name-checking of commercial products, from Twinings English Breakfast Tea to the Eurocopter 135, "the safest in its class" (James, 2012b, p. 329). Alongside the pleasures of sex, the trilogy celebrates the analogous pleasures of consumption. The latter have long been a common co-theme in erotic writing. We saw, for example, how wealth and "opulence" were presented in the Black Lace fiction *Dance of Obsession* (Christie, 1996), and the tradition goes back at least to such Victorian works as *The Pearl* (Anon, 1968) in which sexual indulgence and the contemporaneous bourgeois passion for material consumption are conflated (Sigel, 2002). *Fifty Shades* updates this aspirational theme for the current age of the super-rich with its cold grey aesthetic of glass and steel towers, "impressive, sumptuous" hotel lobbies, black SUVs and giant yachts. Moreover, the theme of consumption is built into the structure of the story as Christian besieges Ana with gifts, an overbearing generosity that she initially resists but gradually yields to. Thus the progressive narrative accretion of material objects marks a second and parallel loss of innocence for Ana. Alongside her transformation into an active subject of "kinky fuckery," she must also overcome her homely middle-class reticence about conspicuous consumption and embrace her newfound status as a billionaire's wife. When the newlyweds set up house Ana struggles to come to terms with the full implications of having domestic "help." Still unable to affect the hubristic nonchalance of the super-rich she modestly scrubs her own butt plug, while inwardly cringing at the thought that the household manager, Mrs. Jones, already sees to the cleaning of their sex room.

Above all, what the Greys' money buys is relative safety and security, the minimization of foreseeable risk being one of the privileges of the contemporary social elite. In the course of the trilogy, Ana is gradually absorbed into the protective material culture of wealth with its exclusive social spaces, architecture and expensive vehicles that separate the rich from the rest of society. Prominent among the supporting cast are Christian's security staff, the ex–Marine Taylor, Sawyer and the others. They have their work cut out protecting the couple from various dark, threatening outsiders: Leila, a deranged stalker, and the villainous Jack Hyde, Ana's work boss who sexually harasses her, until Christian buys the company, sacks him and he resorts to sabotage and abduction. In the asymmetric contest between these puny outsiders and Christian's corporate muscle and security and surveillance apparatus, there seems to be a contemporary resonance with the excess of power with which Western states obliterate potential terrorists.

Like the terrorist, the threat posed by these outsiders functions on a symbolic level. Significantly, what these figures have in common, along with the narrator's *bête noire* Elena, is that they are all unruly sexual deviants: Elena is a dominant woman who had seduced Christian when he was under-age and is therefore a paedophile in Ana's opinion, Leila had been one of Christian's masochistic contractual subs, and Jack exercises abusive power over his female PAs, and turns out to have come from the same foster family as Christian. Jack is thus a dark inversion of Christian, a modern Mr. Hyde in whom sadistic sexual proclivities are not redeemed by a capacity for love, and Leila is a negative, self-destructive version of Ana, pitifully lacking in self-respect or sexual limits. As the narrative progresses it becomes clear that the function of these outsiders is to throw into relief the safely domesticated relationship between sexually submissive female and dominant male, which is forming within the exemplary moneyed haven of Christian and Ana's marriage. Thus a tamed and one-dimensional simulation of BDSM is retrieved from the "outer limits" of Rubin's (1984) "bad, abnormal, unnatural and damned sexuality" and used to re-eroticize the "charmed circle" of privileged heterosexual monogamy. As other's have also noted (Dymock, 2013; Tsaros, 2013), James' kinky fuckery is assimilated to a hetero-normative master narrative.

Conclusion

This essay has argued, in the first place, that the theme of female submission is an historical feature of male pornographic writing and that a female narrative voice was often employed to make the trope appear as an expression of the unmediated truth of female sexuality. Paradoxically, however, following the feminist debates about pornography, when women came to produce and consume sexually explicit literature on a significant scale in the 1990s their fiction often adopted this same trope, as if the female subject were being interpellated into a space already created for them within pornographic discourse. Although many of the more recent contemporary sexual narratives by and for women also employ the theme of female submission, they often do so in ways that might destabilize the clichés of heterosexual eroticism. However, in concocting a hybridized formula that has conquered the market and claimed a mass female audience, E L James has combined two mutually regressive, yet hitherto antithetical, elements: the hetero-normative conservatism of traditional romance and the derogatory essentialism often found in pornographic representations of female sexuality.

Steamy, Spicy, Sensual

Tracing the Cycles of Erotic Romance

KATHERINE E. MORRISSEY

Returning from the annual Romance Writers of America conference in 2013, American author Carolyn Jewel commented, "revolution is not too strong a word for what's going on in the publishing world" (Jewel, 2013). At the 2013 conference, Jewel saw more mid-list romance authors than ever rejecting contracts from big-name publishers and turning instead to digital and self-publishing services. This ongoing movement of mid-list authors, away from traditional publishers and toward smaller digital shops, signals a sea change across the romance market. These changes are indicative of the dramatic impact digital publishing is having on romance fiction.

The shifting of the mid-list is just one piece of a much larger series of reconfigurations within romance publishing. As publishers have gone digital, the availability of certain kinds of romantic content has also shifted. Texts rejected by publishing powerhouses because they do not speak to the largest segments of the market are able to find circulation as e-books online. Romantic sub-genres that once could not compete for space on store shelves are more easily offered in online databases where they do not displace larger selling categories and titles. The growth of the digital market has allowed smaller sub-categories to thrive and enabled the expansion of many niche romance markets.

The seeds of today's revolution were planted long before 2013. In this essay I focus on one area of renegotiation within romance publishing: the boundaries of sexual fantasy. The essay outlines key moments in the history of erotic romance in America, beginning with the "hot historicals" produced (primarily) in America in the 1970s and moving to the production of "erotic" media in America and the United Kingdom in the 1990s. Next, I examine the melding of the terms erotic and romance by American publishers over the course of the late '90s and early 2000s, as well as the debate this provoked among online communities of romance readers at the time. In this history, I will not pinpoint a specific location or origin point for the erotic romance. English-language romance continues to be dominated by international publishers based in New York and Toronto. However, these are texts that have always circulated internationally to English-language readers and beyond. Rather than identifying a single beginning for erotic romance, I argue that the erotic romance sub-genre regularly rises to catch public attention. Each new wave of content signals a moment of reconfiguration within romance, unfolding at the level of industry, technology, and narrative form. The boundaries between romantic, erotic, and pornographic content are lines that are drawn as much by shifting cultural norms as they are by form and content. As social norms regarding gender, desire, and sexual fantasy are periodically renegotiated, the erotic regularly resurfaces in romance publishing.

Today's revolution should be seen as one important point within a broader history: a period where technological and cultural changes intersect to initiate significant shifts across romance publishing. We may also be at a turning point. The shifts from analog to digital and from mass to long-tail markets have profound implications for how popular culture is conceptualized and studied. Analyzing the American romance market in the 1970s and '80s, Carol Thurston outlined a framework for the evolution of popular culture. However, this model does not cleanly apply to today's international digital markets. At least not yet. I conclude this essay by asking where erotic romance is headed next and identifying a set of questions we need to ask as this process unfolds.

The First Erotic Romances?

The term erotic romance has conflicting meanings for academics, readers, and publishers. Explicit sexual content is often said to have first appeared in romance novels during the 1970s, beginning with the American publisher Avon's release of Kathleen Woodiwiss' *The Flame and the Flower* in 1972. *The Flame and the Flower* and the cycle of sexually explicit historicals that followed it have often been described by scholars as the start of erotic romance. In *Fantasy and Reconciliation*, Kay Mussell calls these books "the first erotic romances" (1984, p. 10). In *The Romance Revolution*, Carol Thurston refers to them as "erotic heterosexual romances" (1987, p. 10). In *Desert Passions*, Hsu-Ming Teo identifies the period of the late '70s as the "burgeoning of the erotic romance novel" (2012, p. 156).

Within romance reading and publishing communities, however, these romances are more often referred to as hot historicals or bodice rippers. In the publishing industry, the term erotic romance does not seem to be used as a marketing label until the mid–'90s, roughly two decades after the more explicit romances of the '70s were published. The notion of an entire erotic romance sub-genre took even more time to take shape. *Publisher's Weekly* did not announce that "publishing heavyweights Harlequin, Kensington and Avon all have new erotica imprints" until the summer of 2006, despite predictions in the late 1990s and early 2000s that romance was going to be getting steamier (Patrick, 2006).

The way sexual content is depicted in erotic romances today is also not the same as the bodice-ripping historical romances of the '70s, or the "erotic contemporary series romances" studied by Thurston in the '80s (1987, p. 92). Popular romance bloggers Sarah Wendell and Candy Tan describe the books of the '70s as euphemism filled, "more humpy" than other romances of the day, and "discrete enough" (Wendell and Tan, 2009, p. 12). This is hardly an enthusiastic reinforcement of the books' erotic potential. There are clear links between these earlier works and today's erotic romances, but many readers would be surprised to hear titles from the '70s and '80s described as erotic. When compared to today's erotic romances, their content seems far less direct and explicit.

The 1970s were also not the first time sex became visible within romance novels. Hsu-Ming Teo argues that the erotic historical romances of the '70s trace their origins back to the Orientalist sheik romances that were popular across Western culture in the 1920s. Teo argues, "while the Orientalist romance largely vanished after the 1930s ... it [reemerged] in the form of the historical harem bodice ripper" (Teo, 2012, p. 143). Similarly, jay Dixon observes that the "1920s saw the rise of the bestseller 'sex novel'" (1999, p. 137). According to Dixon, "[s]ex has always been a part of [British] Mills & Boon romances, to a greater or lesser degree, depending on the era, the author and the type of plot" (1999, p. 133).

Rather than seeing the 1970s Avon publications as an origin point for erotic romance, this period should be recognized as a moment where the erotic again becomes visible. Like the sheik romances so popular in America and the West in the 1920s, the erotic romances of the '70s are indicative of a period of reconfiguration across broader Western culture and a moment where the representation of sexual desire in romance was renegotiated.

Nonetheless, the publication of Woodiwiss' *The Flame and the Flower* was important for romance. The book kicked off a cycle of "hot historicals," initiating a trend that continued into the early '80s. Authors like Woodiwiss, Bertrice Small and Rosemary Rogers all published now classic historical romances with Avon during this period. Once the hot historicals established themselves, many publishers began to introduce lines of contemporary romances that also included explicit sexual content. Gradually, sexually explicit content was offered by many different publishers, usually carefully organized within a specific publisher imprint so that readers could find or avoid these stories.

Competition between publishing companies also played a direct role in the move toward more explicit sexual content. In 1972, Avon was a smaller company, "unable to compete with the wealthier paperback houses" of the day (Thurston, 1987, p. 47). Avon turned to paperback originals in a simple attempt to stay afloat, famously pulling *The Flame and the Flower* out of their stack of unsolicited manuscripts (the slush pile) in order to publish it (Radway, 1984, p. 33; Thurston, 1987, p. 47).

At the time, *The Flame and the Flower* had already been rejected by numerous publishers. The book was a publishing risk for Avon, but it paid off. In 1974, following the novel's success, Avon published a second book by Woodiwiss and Rosemary Rogers' *Sweet Savage Love*. While the romance market had been declining in the early '70s, these books drew in both new and existing romance readers. By 1976, the gothic—previously a significant portion of the romance market—had significantly declined in popularity and many other publishers were offering their own hot historicals to compete with Avon (Thurston, 1987, p. 50).

During this period in the late '70s, the romance market was organized around two poles: steamy historicals and sweet contemporaries. Romantic content was available as both single-title and series publications (as it continues to be today). Steamier historicals were often sold as longer single-title publications and sweeter romances typically focused on contemporary women. These were "contemporary sweet romance lines ... generally referred to as brand name, series or category books" (Thurston, 1987, p. 24). Essentially, the more explicit content was kept isolated from the rest of the romance market. These stories were limited to exotic settings and faraway times, presenting sensual fantasy worlds carefully removed from the day-to-day lives of romance readers.

The boundary between explicit content and contemporary settings was again renegotiated in the 1980s when another major industry shift occurred. Looking to consolidate profits, Toronto-based Harlequin took back its American distribution rights from Pocket Books, a division of Simon & Schuster in New York (Thurston, 1987, pp. 51–52). This left Simon and Schuster needing content for their existing distribution chain. Like Avon in the '70s, the company published their own original romances to compensate.

The launching of Silhouette by Simon and Schuster in 1980 shook up the market substantially. Until this point, Harlequin had an "estimated 80–90 percent market share of the series romance" (Thurston, 1987, p. 52). However, as a reprinter of Mills and Boon romances from the UK, Harlequin's content was dominated by British settings and authors. At the time, Janet Dailey was their only American author. Infamously, Harlequin rejected an early manuscript from the (now) wildly successful Nora Roberts during this time, informing Roberts that they already had an American author (Regis, 2007, p. 159). Not only was Harlequin reluctant to introduce more explicit content, the Canadian company also seemed uncertain about incorporating American settings and authors into their publications (Regis, 2007, p. 183).

Quickly after the launch of Silhouette, "the so-called sensuous or erotic contemporary series romance appeared on the market" (Thurston, 1987, p. 53). Another American publisher, Dell, introduced their Candlelight Ecstasy line in 1980. Silhouette introduced Desire in 1982 and Intimate Moments in 1983 (Thurston, 1987, pp. 62–65). These series were as sexually explicit as the hot historicals, but the stories were set in modern times. Slowly, the erotic content of the historical was making its way into settings much closer to readers' lives.

Harlequin did not begin to publish more explicit sexual content until nearly a decade after the first hot historicals were published. The company introduced their SuperRomances in 1980 and finally launched their own erotic contemporary series, the Temptation line, in 1984 (Mussell, 1984, p. 32; Thurston, 1987, pp. 62–65). This made Harlequin one of the last major romance publishers to add a more sexually explicit series.

This slower response from Harlequin is important. Well-established in romance publishing, there was little incentive for Harlequin to shake up its market with potentially risky content. Instead, the newer content provided competing publishers with an alternative product, something that Harlequin did not offer. It was not only the sexy content, however. Harlequin's reluctance to take on American authors meant that there were many American authors sitting on manuscripts at this time, all eager to find a publisher. Seeking new content to distribute, Simon and Schuster was able to take great advantage of these openings. When the company launched Silhouette in 1980, they "made huge inroads into a market that Harlequin had regarded as its own" (Regis, 2007, p. 156). As sexual content made the shift to contemporary settings, "the category or series erotic contemporary ... brought nonseries readers and more nonromance readers into the fold" (Thurston, 1987, p. 187). Shifting social norms created gaps in the market and helped publishers identify viable and distinctive content.

By 1984, the hot historicals trend was beginning to loose its intensity. The market was becoming saturated and readers were beginning to complain about redundant content (Thurston, 1987, pp. 188–89). Broader social changes may have also pointed publishers back toward more conservative content. In 1984, just when Harlequin was finally starting up its steamier Temptation line, Silhouette added a new line of inspirational romances (romances with heavy religious themes). Silhouette did this in response to "the groundswell of conservatism ... that seemed to be emerging after the 1980 presidential election" (Thurston, 1987, p. 190). They also marketed the new Inspiration line heavily in the American South (Thurston, 1987, p. 190). At this point, Harlequin had lost a great deal of its market to Silhouette and other publishers. Finally, in 1984, Harlequin bought Silhouette Books from Simon and Schuster, essentially "buying back most of the market share it had lost" (Thurston, 1987, p. 191).

During the period from the early 1970s into the mid-1980s, romance publishing was bifurcated between more traditional sweet romances and more erotic ones. Then, as the '80s progressed, companies merged, sexual content spread to a broader array of romantic sub-genres, and the genre's content gradually restabilized. Carol Thurston argues that these shifts demonstrate a pattern of disequilibrium followed by equilibrium. She explains that the romance genre only exists in a "state of equilibrium ... when all romance publishers are producing fundamentally similar products" (Thurston, 1987, pp. 213–14). In this state of equilibrium, "one or more publishers can fluctuate products while others do not," and these smaller changes do not destabilize the whole (Thurston, 1987, pp. 213–14). When experiments with genre are successful, these fluctuations initiate a period of disequilibrium, often triggered by social and technological changes.

Thurston uses erotic romance to outline an evolutionary paradigm that regularly resurfaces in popular culture. She argues that the "introduction of a new technique or product may break a kind of social, technological, or economic equilibrium" (Thurston, 1987, p. 211). Thurston's framework provides a rubric for examining how changes unfold in media production and culture. However, the more recent introduction of e-books and e-commerce sites into romance publishing presents significant challenges to Thurston's paradigm.

At first glance, the shift toward digital publishing and the emergence of new publishers and retail sites online seem to replicate past patterns of expansion and disequilibrium in the romance market. Today, the erotic romance category continues to grow and digital publishers are producing content that is far more bluntly sexual than the so-called "explicit" content of the 1970s and 1980s. At times, this content makes its way out to print and the larger publishers. However, digitization seems to introduce greater levels of instability and fluctuation into the romance market. Also, many forms of content are able to remain niche. To better understand the changes unfolding online and their implications for romance, I want to pick up shortly after Thurston's project leaves off. Next, I trace the emergence of "erotic romance" as a marketing term within romance in the '90s and early 2000s.

(Romantic) Erotica

Works like *The Flame and the Flower* were groundbreaking, in part, because they opted not to draw a curtain or close a door when intimacy began. Once sexual content began to appear in both contemporary and historical titles, however, this degree of explicitness became a norm within the genre, rather than constituting an exceptional case. The sexy publishing imprints that once titillated were now part of readers' daily lives.

Even today, sex remains a common component in many, perhaps even most, romantic sub-genres and publisher imprints. In contrast, romances that do not include explicit content may be labeled in ways that set them apart and make them easier for interested readers to find. Terms like inspirational or sweet typically signal much less explicit content. Words like spice, heat, and erotic appear more casually on book covers and content descriptions across many romance sub-genres. Additional sub-category labels like ménage, m/m, BDSM, etc., often flag content that might be getting increasingly niche or explicit.

Sex has now become a common component in many romance narratives. However, it was not until the 1990s that the limits of romance's sexual content began to be significantly renegotiated again. Much like before, the trend began away from core romance publishers, starting this time with the marketing of soft-core and erotic material to female audiences. While this content may not be remarkably different than books labeled erotic romance today, it was not immediately associated with romance. Instead, it was organized into separate erotica or adult literature categories. New lines of "female-friendly" adult and erotic content appeared in print, on television, and in film in the late '80s and early '90s. While adult content had been available for some time, now it began to be increasingly marketed to women.

British publisher Virgin Books launched their Black Lace line in 1992. In America, Alexandria Kendall founded Red Sage Publishing in 1994, and Red Sage began publishing their now classic *Secrets* anthologies in 1995 ("Red Sage Moves to Ebook Publishing," n.d.). On the Red Sage website, the company proudly declares their place in erotic romance's pre-history: "Before there were e-books, before there was something labeled 'erotic romance,' there was Red Sage" ("About Red Sage," n.d.). Company founder Alexandria Kendall explains that the lack of sexually explicit content in romance was a gap Red Sage wanted to address. While attending Romance Writers of America conventions, Kendall "kept hearing ... authors complain about their publishing houses not letting them write the sex they wanted to write in their stories" ("Red Sage Moves to Ebook Publishing," n.d.). Essentially, Red Sage began as a way of creating space for this kind of work.

These more sexual publishing lines in the 1990s appeared in tandem with a wave of soft-core film and television content in America, content also aimed at women. A cycle of soft-core featurettes appeared on premium cable in the early '90s (Andrews, 2006, p. 5). Shows like *The Red Shoe Diaries* (Showtime, 1992) and *Women: Stories of Passion* (Showtime, 1996) positioned themselves as a new kind of female-friendly soft-core programming. Each series focused primarily on female protagonists and heavily promoted their use of women writers and directors.[1]

This influx of adult content aimed at women signals a larger shift happening during the 1990s. Adult content was expanding its market presence and producers were working harder to attract female customers. The kinds of erotic literature being offered by Red Sage and Black Lace gave female readers content that was portable and discreet, but that also could be found more easily at an area bookstore. In moving erotic content from adult video stores and men's magazine racks into television sets and bookstores, erotica was becoming more domesticated (Juffer, 1998).

During this period of the '90s, the labeling of content as soft-core, adult, or erotic signals that a line continued to be drawn between romantic and erotic content, at least for marketing purposes. Once Red Sage and Black Lace began publishing, however, this line seems to fade. Black Lace and Red Sage had ties to the romance industry. Their books were typically marketed as erotica, but frequently included classic romantic elements and themes.

Whether or not this erotic content should be associated with romance was a subject of great debate. In 1996, popular romance web forum and review site *All About Romance* (*AAR*) began hosting regular discussions on the topic. Site founder Laurie Gold observed that "books written by authors such as Thea Devine, Susan Johnson, and Bertrice Small become more erotica than romance" ("At the Back Fence Issue #16," 1996). This prompted her to ask readers:

> Do you like where some of these sexually adventurous authors are leading us? Should they move beyond mainstream romance and have their own category of erotic romance...? Are these authors' books truly even romances or are they erotic fiction, historical erotica or something else altogether? ["At the Back Fence Issue #16," 1996].

In these discussions, members of the *AAR* community actively question and negotiate the boundaries between romantic and erotic content. In several subsequent newsletters, debate on which kinds of content can or cannot be considered romantic continues. *AAR* continued to collect and archive these "Reader Rants about Sexuality" on their website through the year 2000.

Responses from readers were varied and often quite polarized. Nonetheless, more sexual content kept coming from publishers. Well-known romance authors like Susan Johnson and Bertrice Small, both already associated with the hot historicals of the 1970s, continued to publish and push content limits during this time. Johnson, an American author who had been writing for Playboy Press, was recruited to write for Bantam Books in the '90s (Interview with Susan Johnson, 2013). By 1995, Bantam was marketing Johnson to American readers with phrases like "the queen of erotic, exciting romance" on the cover and callingher book *Brazen* a "sizzlingly erotic new novel" (Johnson, 1995). The marketing language on *Brazen's* cover shows the terms erotic and romance slowly coming closer together. And yet, this was precisely the kind of connection that was being debated by members of the romance community online in the late '90s and early 2000s.

Next, another New York publisher, Kensington, began to show interest in testing more erotic content on readers. The company approached Johnson and asked her to write for them instead of Bantam (Interview with Susan Johnson, 2013). Johnson moved over to Kensington and, in 1999, Kensington published *Captivated*, an anthology featuring stories by Thea Devine, Susan Johnson, Robin Schone and Bertrice Small. This was the first in a series of anthologies from Kensington explicitly labeled as "tales of erotic romance" (Johnson et al., 1999). Johnson even recalls debate within Kensington at this time over whether they would dare to "put the word erotic on the cover" (Interview with Susan Johnson, 2013).

When the *Captivated* anthology became a success, Kate Duffy, Kensington's editorial director, predicted to *Publisher's Weekly* that the next big trend in romance was going to be "anything but sweet" (cited in Rosen, 1999, p. 42). Duffy declared, "What I want to read is erotic romance. We're going hot, hot, hot" (cited in Rosen, 1999, p. 42). The company quickly worked to capitalize on this prediction. In 2001, Kensington introduced Brava, a publishing line which promised readers "the best in erotic romantic fiction" (Ramsdell, 2001, p. 153).[2]

Like the sexier Red Sage and Black Lace novels of the '90s, Kensington's publications kept sparking debate among romance readers and writers. In a 1999 review on *The Romance Reader* website, Linda Mowery proclaimed that "[t]hese stories not only push the envelope, they rip it to shreds" (Mowery, 1999). Next, as Kensington prepared to publish Robin Schone's *The Lady's Tutor*, Schone published her essay "Masturbation, Wanton Women, & Other Romance No-Nos" on the *AAR* website (reproduced at "Robin Schone: A Writer Rants About Sexuality," n.d.). Schone argues that explicit erotic content is an important tool for writers. She states:

> Surely there is a place for controversy in romance. Surely there is room for erotica as well as inspirational. For drama as well as lighthearted comedies. For reality as well as fantasy. Masturbation. Oral sex. Anal sex. Sex acts that are not always performed with body parts. These are great tools to advance a plot and develop character. ["Robin Schone: A Writer Rants About Sexuality," n.d.].

This time, debate within the *AAR* community was so heated that the online news website *Salon* eventually published an article on the discussion and the new publications (Gracen, 1999).

During this period, *AAR* was a forum that attracted romance readers, publishers and authors. Their comments were brought together by the site's editor Laurie Gold to represent various perspectives across the romance community. This debate was never clearly composed of one set of stakeholders versus another (for example, publishers versus readers). Instead, there were many different views on the new directions Kensington was pushing romance in. This is also indicative of the different types of romance available on the market at the time, as well as the different comfort levels with the erotic that the romance genre generally accommodates. What is not clear, however, is if nationality or location had any influence on these opinions. Much of this content was being published first in the United States. As an online community, however, *AAR* had the ability to reach English-language romance readers around the world. How quickly did these titles circulate around the globe? What were they marketed as overseas? These are questions I am unable to answer here, but further research would allow romance scholars to trace the "erotic romance" label more precisely and add further nuance to the analysis of online discussions.

While Kensington's new erotic romance publications were particular catalysts for debate online, Harlequin, St. Martins and Berkley also began testing out steamier content during this period. Harlequin's Temptation line, first started in 1984 as a response to the more explicit contemporary romances at that time, introduced a special series called Blaze in 1997 ("Harlequin Temptation Blaze," n.d.). Flagging its content for readers via a special series logo and often accompanied by images of flames on the cover, the Blaze series contained Harlequin's most explicit content to date. Over the next few years, Blaze became so successful that Harlequin announced in 2000 that they were making the series its own imprint (Rosen, 2000, p. 44). Then, in 2005, Harlequin ceased publishing new Temptation titles entirely ("Harlequin Temptation," n.d.). Blaze had, essentially, taken over the imprint it originally emerged from, and became Harlequin's new iteration of steamy content. Two other New York-based publishers, St. Martins and Berkley, got involved as well. Starting in 1999, St. Martins tested a series of sexier anthologies, starting with *Naughty, Naughty,* and Berkley's Seduction line was launched in 2000 (Rosen, 2000, p. 44).

The larger publishers were still moving carefully around the term "erotic," however. To this day, many publishers draw a line between their erotic romances and erotica. For example, while the writing guidelines for Harlequin's Blaze titles call for "fully described love scenes along with a high level of fantasy, playfulness and eroticism," the guidelines continue on to emphasize that "Harlequin Blaze is not ... Erotica. While our books are very sensual, they deliver on the Harlequin promise of one hero, one heroine and an implied committed relationship at the end" ("Writing Guidelines: Harlequin Blaze," 2012). Harlequin's caution seems to be due, in part, to the company's size and the various romance readers it wants to reach. For example, Harlequin has had problems getting Christian bookstores to carry their lines of Steeple Hill inspirational romances (first launched in 1997) because of these booksellers' belief that the company's overall publications are "too racy" (Mantell, 2002, p. 42).

These kinds of publisher balancing acts affect how larger and older publishers like Harlequin organize and market their products for readers.

They lead some publishers to initiate changes with extreme caution. Within digital markets, however, traditional companies compete with digital publishers who do not need to manage so many different audiences and concerns. Digital publishers are typically smaller, selling particular niches of romance directly to readers. Also important, digital publications do not require the same upfront costs as print, reducing the financial risks a publisher faces when publishing less conventional material.

While the "erotic romance" label had already begun to circulate by the early 2000s, at this time larger and more risk averse publishers still hesitated to push content too far. This reluctance provided an opportunity (and an incentive) for smaller digital publishers to explore the erotic aspects of romance even further. This is the publishing environment traditional print publishers faced in the early 2000s as they slowly added more explicit publishing lines.

The Growth of Digital Publishing and the Roman/tica Market

Web-based publishers began to appear in increasing numbers in the late '90s. However, this did not initially lead to dramatic changes in publishing platforms and sales. In its 1998 "ROMstats Report," the Romance Writers of America counted just 95 e-published titles for the year, which constituted a mere 4.8 percent of romances on the market (Hall, 1998). In 2002, however, the RWA announced that a variety of e-book formats were being offered by all major print publishers (Hall, 2003). Availability was increasing, but actual sales numbers remained low.

Romance's e-book sales remained modest until 2006 when, suddenly, the numbers doubled (Romance Writers of America, 2007). At this time, several important technological changes occurred: the International Digital Publishing Forum established .epub as a standard e-book format, Sony debuted its Sony Reader, and Amazon followed with the Kindle in 2007. These changes gave e-books the technological and market support they needed to thrive.

Although 2006 and 2007 were important years for digital publishing, romance had already been building a presence online for some time. As a popular genre with a proven audience, romance was important to many early web-based publishers. Hard Shell Word Factory, Fiction Works, and Dreams Unlimited were all early e-publishers selling romances at least as early as 1998 (Hall, 1998).

Like Silhouette grabbing up rejected American authors in the early 80s, rejections from publishers in the 90s and early 2000s seem to have nudged many authors toward online publication. In a 1999 interview, Hard Shell Word Factory owner Mary Z. Wolfe cited freedom from strict publisher guidelines as one reason for their success attracting authors ("But What She Really Wants to Do is Write," 1999). Wolfe explained, "[w]e have some wonderful books that I'm sure print editors practically cried at having to turn down, not because they weren't written well enough, but because they were too 'different,' ... or just didn't fit comfortably enough into that publisher's line" ("But What She Really Wants to Do is Write," 1999).

Tina Engler, founder of the successful Ellora's Cave website, cites similar factors motivating the start of her company. In the '90s, Engler's writing was rejected by publishers explaining that the writing was strong but "too racy" ("About Ellora's Cave," n.d.). Engler founded Ellora's Cave, in part, because it was a way for her to sell her own work. For authors at the time who were unable to break into publishing through the traditional routes and had manuscripts in hand, web-based publishers quickly became an alternate route to publication.

While the current erotic romance cycle was facilitated by publishers like Black Lace and Red Sage and by Kensington's marketing of erotic romance, early digital publishers were able to push explicit content even further. The comments from Wolfe and Engler indicate that manuscripts were still being rejected as too risky in the late '90s and early 2000s. Smaller online shops could offer niche categories and racier content. Today, the erotic romance label is applied to an ever-expanding array of content online. Sub-categories for erotic romance now include: ménage, BDSM, GLBT, paranormal, interracial, erotic horror, western, older women/younger man, cross-dressing, steampunk.... The list goes on and on.

Digital publishing is also affecting the diversity of romance's relationships. Smaller GLBT, women's and feminist presses have been selling same-sex romances and erotica for years. However, in brick and mortar shops, lower sales numbers limited the availability of these products. Online, however, there's less competition for shelf space and prominent store placement. Large web retailers simply add product listings to their database and coordinate the distribution of products. Websites like Goodreads also help readers find more niche content. Not only is a broader array of stories more accessible online; significantly, these titles often appear in search results alongside more traditional heterosexual romances, disrupting the boundaries between once distinct market categories.

The Internet has also had a major impact on the ways romance authors interact with readers. Throughout the '70s, '80s and '90s, publishers served as a buffer between writers and readers, guiding authors toward content that they felt had the best chance of selling well and pulling authors away from less marketable stories. Similarly, authors were dependent on publishers to market their books: in particular, paying for advertisements and (for a lucky few) prominent displays in bookstores to help make readers aware of new content. In the '90s, authors quickly realized that doing self-promotion online was a way to reach out to readers directly and boost their own sales. By 1997, many romance authors, including well-established American authors Nora Roberts and Debbie Macomber, had begun using websites and online newsletters to communicate directly to readers (Pack, 1997).

Authors in the '90s may have also felt additional pressure to get online and promote themselves. In the early '90s, the "majority of romances ... [were] sold in supermarkets, drugstores, variety stores and mass merchandisers" (Schulhafer, 1994, p. 29). This market was mainly supplied by independent distributors (IDs), "whose primary business is the distribution of dated magazines and periodicals" (1994, p. 29). In 1994, IDs distributed 56.1 percent of romance novels (1994, p. 29). By 1996, however, the independent distributors had begun to consolidate. This lead to "greater returns, less rack space for new authors and intensified competition ... to get books into the slots allotted to the genre" (Mantell, 1996, p. 40). Romance sales during this time continued to grow overall, but "[b]uyers, suppliers and consumers" were more interested in bigger name authors—essentially, guaranteed sellers (1996, p. 41). This left new and mid-list authors in more precarious positions. As the print market continues to fluctuate globally, consolidation within the independent distributors, major bookstore chains, and other mass merchandisers is affecting the success of mid-list authors with larger publishing houses.

Discussion regarding the plight of the romance mid-list has been going on in the pages of *Publisher's Weekly* and on websites like *All About Romance* since the mid–'90s.[3] However, digital publishing seems to be dramatically changing writers' options. This leads directly back to Carolyn Jewel's prediction of a romance "revolution" that opened this essay (Jewel, 2013). The ongoing precariousness of authors' positions with traditional publishers influences the revolution currently underway. Authors, Jewel explains, are no longer accepting the contracts they are offered by major publishers. They often have better options online and they know it.

> The mid-list is walking. I'm not sure it matters, though. Yet. There are still enough writers looking to break in that I don't think publishers are in any

danger of not being able to find books to publish. Yet. Publishers increasingly look to self-publishers as the new slush pile [Jewel, 2013].

Jewel's comments, and her repeated use of the term "yet," signal an unresolved question regarding the future of romance publishing and the growth of erotic romance as a sub-genre. Will this period of disequilibrium come to a close? Will the current changes in romance reach their climax? And, will the genre resettle into equilibrium afterward?

Given the many previous surfacings of the erotic in romance, it is clear that shifting sexual norms often produce gaps which smaller publishers can try to fill. As seen in the '70s and '90s, when particular types of sexual content prove to be successful, publishers are able to adapt their existing publications in response and address a now recognized "need" in the market. After a time, this content becomes more normalized. However, this game of catch-up, as well as its ebb and flow, was particularly bound up with print and the costs involved with circulating physical books. Today's publishing environment may no longer enable the same cycles of disequilibrium and equilibrium. Instead, as niche products increasingly attract readers online, rapid category shuffling and genre expansion may constitute the new status quo for popular culture.

Analyzing romance publishing in the 1970s and early '80s, Carol Thurston argues that the erotic content in the '70s initiated a period of disequilibrium in romance. Thurston claims that periods of market disequilibrium are often initiated by individual companies and small systemic changes. These are connected to broader social, economic, and technological shifts. But Thurston outlined a process that inevitably settled. In this paradigm, new content and methods are reincorporated into the whole, new norms are established, and the market returns to equilibrium (Thurston, 1987).

Compared to the periods of disequilibrium of the past, today's romance market is a near riot of options in terms of sub-genres, kinks, and writing quality. At this point, there are so many different digital publishers, and so many ways for authors to publish, it is nearly impossible to map the boundaries of the romance genre today. Within this environment, what constitutes an equilibrium? As the new slush pile for large publishing houses, digital sales have become something major publishers can watch and use to identify content suitable for print as well as for translation and international circulation. Digital publishing facilitates the constant "discovery" of unaddressed content categories and new voices in romance. This seems, at least on the surface, to trigger an expansion of the kinds of intimate relationships and sexual fantasies that are acknowledged as "romantic." It may be more accurate, however, to describe today's romance genre as a series of intersecting markets and sub-genres, with particular titles and authors making their way from one layer to another and from one reading community to another.

Digital publishing does not require the same degree of market safety for a publisher to invest in an author. It also does not rely as heavily on clearly bounded sub-categories to test and market content. The database driven models of bookselling seen on sites like Amazon.com facilitate the blending of romance categories and audiences which were once carefully isolated from one another. Coupled with social tagging features that allow readers to tag, list, and organize their own genre and sub-genre categories, the ways the romance genre is rendered up to individual readers on an online bookstore looks very different than the pre-determined selections of romance paperbacks available at the local bookstore or in a pharmacy's magazine section. Sub-categories, the publisher constructed silos of the past, may continue to guide readers toward new content. However, digital interfaces simultaneously support and break down these categories through user-generated searches, tag browsing, and algorithmically generated recommendation lists.

These interfaces significantly change the ways readers encounter new content. It may make it easier for romance publishers and authors to represent various forms of intimacy in romance, facilitating an ongoing expansion of romance's erotic boundaries in ways that print could not. However, digital publishing is also becoming a production zone that continually tests broader acceptance of certain types of relationships. Scored and tracked in databases, genre sub-categories and reading audiences are assigned ranks and market values. These numbers then determine if and how content is made visible to Internet users. These rankings also shape which content is picked up for the broader market, translated, and allowed to circulate globally.

All of this raises significant questions about the future of romance and how it is studied. Genres are shaped as much by cultural norms and capital as they are by aesthetics. How do we begin to explore the social limits of genres in a production environment that is designed to circumvent boundaries and enables so many versions of romance and of the erotic? What are the long-term implications of this for the ways that romance is defined and organized?

Rather than slower cycles of disruption followed by reintegration and calm, we may now be seeing new types of stratification and siloing within popular culture. In this publishing environment, there are tiers forming between individual authors, smaller digital-only publishers, and larger global digital and print marketplaces. At the individual level, online publications come out quickly and the range of content is broad. However, these titles may only ever be seen by a small niche of readers.

We need to think about the broader implications these layers of niche and mass content have for the representation of desire and sexual fantasy in broader media culture. How does the current system construct silos for romantic and erotic content? Simply because a greater array of material might be found online by individuals in the know (or with the right cookies and trackers in their web browsers) does not mean this content can be said to be circulating freely or be readily available. How are rankings determined in today's review-saturated websites? What role do aesthetic critique and discussions of "quality" versus "amateur" writing play in shoring up norms and reinforcing older stigmas on romance and female desire? Which types of fantasies are permitted to flow outward, circulating globally beyond the English language market? What constitutes "market value" in this environment? Also, when new forms of erotic content are "discovered" by the media, how are they represented? Are they strange phenomena to be marveled at or are they treated as natural and unsurprising aspects of popular culture? Does the origin point for a text play any role in a book or author's ability to gain broad recognition?

These are just some of the critical questions that need to be asked in relation to romance, erotic romance, and digital publishing today. It seems, for the moment, that expansion and genre hybridity are central elements in the new status quo. Writers continue to experiment with new kinks and new niches, and push the boundaries of what the "erotic" in erotic romance refers to. This has the potential to open up new possibilities for romance and the expression of desire, but just how broadly are these titles able to circulate and what framework for cultural production are we watching unfold?

Notes

1. For more on this trend see Juffer, 1998; Backstein, 2001; Andrews, 2006; Martin, 2007.

2. Many thanks to Sarah Frantz for her help collecting images of the original covers from these novels.

3. For more on this see: 'At the Back Fence Issue #10'; Mantell, 1996.

Refiguring Penetration in Women's Erotic Fiction[1]

Amalia Ziv

Ever since Ancient Greek civilization, Western culture has regarded subjecthood as premised on bodily autonomy, and bodily autonomy as incompatible with sexual penetrability.[2] In the modern state, where the body of the citizen is no longer seen to represent the body politic, and where women have achieved full citizenship, penetrability is no longer seen to conflict with political subjecthood, but the conception of sexual penetration as antithetical to sexual subjectivity endures. This conception finds expression most notoriously in mainstream heterosexual porn—in which penetration often figures as an act of domination or humiliation, and women are reviled for "wanting" or "needing" penetration—but also in diverse theoretical writings, such as those of Georges Bataille, Leo Bersani, and Andrea Dworkin, the latter of whom both provides a rich record of the pejorative significations of sexual penetration across a broad range of cultural spheres, and endorses the notion that penetration is incompatible with subjecthood.[3]

This enduring sense of sexual penetration as inimical to subjecthood presents a significant stumbling block for regarding women as sexual subjects. In this essay, I would like to examine the ways in which erotic fiction by women inspired by the vision of pro-sex feminism tackles the issue of sexual penetration and resignifies its dominant cultural meanings. I begin by situating erotic fiction by women in the context of the project of feminist porn and underscoring this project's preoccupation with the problem of female sexual subjectivity. I want to suggest that many feminist discussions of pornography tend to foreclose the radical possibilities of pornographic material because they fail to question the dominant conceptualization of subjecthood as antithetical to penetration. The erotic writing which I then go on to analyze does much to challenge this conceptualization, and thus invites us to think again about the radical potential of porn.

The 1980s saw the emergence (mostly in the U.S. but in the U.K. and elsewhere too) of a new and intense engagement by women with the field of sexual representation—both, increasingly, as consumers of explicit materials, and as makers of erotic fiction, sexual imagery, and video porn, who appropriated the discourse of pornography with the aim of changing women's relation to sexuality and providing an alternative to mainstream porn.[4] This wave of pornographic production by women went hand in hand, and at times overlapped, with women artists' growing preoccupation with the body and with sexuality, a preoccupation that had its roots already in the 1970s feminist art movement.[5] Before the advent of the Internet that created new modes of publishing and circulation, and minimized the mediation between authors and their public, erotic fiction by women was published usually in the form of anthologies, such as *Herotica, Best Women's Erotica,* or *Best Lesbian Erotica.* Such collections came out of feminist and LGBT presses like Cleis or Alyson books, and were available not only in women's and gay bookstores but on wider distribution as well. This kind of literary production is closely linked to feminist pro-sex and anti-censorship activism and writing, which sprang up in the 1980s in response to the feminist anti-porn movement. Indeed, the editors of the recently published *Feminist Porn Book* even prefer to speak of a forty-year-long *feminist porn movement* that unites "thinkers, viewers, and makers, grounded in their desire to use pornography to explore new sexualities in representation" (Penley et al., 2013, p. 13). Feminist porn is for them both "a genre and a political vision," or a genre motivated by a distinctive political vision (p. 18). And indeed, many authors and editors of women's (or lesbian, or queer) erotica, such as Susie Bright, Carol Queen, Pat Califia, and Tristan Taormino, are equally known as pro-sex activists.

There are also other, more commercial, venues for erotica by women that emerged in the 1990s, for example, the Rosebud imprint of lesbian erotica by Masquerade Books, and Virgin Books' Black Lace imprint of "erotic fiction by women for women" launched in 1993 and active to this day. In her discussion of the latter, Esther Sonnet argues that while this series situates itself against pornography created by men for male consumption and claims to provide a woman-defined space for the enjoyment of sexually explicit material, in fact its address to its public is grounded in a post-feminist discourse of personal empowerment that regards sexual pleasure as a form of capitalist consumer entitlement, and cuts off sexuality from the realm of the political (Sonnet, 1999). Further, she argues that while the series "announces itself as a 'safe' space for a constructive revisioning of pornography for women readers," this promise rests on an essentialist and naïve notion of female authorship as guaranteeing "female authenticity."[6] Both she and Simon Hardy, who analyzes the sexual scenarios in a sample of Black Lace books, note the predominance of narratives of surrender and abnegation of responsibility for sexual pleasure. Also, Hardy observes that in many of the fictions a journey of sexual exploration leads to "crossing a threshold of submission, in which the woman's social self must yield to the natural 'truth' residing in her body" (Hardy, 2001, p. 442).

I agree with Hardy and Sonnet's critique that female authorship alone is not enough for erotic fiction to count as a feminist intervention, and that the discourse of female authenticity can serve to uphold conventional erotic meanings. However, I strongly contest the implication in Sonnet's article that the project of female erotica is essentially a "post-feminist" one.[7] An investment in the production and consumption of erotica need not signify a "return to feminine pleasures," and need not be grounded in a sense that feminist goals have already been achieved thus opening the way for women to redefine their relation to sexuality in terms of consumer entitlement (Sonnet, 1999, p. 170). While this may be the case with the Black Lace series (with which I am not familiar), erotic fiction by women, especially when it is more directly informed by feminist ideology, is often engaged not only in reclaiming the field of sexuality for women or asserting women's right to sexual pleasure but also in redefining female sexuality.

I would suggest that part of the project of feminist literary erotica and feminist porn in general has to do with the struggle to construct women as sexual subjects. Women's partial exclusion from the sphere of sexuality and their traditional portrayal as lacking autonomous desire and sexual agency make it difficult to conceive women as sexual subjects. The problems arise around the dominant constructions of sexual desire and sexual agency, which are congruent with normative conceptions of male sexuality but conflict with those of female sexuality. Desire is normally understood as desire *for an object* (rather than desire for a setting or a script or auto-erotic desire), desire to *possess* the object (rather than to be possessed), and to *act upon* the object (rather than be acted upon). Agency is identified with the active pole in the active/passive or active/receptive divide (receptivity being usually conflated with passivity). If "fucking" is regarded as the ultimate expression of sexual agency, the action denoted by the verb "to fuck" is usually construed as transitive and unilateral, a transitivity of which women can only be the object, not the subject. Finally, a disruption of bodily boundaries, that is, sexual penetration, is regarded as antithetical to subjectivity.

I ought to clarify here my usage of the term "sexual subject." Hardy observes in relation to the Black Lace series that it may be seen to establish a female subject both by providing a platform for women's authorship of erotica, and by constructing its readers as "sovereign recipient[s] of individual rights, including the right to the pleasure of consuming explicit sexual representations" (Hardy, 2001, p. 449). As he notes, if we understand "subject" simply as the interpreter and/or producer of symbolic meaning, then women's new positioning in the field of erotic meaning as authors and addressees sets them up as subjects. Hardy sees women, as a social category, as in the process of becoming erotic subjects, and raises the question of whether this emergent female subject can produce new patterns of erotic meaning. I, on the other hand, do not see sexual subjectivity as residing merely in women's relation to erotic discourse. Rather, I understand the very notion of sexual subjectivity as a discursive construction—that is, as itself part of the realm of erotic meaning—hence as amenable to resignification by women in the field of sexual representation. In other words, as women struggle to construct themselves as sexual subjects they need to overcome the conceptual hurdles posed by the dominant constructions of desire and agency, and by doing so they resignify the very notion of sexual subjectivity.

In this essay, I examine how erotic fiction by women tackles one of these hurdles—the view of penetration as incompatible with sexual subjectivity. Yet, before going on to conduct close readings of erotic stories, I would like to dwell in more detail on the radical feminist analysis of sexual penetration as it was developed by Andrea Dworkin. While Dworkin's work may seem dated and too "extreme" even to present-day anti-porn feminists,[8] she is nevertheless one of the central voices of anti-porn feminism. In this sense, she exerted a formative influence on anti-anti-porn or pro-sex feminism, which emerged as a response to the anti-porn analysis. Secondly, in her book *Intercourse* (1987), the most sustained—and notorious—feminist critique of heterosexual intercourse, Dworkin offered what is probably the most elaborate and poignant contemporary articulation of the view of penetration as antithetical to subjecthood. I believe that this articulation is important for gaining an understanding of the nature of the problem that feminist erotica is up against.

Intercourse is concerned with the cultural meanings of heterosexual intercourse "in a man-made world," that is, under conditions of male domination. Dworkin extracts these meanings from a broad range of cultural texts—fiction, religious and legal literature, and sexological texts—as well as through a more general cultural analysis. From all these sources she derives an equation of intercourse with possession, domination, ownership, invasion, and violation, entailing for the woman a loss of identity, integrity, and privacy.

Dworkin is ostensibly recording cultural meanings—intercourse as it is "commonly written about and comprehended"—but she is also making claims about the experiential reality of both participants in the act: "alone together, a man fucks a woman; he possesses her; the act is an act of possession in and of itself; the man and the woman experience it as such" (1987, p. 79). And similarly,

> women feel the fuck—when it works, when it overwhelms—as possession; and feel possession as deeply erotic.... And therefore, being possessed is phenomenologically real for women; and sex itself is an experience of diminishing self-possession, an erosion of self [Dworkin, 1987, p. 67].

This equation of male-defined cultural meanings and women's subjective experience of sexuality is explained by the fact that, in a male-dominated society, these meanings both echo women's total social experience of being dominated, and inform and saturate actual sexual practice. They are transmitted via this practice, thereby shaping women's sexuality, and forging intimate links between the experience of sexual pleasure and the sense of being possessed.

Dworkin draws attention to the political dimension of intercourse—its "exemplary" function as an expression, assertion, and rationalization of male dominance, its role in communicating to women their inferior status. She underscores the highly codified and regulated nature of this allegedly private act, thus revealing society's role both in prescribing the practice and backing its meanings. Yet while, on the one hand, she seems to attribute the cultural meanings of intercourse to the social reality of male power, on the other hand, she voices the suspicion that the act itself is incompatible with women's freedom and equality, and further—might even be "a basis of or a key to women's continuing social and sexual inequality" (1987, p. 128). Efforts to reform the circumstances that surround intercourse, she warns, still fail to "address the question of whether intercourse itself can be an expression of sexual equality" (1987, pp. 126–27). This suggestion that intercourse is un-amenable to reform because it is inherently hierarchical and opposed to women's humanity, runs counter to Dworkin's initial line of argument that exposes the arbitrariness of equating intercourse with the man's possession of the woman:

> Remarkably it is not the man who is considered possessed in intercourse, even though he (his penis) is buried inside another human being.... He is not possessed even though he is terrified of never getting his cock back because she has it engulfed inside her, and it is small compared with the vagina around it pulling it in and pushing it out.... He is not possessed even though he rolls over dead and useless afterward, shrunk into oblivion: this does not make him hers by virtue of the nature of the act [Dworkin, 1987, p. 65].[9]

In this passage, Dworkin underscores the tendentiousness of the normative reading of intercourse, and seems to suggest that bodily acts are amenable to divergent and competing interpretations, the prevailing interpretation being the one that is backed by social power. However, in a later chapter, she does select one feature of this corporeal interaction—the penetration of the woman's body, and *not* the anxiety-evoking engulfment of the penis—as paramount for defining the meaning and significance of the interaction, and sees it as bearing an inherent meaning integral to the bodily experience itself.

The disruption of corporeal boundaries is described by Dworkin as essentially invasive and abusive, incompatible with the standard of humanity and citizenship:

> A human being has a body that is inviolate; and when it is violated, it is abused. A woman has a body that is penetrated in intercourse: permeable, its corporeal solidness a lie....
>
> She, a human being, is supposed to have a privacy that is absolute; except that she, a woman, has a hole between her legs that men can, must, do enter. This hole, her hole is synonymous with entry [Dworkin, 1987, p. 122].

Dworkin is right of course to object to the definition of women as made to be entered—their anatomy prescribing their "use" (while the rectum, the bodily orifice common to both sexes, is not regarded as "synonymous with entry"). She also rightly criticizes the double standard of humanity, according to which what is considered a fundamental violation of bodily integrity for human beings in general is regarded as not only the "normal use" of women but also the affirmation of their human potential. However, there are questions to be asked concerning the equation of bodily integrity with impermeability, an equation that relies on an image of the human body as a closed unit, with every disruption of its contours spelling danger and disaster. For the construction of the female body as a hole, Dworkin substitutes a construction no less imaginary and normative of the properly human body as a hermetically closed unit.

If one's sense of integrity, autonomy, agency, and self determination all depend on an experience of bodily inviolability, understood as impermeable boundaries, then genital penetration inevitably has destructive consequences for women's subjectivity. It also has inevitable implications for women's political status, leading Dworkin to ask, "Can an occupied people—physically occupied inside, internally invaded—be free" (1987, p. 124).

In fact, Dworkin's equation of intercourse with possession is subject to two major critiques: 1. that by affirming that penile penetration in and of itself *is* indeed possession and violation, that is, that it achieves in fact all that dominant ideology attributes to it, she is unwittingly subscribing to the heroics of a phallic mystique; and 2. that her view of penetration as loss of self relies on a masculinist model of the subject. This latter critique is directed by Drucilla Cornell (1991) at Catherine MacKinnon, Dworkin's partner in the battle against pornography, who acknowledges Dworkin's influence on her thinking on sexuality. In response to MacKinnon's rhetorical question "whether a good fuck is any compensation for getting fucked," Cornell poses the opposite question: "but why is it the end of the world 'to be fucked'?" (Cornell, 1991, p. 153). Her answer is that the catastrophic view of being fucked is a specifically male one, stemming from the fear of having the attributes of a woman in a system of gender opposition and hierarchy. In such a system, the subject is defined 'from the side of the masculine,' as seeking freedom rather than intimacy, and the body is figured as impermeable and imperiled. It is this masculine notion of subjectivity, claims Cornell, that MacKinnon—following Dworkin—adopts:

> Under MacKinnon's view of the individual or the subject, the body inevitably figures as the barrier in which the self hides and guards itself as the illusionary weapon—the phallus—in which "it" asserts itself against others. But why figure the body in this way? Why not figure the body as a threshold or as a position of receptivity? As receptivity the body gives access. To welcome accessibility is to affirm *openness* to the other. To shut oneself off, on the other hand, is *loss* of sensual pleasure ... it is only if one accepts a masculine view of the self, of the body and of carnality, that "being fucked" *appears* so terrifying [Cornell, 1991, p. 154, italics in the original].

MacKinnon and Dworkin select the wrong target for attack when they reject the practice itself rather than its cultural significations, thus embracing a masculine model of subjectivity that upholds autonomy and impermeability over intimacy and accessibility.

Dworkin impugns intercourse as a phenomenological whole, without attempting to separate the bodily practice from the political context in which it takes place or from the cultural meanings that inform and shape it, and also without subjecting the corporeal practice itself to more careful scrutiny. Consequently, she fails to make some not so negligible distinctions regarding what it is exactly that she indicts in the practice known as heterosexual intercourse. Dworkin refers occasionally to the hierarchical topography of the missionary position, but rejects the sexual position of the woman on top as a fake alternative which does not affect the basic power relations of the act; she mentions Shere Hite's suggestion of intercourse without thrusting (presumably to minimize the invasive and aggressive dimension of the act) but dismisses that too as one of the utopian programs for reforming intercourse that women conceive. Her text indicates quite clearly that she regards penetration itself to be the chief evil, but she does not specify whether the problem lies in the vulnerability that attaches to the very experience of having a bodily orifice penetrated by another person, or whether it has to do more specifically with the fact that the pleasure of the male partner is taken to be the chief motive for the act, thus turning the penetrated woman into a mere vehicle for penile pleasure. In the context of heterosexual intercourse, orthodoxly defined as the insertion of the penis into the vagina ending in ejaculation, this distinction is indeed immaterial—since penetration is tantamount to penile penetration, every other form of penetration is seen as either heralding penile penetration or imitating it. But once we move beyond the heterosexual context or even beyond the orthodox definition of heterosexual sex, the distinction between penetration as selfishly motivated or altruistically motivated, penetration as taking or as giving, does acquire significance and opens the way for rewriting the cultural significations of penetration, which Dworkin regards as immanent and immutable.

As we have seen, Dworkin's endorsement of the cultural equation of penetration with possession, violation, powerlessness, and loss of self has been contested by other feminist critics. This equation has been challenged from another direction as well, namely, pro-sex feminism and the sexual representations it gave rise to. In the remainder of this essay I examine how erotic fiction by women attempts to resignify sexual penetration. I focus on the issue of heterosexual penetration, since in lesbian sexuality the meanings of sexual penetration are considerably different. Whereas in heterosexual discourse penetration is practically synonymous with penile penetration, in a lesbian context this equation is obviously broken down. Since penile and non-penile penetration involve different balances of pleasure and power between the sexual partners, the absence of a penis of necessity effects a rearticulation of the significations of penetration. As Ann Cvetkovich points out, "if the 'top' penetrates the bottom with a penis, then the 'top's sexual pleasure might be assumed to be central. In contrast, if the 'top' penetrates with a finger, fist, dildo, or other nonorgasmic object, then the bottom might be considered to be the partner whose sexual pleasure is the primary goal" (Cvetkovich, 1995, p. 134).

It may be objected that the fantasy positions associated with penetration are unrelated to the anatomy of the participants, hence that the meanings of penetration in a lesbian context are not radically affected by the absence of genital pleasure for the penetrator. While I agree that sexual pleasure cannot be reduced to genital pleasure, that the phantasmatic dimension is central to sexuality, and that lesbian sexuality is inflected by the heterosexual imaginary, nevertheless one mustn't lose sight of the embodied character of sexual experience. The presence or absence of genital pleasure for the penetrator cannot but have some kind of psychic registration.

The fact that penile penetration is at least largely *assumed* to be motivated by and geared toward the genital pleasure of the penetrator gives scope to the meanings—both cultural and lived—of objectification and abuse that attach to it. In a lesbian context, on the other hand, the structural impossibility of penetration with an "orgasmic object" predefines penetration as altruistically rather than selfishly motivated, which taken together with the lack of gender hierarchy between the partners eliminates most of the problematic significations of heterosexual penetration and opens the way for radical rearticulations.[10] Here, however, I want to explore how women can resignify penetration even on the terrain of heterosexual sexuality.

My chosen corpus is one of the classic series of women's erotica, *Herotica*, first published by the independent Down There Press, and subsequently taken up by Plume, a division of Penguin books. The series comprises seven volumes to date, but I will focus on the first three, published in 1988, 1992, and 1994, and edited by Susie Bright (the second volume was co-edited with Joani Blank).[11] Bright is an author, editor, and sex educator, and one of the figures most identified with pro-sex feminism. In the volumes she compiled Bright professes an editorial policy of selecting erotic stories that are "female-centric" (Bright, 1991, p. x). For her, the two hallmarks of women's erotica are, first, the narration of the sexual encounter from the female protagonist's point of view, that is, a focus on *her* sexual experience; and second, what she names "femmechismo"—the depiction of women's sexual courage, pride, and adventurousness or, in other words, the portrayal of women as sexually powerful and agentic (Bright, 1991, pp. x–xii). The first thing to note is that in these collections penile penetration is generally demoted from its privileged status. In *Herotica 2*, for example, out of sixteen stories that feature heterosexual sex (the volume as a whole includes twenty-six stories, eight of which are about lesbian sex and two about masturbation), only nine represent penile penetration, vaginal or anal—either actual or fantasized; in the other stories, men pleasure women through oral sex and finger fucking (and even in one case toe-fucking). In two of the stories the male protagonists are even incapable of penile penetration.

Assuming that these statistics reflect not only a conscious or unconscious editorial choice, we can note a tendency in contemporary erotic writing by women to counter the prevailing cultural assumption according to which heterosexual sex equals penile penetration, or at least penile penetration is its defining core (all "the rest" counting as foreplay, unnecessary frills, concessions to female demands, or simply perversion), and female sexual gratification is incomplete without it. A first strategy for dealing with the problematic significations of penetration then is to downplay its centrality, that is, reveal penile penetration as inessential to women's sexual gratification and not defining of heterosexual sex.

In one of these stories where penile penetration does not occur, "Taking Him on a Sunday Afternoon," the woman protagonist, who initiates the sex, goes down on her boyfriend while fantasizing that *she* is anally fucking *him* with an imaginary cock.[12] In the discourse of penetration, oral sex represents a special case, since it disrupts the neat alignment of the inserter/insertee division with the active/passive binary. In oral sex it is the receptive partner (the one who takes in his/her partner's penis) who is usually the more active one.[13] Heterosexual erotic stories by women, like this one, often stress the active aspect of giving head—the sense of agency and control of another's pleasure, thus removing it from the frame of penetration and resignifying it as a form of active fucking. The active penetration fantasy in the story can be understood, then, as lending a culturally legible expression to the protagonist's sense of sexual aggression, which she finds difficult to articulate from a feminine position. Interestingly, the switch point to the fantasy occurs when she tries to insert a finger into her lover's anus, and he clinches his muscles and repulses her. It is at that moment that she fantasizes having a cock that would enable her to possess him and overcome any objection:

> The thought pops into my mind that if I had a dick ... I would wear him out. I would stay in that puckered, slippery, sex-smelling ass as often as I could. I would dominate him ... I would be the aggressor, and he could not ask sex

of me: only I would be allowed to initiate ... I would fuck him from behind ... the completion of his pleasure at my bidding alone ... his eyes closed, throat exposed ... allowing me to do with him as I chose [Michaels, 1991, p. 19].

Penile penetration is associated here with sexual aggression and domination—the power to initiate, and to control the very occurrence, duration, and form of the sex; the ability to take one's pleasure *from* the other, as well as to control the other's pleasure; and the insertee's position is posited as one of exposure and vulnerability. In the narrator's mental picture of the act, her lover is docile and submissive, and she is dominant and aggressive. In this fantasy of turning the tables, the female narrator imagines penetrating her lover with a penis as a way to possess, dominate, and overwhelm him sexually—thereby affirming the prevailing cultural meanings of penetration. In this sense, the story has a double impact—on the one hand, it affirms women's active and aggressive desires in the context of heterosexual sex; on the other hand, in order to express these desires in a culturally legible way it has recourse to the trope of penetration, thus reinforcing its traditional cultural significations.

If one strategy is to downplay the importance of penile penetration in heterosexual sex, stories that do represent it often contest its dominant meanings and suggest alternative ones. Such is the story "Claudia's Cheeks" by Catherine Tavel (1991), in which it is the female protagonist who asks her male partner to penetrate her anally and who directs and controls the sex. As the story tells us, this instance of anal sex functions to rectify a previous traumatic experience of painful and non-consensual anal sex with an inconsiderate and brutal lover. Whereas in the early encounter between the inexperienced eighteen-year-old Claudia and her older lover, Claudia was passive, helpless, and coerced, and derived no pleasure from the act, in the later encounter she is in command and enjoys a powerful orgasm while her partner's climax receives no mention. The differences in power relations correspond to and are manifested by differences in physical position: unlike the first encounter when she was in her partner's grip, her motion restricted while he thrust into her, and her face pressed to the mattress making it difficult for her to breathe, in the second encounter it is Claudia who moves on her partner's penis while he remains motionless. And the text states that "for the first time in her life, she felt that *she* was doing the fucking and not getting fucked. And Claudia liked it. She liked it a lot" (Tavel, 1991, p. 181). Significantly, while Dworkin dismisses both the woman-on-top position, and the option of intercourse without thrusting as ways of altering the significance of penetrative sex, the story suggests that the factors of posture and movement do make a difference in terms of the experienced meaning of the act.

After describing Claudia's climax, the closing lines of the story state, "And do you know what it felt like? It felt like power. You see, Claudia had finally learned how to get on top using her bottom" (Tavel, 1991, p. 181). The depiction of being penetrated in terms of activity and power is even more striking because it is anal penetration at stake. Since anal penetration does not involve direct genital stimulation for the female partner, it is often represented in pornographic literature (and in culture in general) as abusive, sadistic and humiliating,[14] that is, as carrying to extreme the negative connotations that attach to penetration in general.[15] Hence, representing anal penetration as not only enjoyable but also empowering is a gesture that contests the penetration=violation equation by reclaiming the most infamous and abjected type of sexual penetration.

A central theme of the story is Claudia's continual objectification owing to her "Big, bouncy, beautiful ass," which is the part of her that attracts most attention from men to the neglect of her other qualities. Repeatedly subjected to a fragmenting, fetishizing gaze that often translates into a corresponding sexual practice in the men she sleeps with, Claudia nevertheless manages in the final sexual encounter to attain sexual agency. Unlike traditional male-authored pornography, "Claudia's Cheeks" does not depict its protagonist as perfectly happy with her sexual objectification, nor does it offer a utopian view of heterosexual sexuality. It does depict and problematize sexual objectification, and it does represent a particular instance of sexual penetration as abusive and violating; yet, as opposed to such an experience, it delineates the possibility of experiencing penetration as empowering even within the frame of a predominantly sexist culture.[16] Against the reified view proposed by Dworkin, which sees sexual penetration as signifying always and only possession and domination, the story suggests a more nuanced understanding of the acts that takes into account a whole array of contextual factors, such as consent, consideration, the power differential between the partners, the power balance within the act itself (who initiates and directs the act, sexual posture, freedom of movement, thrusting, etc.), and the balance of pleasure.[17]

Another story by Catherine Tavel (1994), "About Penetration," which appears in *Herotica 3*, tackles the subject of penetration from a different angle. "About Penetration" is in fact a story about penetration that does not occur, and it is through this central absence that the text discusses the meanings of sexual penetration. The text tells the story of an extra-marital affair between Diane, the protagonist, and Thomas, both married. The two, who develop a deep intimacy, have phone sex and a few spells of partial sex, especially joint masturbation, but Thomas refuses to sexually penetrate Diane "with his finger, his tongue or his penis," so as not to be unfaithful to his wife (Tavel, 1994, p. 64). Diane is tormented by this refusal but accepts it. In the closing episode of the story, Thomas agrees to meet Diane in the company of his friend, Kenny. After dining together the three go to Kenny's house, and at Thomas' prompting Diane and Kenny have sex as he watches. The text makes it clear that Kenny is acting as a proxy for Thomas, and that Diane and Thomas experience the interaction as a mediated sexual encounter between the two of them.

Thomas' refusal to penetrate Diane is presented as an attempt to avoid full commitment and loss of control. The rationale behind it is that no penetration equals no adultery. Yet Diane, who experiences his refusal as a rejection, also suspects that Thomas is enjoying the power his refusal gives him over her, and compensates himself in this way for his wife's sexual rejection of him: "it was pretty wonderful to make another woman wet, to make her squirm for you, even in her sleep, wasn't it? All that, without technically committing adultery" (Tavel, 1994, p. 66).[18] To make up for the absence of sexual penetration, Diane and Thomas' relations contain other forms of symbolic penetration. Diane has a pair of matching earrings made for Thomas and herself; to wear hers, she gets her ear pierced, and the text comments: "the piercing was intensely painful yet seemed significant." When Thomas finally agrees to accept his earring and puts it through the hole in his ear, it is "almost a religious experience" for the two of them (Tavel, 1994, p. 66). Beside this ceremonial act, the major form of penetration in the story is ocular. Diane and Thomas' mutual passion is expressed by the way they penetrate each other visually: "whenever they were alone, or even in a crowd, their eyes would bore holes through each other" (Tavel, 1994, p. 65). The exchange of gazes in the final episode is especially charged. On the one hand, it is Diane who is particularly vulnerable in this interaction: she is doubly penetrated—genitally by Kenny, and also by Thomas' gaze—and she is both physically and mentally exposed. On the other hand, she manages to dislodge Thomas from his initial impassive stance, affirm her emotional hold over him, and involve him in the interaction by looking into his eyes. The change in the power balance comes about through Diane's first orgasm, which empowers her:

> That was the moment Diane realized her own strength. She would penetrate Thomas without even touching him. She would penetrate him with her eyes and with other things. She would take him inside that way. She would use the power generated by her orgasm to pierce him [Tavel, 1994, p. 68].

The fact that she has managed to accomplish this is confirmed at the end of the story by Thomas, who admits that she has penetrated him with her heart, her mind, and her eyes.

The story thus reverses some of the meanings conventionally attached to sexual penetration—rather than being an expression of aggression, hostility, and subordination, sexual penetration is represented as an expression of intimacy and commitment, and as implying self-exposure and risk not only for the receptive partner but for the penetrating partner as well. In refusing to penetrate Diane, Thomas refuses not only to possess her but also to be possessed himself; in refusing to "take" her, he refuses to give of himself. Contrary to the picture painted by Dworkin, Thomas wields power over Diane not by fucking her but by abstaining from doing so, and it is this abstention that she experiences as cruel and aggressive.

Further, the type of erotic possession and intense emotional connection accomplished by sexual penetration can, as Diane proves, be achieved through other means too. Similarly to Claudia in "Claudia's Cheeks," Diane feels sexually empowered in a situation that on the face of it could seem humiliating or exploitative; she attains the strength that allows her to "penetrate" Thomas by making herself open and vulnerable. The story thus makes a triple statement concerning heterosexual penetration: penetration is seen as an act through which the penetrating man is possessed by the penetrated woman no less than the other way round; far from experiencing subordination, the female partner's experience is revealed to be empowering; and finally, sexual penetration is demoted from its exclusive status as the sole means of erotic and emotional possession. The story's resignification of penetration in terms of (denied) intimacy and commitment, and its valorization of sexual receptivity as openness to the other, echo Cornell's notion of the body as threshold and a position of receptivity. Like Cornell, the story figures sexual receptivity as a libidinal position that also implies a valorized ethical position: Thomas' refusal to penetrate is revealed as tantamount to an avoidance of being emotionally penetrated—a defensive stance of withdrawal from the other.

Another strategy for resignifying sexual penetration involves phantasmatic identification with gay male sexuality. This strategy is more commonly found in lesbian erotic fiction, but occasionally it can be noted in heterosexual or bisexual erotica as well. Carol Queen's "Sweating Profusely in Mérida: A Memoir" is a case in point (Queen, 1994). The text tells the story of a sex vacation that the narrator and her lover, whom the story designates only as "Boyfriend," take in the Mexican town of Mérida. Boyfriend is bisexual though his cruising efforts are directed mostly toward men, and their relationship, far from being a conventional monogamous one, revolves around sex parties and threesomes with other men. Mexico is chosen as a holiday destination owing to Boyfriend's obsession with uncircumcised men, and the assumption that Mexican men "will play with men, too ... especially if there's a woman there" (Queen, 1994, p. 191). The highlight of this vacation is an orgy with four Mexican men at the local bathhouse, the narrator being the only woman. During this session she is vaginally and orally penetrated many times until in the end the floor of the room is littered with condoms, and she has to be supported to the shower. While it is evident that she is the epicenter of the sexual encounter, and that at least for three of the men her presence is essential for them to engage in male-male sex, nevertheless she makes it clear that for her the encounter is mediated through her identification as a gay man: "I was finally in a bathhouse doing what I had always wanted to do and feeling more like a faggot than like a beautiful *gringa*" (Queen, 1994, p. 194). She notes that most of their shared sexual partners classified her as a "beautiful girlfriend," but contests the adequacy of this label remarking, "I had a feeling most men couldn't keep up with a girlfriend who was really a faggot, or a boyfriend who was really a woman, or whatever kind of fabulous anomaly I was" (p. 194). She also observes that part of the thrill of the experience for her lies in venturing into exclusively male territory—"a place no woman I knew had gone before" (p. 194).

But in what way does a phantasmatic identification with gay male sexuality resignify the sexual encounter? How is having group sex as a faggot different from having sex with a group of men as a woman? The answer seems obvious enough. First of all, group sex involving a woman and multiple men is usually associated with exploitation and coercion; and when free will is assumed on the part of the female participant she is most likely to be branded a slut, since promiscuity in women is always condemned. However, with the narrator as a "faggot," the encounter becomes one of group sex between equal status partners, eliminating the suggestion of exploitation that results from the construction of heterosexual sex as a fundamentally unequal exchange between hierarchically positioned partners.[19] Moreover, while heterosexual sexual morality evaluates promiscuity according to a double standard that censures it in women but condones or even applauds it in men, gay male sexual culture is not only based on a positive valuation of casual sex, multiple partners, and anonymous sex, but has also developed institutions specifically designed to facilitate such encounters, of which the bathhouse is one. Though the bathhouse in Mérida is not the standard gay bathhouse, and perhaps not a gay bathhouse at all—it does not exclude women, and sexual encounters seem to take place there only on a commercial basis—for the narrator it fulfils the fantasy of being in a gay bathhouse and having sex in the mode that such an institution designates. Having sex as a faggot stands for the ability to be lustful with men without opprobrium, and to evade the heterosexual construction of sex as an exchange in which the main beneficiary is the male partner.

The phantasmatic identification with gay male sexuality also works to counter the traditional connotations of sexual penetration. To understand how it does that, we need to take a brief look at the signification of sexual receptivity in contemporary gay male culture. While traditionally homosexual culture shared the equation of penetration with feminization—and accordingly the view of homosexuals as feminine—since the 1970s gay male culture has undergone a marked process of "virilization," that is, attachment to and appropriation of symbols and styles of hypermasculinity.[20] As part of this process, getting fucked and the desire to get fucked were recast in a lot of gay porn *as* masculine. Bottoming as masculine is a commonplace notion particularly in s/m or leather-oriented porn. In this kind of porn, the sexual exchange is often conceived on the model of an initiation rite, in which it is the older or otherwise senior partner—who is also the more masculine man—who fucks the younger or junior partner, thus in a sense imparting some of his masculinity to him, and "making" him (more of) a man.[21] Beside the masculinizing influences of male-male interaction in general, the penetrator's penis and his semen always function as synecdoches of his masculinity. The penetrator's semen is often conceived as the "essence" of his manhood, and its oral or anal reception by the bottom figured as a kind of communion in which this essence is internalized. Similarly, since the penis is seen to stand for the top's virility, taking it in is understood as an assimilation of his power and agency or, in other words, an assimilation of the phallus. Finally, taking in the penetrator's penis is often figured as an arduous task, which tests the insertee's endurance, self-control, and discipline, so that submitting to it successfully is itself a proof of masculinity. Thus, the refrain "take it!" so often addressed by the top to the bottom in gay porn during the sexual act conveys the compounded sense of the literal imperative to take in the penis, and the challenge to endure the rigors of penetration. The masculine construction of penetration is certainly not unique to porn, nor is it exclusive to leather culture, and can be found in various segments of gay male culture, alongside the enduring opposite construction of penetration as feminizing.

Gay male culture since the '70s has managed, then, to undermine the symbolic equation of sexual receptivity with both femininity and non-subjecthood. By drawing on this alternative symbolic construction women too can inscribe themselves as sexual subjects even when occupying the object position, and even when enjoying penetration. Most heterosexually identified women would probably not conceive themselves as assimilating the penetrating male's manhood, but they can certainly embrace the construction of bottoming as a site of sexual agency involving skill, expertise, and endurance. The narrator's boastful tone in reporting about the condom-littered floor and having to be supported to the shower displays precisely such a bottom's braggadocio.

An identification with gay male sexuality works as a phantasmatic strategy that enables women to recode their sexuality and thus gain symbolic access to sexual subjectivity. The disjuncture between anatomy or biological function and sexual aim allows the male homosexual subject to symbolically maintain sexual agency even when forfeiting phallic power. Hence, when so-called "feminine," that is, passive or receptive desires in women are mediated through a male subject position they acquire a transgressiveness that they lack when seen as biologically determined, and allow for a sense of agency predicated on the paradigm of choice implicit in gay male subjectivity, and allegedly absent from female heterosexual subjectivity.[22]

To sum up, in the stories collected in the first three volumes of the *Herotica* series, we find several different strategies for tackling the prevailing cultural meanings of penetration and the problems they pose for an attempt to construct women as sexual subjects. First, we see a de-centering of penetration in heterosexual sex through representations of women obtaining sexual gratification through various forms of non-penetrative sex with men. Secondly, as in the story "Claudia's Cheeks," we see representations of a range of experiences with sexual penetration—that run the gamut from objectification, helplessness, and abuse to a sense of power and control—depending on a variety of factors and circumstances (including posture, readiness and arousal, the partner, his level of skill and consideration, and the woman's sexual experience and ability to communicate her preferences and shape the sexual interaction according to them). The depiction of a range of experiences contests the ascription of a single, uniform and unvarying meaning to the practice and experience of penile penetration, and lays stress on the multiple elements that shape women's experience of penetration. In the context of an intimate relationship penetration is shown, as in the story "About Penetration," to function as an expression of intimacy and trust, and entail vulnerability for the penetrating partner too—so that the possession effected by the act is reinterpreted as mutual possession, the penetrator's boundaries being disrupted as well. Finally, women can resignify penetration through phantasmatic identification with gay male sexuality, which lends them access to the recoding of penetration in gay male culture. All these representational and phantasmatic strategies for contesting, supplanting, inverting, broadening, and qualifying the dominant meanings of heterosexual penetration testify both to the enduring problem that the latter pose for the project of articulating female sexual subjectivity, and to women's creativity in resisting them.

NOTES

1. An expanded version of this essay appears in Amalia Ziv, *Explicit Utopias: Rewriting the Sexual in Women's Pornography*, published in 2015 by the State University of New York Press. This version is published with permission from the State University of New York Press.

2. As David Halperin explains in his discussion of prostitution in classical Athens, the body of the male Athenian citizen was sacrosanct, protected from any kind of violation. This corporeal autonomy and integrity served as the basis of the citizen's political privileges, and any citizen who voluntarily compromised his bodily integrity, for instance by engaging in prostitution, was to be excluded from political participation. Women, even those of the citizen class, did not enjoy political citizenship (Halperin, 1990, pp. 88–104).

3. Bataille, who elaborates a notion of eroticism in which violation and self-loss are defining features, likens heterosexual penetration to ritual sacrifice: "The lover strips the beloved of her identity no less than the blood-stained priest his human or animal victim" (Bataille, 1986, p. 90). And Leo Bersani, writing in a different cultural context and from a psychoanalytically inflected perspective, celebrates the subversive force of male anal receptivity as an antidote to "the masculine ideal of proud subjectivity" (Bersani, 1987, p. 222). Andrea Dworkin's critique of heterosexual intercourse will be discussed at length shortly. It is interesting to note, however, that while she and Bersani both see the hierarchical and destructive conception of penetrative sex as lying at the root of sexism and homophobia respectively, Dworkin condemns the practice, which she sees as responsible in large part for the low status of women in patriarchal society, while Bersani suggests that the value of sex lies precisely in its negative, self-shattering aspect.

4. In the adult video industry, the 1980s gave rise to two women-owned and run companies: "Femme Productions" established in 1984 by former porn start Candida Royalle, which targeted a heterosexual female audience and set out to create porn from a woman's point of view, and "Fatal Video," established in 1985 by Nan Kinney and Debi Sundahl, that produced lesbian porn.

5. Thus, for example, Annie Sprinkle's work after she quit the mainstream porn industry blurs the boundaries between performance art or body art and alternative porn. The convergence between the projects of feminist art and feminist pornography is instantiated by the 1991 anthology *Angry Women*, that consists of interviews with feminist thinkers, writers, and performance artists, and includes among them Annie Sprinkle and Susie Bright.

6. Concurring with Sonnet, Simon Hardy notes that the discourse of the series assumes that sexual fantasy is the expression of an inner essence, ignoring "the possibility that the 'truth' the subject speaks does not really emanate from within but is prescribed by the given parameters of the existing erotic discourse" (Hardy, 2001, p. 450).

7. Sonnet writes, "post-feminist representations of sex (and readings of them) will inevitably bear the traces of both a feminist past—which will insist that there are no spaces outside of unequal heterosexual power relations—and a contemporary desire to move beyond that impasse into a place where women's enjoyment and pleasure are paramount" (p. 184). This setting up of the opposition between the radical feminist analysis and pro-sex feminism in temporal terms, and the equation of the first with feminism *per se*, is analytically and historically unjustified. The feminist pro-sex position that called for a feminist politics that views sexuality as a site not only of danger for women but of pleasure as well, began to crystallize already in the 1981 sex issue of *Heresies*, and the 1982 Barnard College Conference on Women and Sexuality, and was formulated in two collections of essays, *Powers of Desire* published in 1983 and *Pleasure and Danger* published in 1984. For a full chronology of the feminist sex wars, see Duggan and Hunter, 1995.

8. E.g., Pamela Paul, author of *Pornified*, elliptically refers to "feminist hardliners" who claimed that "all women are victims and all sex is rape," and alienated through this extreme position "what may otherwise be a natural broad-based following among women" (Paul, 2005, pp. 258–59).

9. Note the rhetorical conflation of the man with his penis in this quote.

10. For a discussion of how sexual receptivity is experienced and conceived in writings by lesbian femmes, see Cvetkovitch, 1995; for discussion of rearticulations of penetration in lesbian s/m porn fiction see Ziv, 2015.

11. The subsequent volumes were edited by Marcy Sheiner.

12. Indeed, some representations of heterosexual sex turn the tables completely and figure women penetrating their male lovers. This is the theme of the video *Bend Over Boyfriend 2* by S.I.R. Productions, which features several episodes of heterosexual sex in which women anally penetrate their male partners with a dildo. It is probably no coincidence, however, that S.I.R. Productions is owned and managed by a lesbian couple and produces mostly lesbian pornography.

13. John Boswell notes that the active/passive division current in the modern West has displaced the donor/recipient distinction, i.e., the giving versus receiving of semen, which predominated in classical antiquity. Boswell speculates that it is this shift of paradigm that has made the Christian West more tolerant of fellatio than the ancients, since while the fellator occupies the ignoble pole in the donor/recipient divide, he escapes the charge of passivity (Boswell, 1989, pp. 33–34). In contemporary pornography, the practice of face-fucking (as opposed to regular fellatio), and the increasingly popular practice of "gagging" seem to be intended to realign active/passive with donor/recipient.

14. See especially the prominent role of anal sex in the Marquis de Sade's novels, or its depiction as violent and violating in Pauline Réage's *Histoire d'O*. The transgressive status of anal sex has of course a lot to do with the Christian prohibition on sodomy and its status as mortal sin. Many non-religious discourses also reject anal sex owing to the dual charge of its non-generativity and scatological associations.

15. Cf. Ann Cvetkovich (1995) who, comparing the status of penetration in lesbian and in gay male culture, offers that "the penetration of the anus is perhaps even more culturally freighted as a signifier of power than the penetration of the vagina" (p. 136).

16. It may be argued, however (as did some of my students who were assigned the story), that while the story does describe the adverse effects that objectification has on women, the solution it offers consists in a change of mental attitude by the woman. In this female empowerment narrative, Claudia's empowerment consists in learning to accept and enjoy being reduced to a body part by casual men: "instead of feeling angry or hurt, Claudia felt proud" (p. 180), and to translate it into a sense of sexual power. Yet, her body and her control of her body are still her major source of self-esteem.

17. Gayle Rubin, arguing against all systems of sexual judgment that produce hierarchies of sexual value, has similarly suggested that rather than ranking sexual acts in advance as good or bad, normal or abnormal, "a democratic sexual morality should judge sexual acts by the way partners treat one another, the level of mutual consideration, the presence or absence of coercion and the quantity and quality of the pleasure they provide" (Rubin, 1984, p. 15).

18. Thomas wields control over other aspects of the relationship too—only he can contact Diane since she does not know his phone number or address.

19. Needless to say, however, not all gay encounters take place between partners of equal status; same-sex interactions may be inflected by other social power differentials, such as race, class, etc. Indeed, in the sexual encounter depicted in the story, the neutralization of the gender hierarchy depends to a large extent on its replacement by the postcolonial power relations that obtain between the (presumably white) American couple and their Mexican and Chicano partners. The narrator herself situates the encounter within the frame of global economic exploitation and U.S. cultural hegemony. At the end of the story, after blithely noting how shockingly cheap the transaction has been, she muses, "I wondered if this was how Japanese businessmen in Thailand felt. Was I contributing to the decline of the Third World?" (p. 195). But this thought does not mar the jubilant note of the closure; and moreover, the comparison to Japanese sex tourists only serves to reinforce her masculine positioning by marking her as a sexual consumer rather than a sexual commodity.

20. The earliest manifestation of this process can be found in Tom of Finland's graphic art, and its most common contemporary symptom is the figure of the gym clone.

21. Male-male sex as a male initiation rite has, of course, a long and venerable history. The institution of pederastic love in ancient Greece is one of its more sublimated manifestations, while initiation rites for young warriors in New Guinea included daily oral insemination by older warriors, the ingestion of semen being thought to counter the feminizing influences of birth and rearing by women (Herdt, 1981). For a discussion of Greek pederasty as initiation, and comparisons to other initiation rites involving male-male sex, see Halperin, 1990.

22. Of course, sexual agency does not exist independently of the actual power relations within which sexual interactions take place. However, inasmuch as the notion of sexual agency is also an ideological construct, this kind of phantasmatic cross-gender identification can open the way for different interpretations and valuations of heterosexual female sexuality, that circumvent its alleged incompatibility with sexual subjectivity.

Erotic Pleasure and Postsocialist Female Sexuality

Contemporary Female "Body Writing" in China

Eva Chen

Erotic writing and art have a long tradition in China. Though remnants have been found dating back to the first century, erotic wall murals found at the Dunhuang Buddhist grottoes suggest a flourishing erotic art scene around the tenth century. The late Ming Dynasty in the seventeenth century saw a peak of erotic poetry and fiction, as well as erotica portrayed in "pillow books" and Taoist treatises on effective sexual techniques for maximizing life energies (van Gulik, 1974). Much erotica of the period also focused on female foot-binding, a practice started among court dancers in the tenth century which later spread to gentry families, brothels and even peasant households, and functioned both to signify female virtue and domesticity and to appeal to male fetishistic pleasure (Ko, 2005). Attitudes hardened from the time of the Qing Dynasty in the eighteenth century with the resurgence of Confucian moral conservatism, all but bringing to an end a thriving tradition of erotica. Much of this erotica was written from a male point of view for a predominantly male audience, while the vast majority of Chinese women were confined by Confucian gender prescriptions of subservience and domesticity.

The Western understanding of sexuality as an essential, intrinsic component of personal identity first entered China in the late nineteenth and early twentieth centuries, when national humiliations at the hands of imperial powers drove many elite Chinese to emulate Western ideas and distance themselves from the Confucian patrilineal heritage. An idea of woman (*nüxing*) based not on Confucian kinship roles but on physiology, couched in the rhetoric of Western sexual and eugenics theories, was a new concept introduced in elite circles, along with other concepts like "the individual" and "the citizen." This concept imagined a link between social or national progress and the liberation of women as autonomous, heterosexual subjects (Barlow, 2004). However, this sexualized female subject was not celebrated for its own sake but was, rather, invoked as the binary opposite of a Westernized, masculine self that needed to be cultivated to "upend" Confucian kinship categories (Barlow, 1994, p. 266). The origin of this idea in the Western, humanist understanding of an essential human nature, of which sexuality is an inalienable part, partially explains the later socialist criticism of this idea as bourgeois. When the Maoist party swept into power in 1949, the socialist state began to promote a new concept of woman (*funü*), emphasizing collectivist public roles rather than sexual difference, along with other statist categories like the worker and the proletariat. The state advocated gender parity on the political and social level but erased signs of femininity and sexual difference in the official celebration of the androgynous, public-spirited, asexual female factory worker enthusiastically working alongside men for the public good (Evans, 1997). While the new Marriage Law instated a legal form of female sexual agency by providing for a woman's right to choose a husband and her right to divorce, the state's simultaneous policy of puritanical collectivism suppressed the private and the individual, and treated sex only in terms of a scientific physiology stressing reproduction and sanitation.

It is in this light that the postsocialist celebration of the body, sexuality and "natural femininity" since the market reforms in the 1980s needs to be understood: as a reaction to the perceived socialist distortion of the "natural," gendered human self with its individual emotions, desires and needs. In literature, female sexuality recurred as a favorite trope in the work of male writers as a means of celebrating emotion and an unshackled human nature, as women were linked with irrationality and irrepressible nature (Barlow, 1994). In the mid–1990s, however, a new wave of female-penned literature serving a predominantly female readership commanded public attention. Aptly termed female "body writing," it celebrated female sexuality, female empowerment and a salacious commodification of the female body that was also becoming ubiquitous in advertising and mass culture, and played on what Yang calls the "blurred boundary" between literature and mass market fiction (2011, p. 4). By the end of the decade the genre was being dubbed "beauty writing" and was beginning to be dominated by younger female writers who capitalized on the rising neoliberal commodity culture and utilized its rhetoric of freedom of expression and individual desire. These writers traded on their looks and sexualized body images and cultivated a highly bankable notoriety to launch careers as bestselling authors. The language of this genre is more explicit than earlier postsocialist erotic writing, and it portrays a wider and more controversial range of female sexual experience. These bestsellers often claim a high degree of autobiographical authenticity, celebrate female sexual agency in the consumerist terminology of choice and freedom, and emphasize participation in, rather than resistance to, mainstream beauty culture.

It would be naïve to conceptualize the evolution of postsocialist female sexuality in China simply in terms of a repressive state versus a people clamoring for liberation. The re-feminization and sexualization of women in both literature and popular media culture has to be understood in the context of a national push to undo past socialist wrongs that are said to have shackled people and mired China in isolation and underdevelopment, a desire to reinstitute "inalienable" human rights and re-launch China into a globalized modernity of universal values. In this postsocialist context, feminist criticism has become difficult and, to some extent, there has been a backpedalling on women's political and social rights and a return of sexist gender categories viewed now as "natural." This re-feminization of public images of women has certainly been promoted by the flourishing commodity culture, but the state has also played a part in this process. As Lisa Rofel points out, the state has been responsible in adopting a neoliberal policy of marketization and privatization and publically promoting the construction of a new type of Chinese citizen who aims to satisfy his/her "natural" sexual and material desires as long as these are directed toward consumerist goals (Rofel, 2007, p. 13). Here we can see how neoliberalism, in its emphasis on "the market in human nature" which should not be obstructed (Read 2009, p. 26, citing Fredric Jameson), converges in the postsocialist context with a long-felt need to restore and liberate the "natural," "free" human self. The state's role is thus ambivalent. In relation to female sexuality, this is evident when the state both tolerates and even encourages the commodification of a "freed" female sexuality, but also worries about the possible socio-political dangers of unruly sexual energies, resorting to censorship and campaigns against what it terms Western pornography and vulgarity.[1]

The female-penned "body writing" has been able to exploit this complex interplay of postsocialist politics, neoliberal commodity culture and Confucian gender heritage, thus generating a distinct representation of postfeminist female sexuality. This writing presupposes a female reader who actively desires and is sexually uninhibited. It promotes female individualism and sexual empowerment based on the idea of a self-interested, neoliberal subject who equates agency with active participation in commodity culture. These traits do link this Chinese writing to the erotic fiction which has emerged in the West in the same period which, as Esther Sonnet describes, employs the language of postfeminist female sexual empowerment (1999, p. 170). At the same time, while Western postfeminist erotica is circulated in a social context where feminism has been greatly successful and as a result is, to some extent, taken for granted, postsocialist Chinese culture has just emerged from a socialist legacy that only instated nominal gender parity at the political level and is now largely associated with unnatural gender distortion. Chinese female "body writing" thus makes much greater reference to a generalized human nature in need of liberation, of which the female sexual self is an intrinsic part, rather than to an oppositional concept of female liberation. This explains the predominant tone of individual liberation and freedom of speech characterizing much of this female writing. In this sense it both works with the postsocialist discourse of a liberated, masculinist human nature, and also sometimes against it when it asserts a distinctly female sexuality.

This female "body writing" has been the focus of major public controversy from the 1990s and well into the new century, galvanizing public attention toward female sexuality, freedom of speech, individual rights and the boundaries between the private and the public. Often the target of censorship, and of public criticism from what Farrer calls "state-affiliated actors" like government administrators, media representatives, psychologists and university professors (2007, p. 9), it acts as a landmark in postsocialist Chinese sexual politics where movements toward greater plurality are often recuperated into the service of state power. This entails a crucial public and social impact that distinguishes the Chinese writing from most contemporary female erotica in the West. However, this political urgency has partly diverted attention away from other aspects of female body writing. These include its stress on the female point of view and the need for women to express their own sexuality, and its celebration of female sexuality for its own sake rather than as a symbol of postsocialist liberation. The discursive emphasis on liberation should not blind us to the power relations at work in the construction of this newly agentic female sexuality, nor to its potential complicity with the neoliberal state. This essay discusses Weihui's *Shanghai Baby* (2000) and Muzimei's sex blogs, later published as *Left-over Love Letters* (2003), as these texts figure crucially in two major public controversies concerning this Chinese female "body writing," and as such represent important stages in the evolution of postsocialist Chinese female sexuality.

Shanghai Baby *Goes to the Market*

With her bestseller *Shanghai Baby* (2000), Weihui became the most famous of the new, more commercialized group of "beauty writers" at the turn of the century. The novel records the love life of a young Shanghai journalist named Coco who moves in a glamorous cosmopolitan scene of artists, writers, rich entrepreneurs and Western expatriates. Unlike the mid–1990s "high literature" female "body writing" of authors like Chen Ran (S. Zhao, 2001), Weihui unabashedly courted publicity and mass sales by playing on the border between literature and erotica, and emphasizing her status as both a well-educated writer and also a physically attractive young woman. Weihui designed the book cover of *Shanghai Baby* herself; it features a seductive, close-up photo of herself dressed in an off-the-shoulder tank top. Captions on the cover suggest that it is intended to appeal to both sexes. Words like "an alternative erotic novel set in the secret garden of Shanghai" seem to invite a male voyeuristic gaze, while "a novel by a woman for other women, on the female body experience" stresses a need to articulate female sexuality from a female point of view in contrast to previous masculinist representations. During her nationwide book tour, Weihui managed to grab tabloid attention by implying that she might go naked to boost sales—"let them see the breasts of the Shanghai Baby" (Shao, 2005, p. 17). A national uproar soon followed, and the novel was subsequently banned by the Press and Publications Bureau in Beijing in May 2000 on the grounds that the novel contained "unhealthy and obscene contents" and "typified corruption and decadence and cultural poisoning by the West" (Tan, 2000, p. 1). Her publisher, ordered to suspend its operation for three months, complained of Weihui's "over-the-top" stunts. But Weihui herself emerged unscathed and ever more prosperous, reaping huge gains from the black market sales and overseas editions, and topping the national list of most wealthy writers (Shao, 2005). The novel quickly sold millions of copies and its website received millions of hits. Imitations followed in the ensuing years, with a "Baby" series and "Pink-collared Beauty" series set in other big cities and featuring young urban women similarly bent on sexual and consumerist gratification (E. Chen, 2012).

The huge success of *Shanghai Baby* led to a heated public debate in which the bulk of domestic commentators, comprising mostly literary critics and social commentators, decried its "immoral," "vulgar" explicitness and "decadence" (Yu, 2002), while Western media responses celebrated Weihui for challenging draconian Communist taboos and writing about a "people determined to break free," about whom "the Chinese government does not want Westerners to read" (Smith, 2000, p. A4). However, behind this liberation versus repression tug-of-war, what makes this novel different is not just its controversial nature and hence its ability to force public attention on sexuality, but its celebration of female sexual desire from the female point of view and in terms of empowerment and independence. By taking female sexual desires seriously, this female-centric emphasis suggests a feminist belief in the need for women to "speak" sex in a manner which is authentic, that is, non-male mediated or "non-colonized" (Sonnet, 1999, p. 173). This style of writing does point to a more agentic female self than the postsocialist trope of "naturalized" femininity constructed as the inferior other of a masculinist self. The heroine, Coco, characterizes herself as a modern woman with a solipsistic and pleasure-seeking approach to sexual desire. She announces that she represents a new generation of Chinese women who have "more freedom than women of fifty years ago, more beauty than women of thirty years ago and a greater variety of sexual orgasm than women of ten years ago" (Weihui, 2000, p. 118). In other words, Coco is well-educated and economically independent in ways that were denied to presocialist women of Confucian gender subordination, and possesses a re-"naturalized" femininity and beauty denied to socialist women of androgynous distortion. She enjoys a more liberated sexuality that is, however, not credited to feminist struggles but to a neoliberal commodity culture accelerating since the 1990s.

    This idea of an evolution of female empowerment from the more socio-political area of education and employment to the private and individual area of love, beauty and sexual pleasure reflects the unique Chinese reaction against past socialist distortion. However, it also matches the general trajectory of postfeminist development in the West. *Shanghai Baby*'s celebration of Coco's new assertive, uninhibited, "bad girl" sexuality seems to be the linchpin wherein lies Coco's generational difference from her "soft and haggard-looking" mother, who has "spent her whole life ironing shirts for her husband" (Weihui, 2000, p. 25). This celebration is also accompanied by the portrayal of a wider range of female sexual experiences. For instance, Coco masturbates daily when she is with her impotent boyfriend, something seldom portrayed in detail or without stylization in Chinese literature. When she comes home after performing a striptease dance and is unable to be satisfied by her boyfriend, she describes her orgasmic flights into ecstasy through the help of her "long, delicate fingers" "time and time again" (2000, p. 22). On one occasion she has an intense, same-sex erotic episode with her friend, Madonna, in a context that suggests her ongoing journey of sexual exploration (pp. 161–62).

Few of the "liberation-versus-repression" responses to the novel have focused on an analysis of the representation of female sexuality *per se* or its inherent problems. The most controversial aspect of the novel is the representation of Coco's heterosexual encounters, involving violence and sadomasochism, with her domineering German lover. While elsewhere Coco celebrates her sexual agency, here she succumbs to the "radiating," commanding power of the German lover "like a prey" (2000, p. 41). When she first sees him, he is described as having "eyes like a predatory animal lurking on the sly in the bush" and a body sleek and erect like a "brand new umbrella" (p. 41). "Wonderfully strange feelings" and intense "masochistic pleasure" sweep over Coco's body despite the protests of her rational mind (p. 41). When he subsequently makes love to her "without mercy" and "non-stop" (pp. 82–84), excruciating pleasure mingled with pain conquers Coco, as she imagines him as a "German Nazi," "cold and beastly" in his Nazi uniform, boots and leather coat, "occupying and abusing" her but also mesmerizing her (p. 84). This tone pervades all their subsequent sex scenes as she finds herself increasingly addicted to the affair, and culminates in the final goodbye before the German leaves China, where Coco feels both like a battered and "raped dummy" but also "mesmerized," completely given over to intense orgasm (pp. 326–29).

In the context of the novel's general tone of liberation, supported by quotes from Western rebels ranging from Ginsberg to Madonna, this portrayal of female masochistic desire suggests the belief that all female sexual desires, including masochism, should be celebrated as authentic expressions of female sexuality. The issue of masochism has figured crucially in Western feminist debates on female sexuality, particularly between so-called "anti-porn" feminists and "sex-radical" or "pro-sex" feminists. Whereas anti-porn feminists have repudiated masochistic representations, arguing that they eroticize male domination and violence (C. MacKinnon, 1989), pro-sex feminists believe that women should eliminate inhibitions and embrace the whole range of their sexual desires (Califia, 1996). Furthermore, post-structuralist understandings of the self as no longer fixed or essential but as fluid and performative challenge feminist approaches to sexuality based on binaries of male or female, abjection or aggression. Such an approach also suggests that it is problematic to accept female sexual desires as valid simply because they are "natural." As Sonnet argues, sexual desires are never just natural, but socially constructed (1999, p. 180). Any celebration of non-normative sexuality such as masochism needs to also involve a critical examination of the underlying links between female masochistic desire and male-dominance in the broader culture. In this sense, *Shanghai Baby*'s general rhetoric of emancipation and rebellion against a perceived legacy of repression and distortion may mask an inadequate critical consideration of the nature of that sexual rebellion per se.

Another crucial side to *Shanghai Baby*'s celebrated female sexuality is that this female empowerment is often expressed in neoliberal consumerist terms (E. Chen, 2012). Coco, for instance, equates her own sexual attraction with a capacity for unlimited consumption, comparing her confident beauty to "a credit card with a high credit limit that can be used for a very long time without having to worry about the bill." She commands unrivaled sexiness, for "none of the dazzling neon street lights could outshine me," "nor is the ATM machine as rich as me" (Weihui, 2000, p. 253). When her cousin, Zhu Sha, divorces her boring husband for a sexually gratifying relationship with a younger man, Coco applauds her sexual awakening and compares her to a "model stepping forward from a Paris Printemps billboard" (p. 133). Like Coco, Zhu Sha is now aspiring toward the ideal of the "modern, independent, new woman" who has "much greater freedom in independently choosing how to live their own lives." The diamond ring-flashing, confidently-smiling, professional woman in the De Beers ads speaks to their hearts, and so does the male voice-over "shining with confidence and sexual attraction" (p. 256).

This consumerist version of female sexual agency evokes the neoliberal subject, interpellated as an entrepreneur of his/her own human capital and making free choices based on his/her own marketized self-interests. However, as Nicholas Rose writes, following Foucault, neoliberal freedom and agency is never absolute or unlimited freedom but rather the ability to willingly and actively choose the maximum material benefits for self-actualization (Rose, 1999, p. 137). The path most conducive to self-interest often turns out to be the normative one for which the state has provided the best conditions. In the case of *Shanghai Baby*, this means that the neoliberal subject of agency is complicit with and enabled by the state, particularly the Chinese state's policy to direct its citizens' newly "freed" sexual and material needs to consumerist purposes. Despite *Shanghai Baby*'s much touted rebelliousness, Coco and her liberated female friends function as privileged women whose success and confidence is predicated on their ability to profit from a market economy that the postsocialist state has enabled and promoted. Coco, based on Weihui herself, reaps great financial benefit by writing bestsellers about her unbridled sexuality, and her cousin's sexual awakening and decision to divorce her husband is buttressed by her economic independence facilitated by her managerial job at a multinational corporation. They represent a new generation of young, successful and well-educated urban Chinese women vastly different from the majority of older, poorer women excluded from that neoliberal "choice" and "freedom." In *Shanghai Baby*, these less "free" and much more constrained women take the form of laid-off female workers from the inefficient, state-owned textile factories who are forced to move to the outlying suburbs, women who Coco describes condescendingly in a passing reference as "rejected by the young and fashionable" (Weihui, 2000, p. 75).

That neoliberal freedom and empowerment actually entails hierarchies and exclusions takes a further spatial form in the novel. Shanghai is credited in the novel with giving Shanghai women that extra sexiness and erotic appeal over the bulk of less fashionable Chinese women. It owes that reputation to its status as the most prosperous Chinese city and the success story of the Chinese state's market reform policy. Thus, when Coco takes off her clothes in the dark and dances in her underwear in the shaded rooftop of a hotel along the skyscraper-lined riverfront, the Shanghai Bund, it is the phallic Pearl of the East tower at the Putong New Economic Area that she dances to, ecstatically aroused by and paying erotic homage to this most emblematic landmark of China's new economic success and national pride, this "energetic force the bustling metropolis emits" (Weihui, 2000, p. 23). This complicity with the neoliberal state indicates the need for a critical interrogation of the ideological function of *Shanghai Baby*'s famed breaking of taboos and celebration of a liberated female sexuality.

Muzimei and Everyday Sex Blogging

Shanghai Baby may be explicit and controversial, but it is still stylized literature with some self-conscious claims to avant-gardism, evidenced by its many quotes from Western writers and rebels. In 2003, another major controversy arose involving the candid sex blogs by a young Canton journalist pen-named Muzimei. Muzimei's blogs brought an immediacy to female erotic writing in China and sparked a previously unseen level of popular participation. What is important about this so-called Muzimei phenomenon embroiling much of China's public discourse in 2003 and 2004 is not just the explicitness and unmediated authenticity of the female sexuality presented, but also the social media format of this writing and the huge level of ordinary netizen response and participation afterward.

Blogging was officially introduced in China in 2002, to a rather lackluster start, when two male founders established Blogcn.com in August (J. Chen, 2004). On June 19, 2003, Muzimei started to post on Blogcn.com a diary of her sex adventures with numerous men. It received little attention until August, when she published the real name of one of her one-night-stands, a rock star of some reputation in Canton. Uproar ensued, and 20 million visitors accessed her diary in one day (Pomfret, 2003), making her blog the most trafficked in China. Muzimei is thus credited with kick starting the Chinese blogging revolution by galvanizing national attention on blogging itself as a new form of online communication. Currently there are 181 million bloggers and 300 million microbloggers in China (Leibold, 2011, p. 1023). After three major Internet news sites reported on her blog, a national debate on sex, morality and sexual liberation ensued, some of it in mainstream media, but primarily online in the form of responses and counter-responses posted on her blog and other Internet sites by ordinary netizens. In October, Muzimei's blogs were published as a book entitled *Left-over Love Letters*, and her true identity was revealed as Li Li, fueling further speculation over the identities of her many lovers and greater interest in her as a celebrity. Li's face appeared on the cover of three magazines, and a number of copycat blogs sprung up, with women such as "Big Sister Furong" and "Hooligan Yan" disclosing their sexual experiences and even posting their naked photos (*Sina News*, 2005). After the Ministry of Propaganda issued a nominal ban on her book, Li resigned from her job at a Canton magazine and shut down her blog. However, Internet versions of her book and diaries are freely available, and Li now works as a full-time blogger under a different name.

The Muzimei phenomenon represents a new phase of female "body writing" in China, dominated by online sex writings by ordinary women. Weihui still needed the approval of editors and publishers as figures of literary authority in order to get published and take care of the logistics of printing and promotion. All this seems to have been bypassed in Muzimei's meteoric rise to fame, largely because of the revolutionary nature of online blogging. As a form of self-publishing with a low entry threshold, low costs, instant impact and interactive nature, blogging has proven particularly attractive to women compared to other forms of online communication like discussion forums or chatrooms. The intimate, personal and confessional nature of blogging links it to traditional women's genres like autobiography and diary writing and potentially allows a greater degree of frankness and explicitness (Attwood, 2009, p. 6). The Chinese Internet is a highly controlled environment where the state maintains a sophisticated Golden Shield surveillance system, banning access to Western websites and politically sensitive information. But while the state routinely removes and campaigns against pornographic images and what it dubs "the Cyber Yellow Disaster" (Jacobs, 2012, p. 27), sex blogs and online private diaries have enjoyed much greater freedom as netizens reveal their sexual experiences or openly search for sex partners without censorship or harassment (Chien, 2005). This DIY form of written erotica is particularly dominated by women, and suggests a more emancipated female sexual expression and more heterogeneous representations of erotic desire. However, I argue that this expression of female sexuality should also be analyzed closely and in the context of its categorization as female "body writing" in China. Like its predecessors, this new phase of female erotica is blatantly commodified, with many female bloggers seeking a financially lucrative notoriety. What is different is that Muzimei and the other bloggers do not possess the beauty which Weihui and the other "beauty writers" utilized to great commercial success. The female sexuality they portray is also rather "masculine," in that emotional involvement is often divorced from sexual pleasure and casual sex is promoted. This is what proves most upsetting and threatening to many reviewers. Finally, these women may command a wider public interest as a result of their adroit use of the Internet to maximize individual expression, but they are also subject to greater abuse and opposition, often from a masculinist Internet public.

Muzimei's real identity was revealed after her blogs were published as a book. Online netizen criticism shifted immediately from scandalization over the blogs' explicitness to scathing mockery of her ordinary looks. This criticism, compared with the previous fanfare and publicity over the "beauty writers'" looks and sexiness, suggests that public attention to female sexuality is still motivated largely by a voyeuristic gaze that desires only young, beautiful women, a gaze that is further titillated when the women in question have the relatively rare credential of being privileged and thus not easily accessible. Muzimei is at least young. Other female erotic bloggers, like the middle-aged, working-class Hooligan Yan, are also humiliated for daring to post naked photos of their aging and overweight bodies. This response highlights the normalizing process which determines who is "qualified" to represent themselves in public as "sexual agents" (Farrer, 2007, p. 22). It further exposes the exclusions and hierarchies behind the sexual agency and freedom touted in *Shanghai Baby*, agency that seems to be limited to young, conventionally beautiful and well-off women.

What is most noteworthy about the concept of female sexuality expressed in these sex blogs is its "unfeminine" nature and its challenge to traditional ideas of emotion or love-based female sexuality. Patriarchal norms teach that men and women are physiologically different and that women, unlike more aggressive men, experience arousal only when emotionally invested. This idea finds an interesting echo among some cultural feminists like Carol Gilligan (1982). But such criticism of oppressive heterosexuality and celebration of female sexual experiences that only lead to nurturing, harmonious or emotionally fulfilling results could also end up sanctioning certain forms of sexual desires to the exclusion of other, less normative or deviant ones. It may help to reinforce the impression that women's sexual desire is primarily emotion-based. In Muzimei's case, however, she seems to have an aggressive, casual approach to sex normally linked with the masculine, treating her one-night stands simply as sexual objects for pleasure, and flaunting her ability to invest no emotion in the liaisons.

Muzimei claims to have slept with more than 70 men, most of them one-night stands she picks up at bars and clubs. She catalogues them according to their sexual prowess, particular fetishes and decency both in bed and afterward. They are stored in her smart phone-like CDs in her desk, checked out and selected according to her moods and put away and forgotten afterward. None of them engages her emotionally, and she blogs about their sexual performances and fetishes in a blunt, wryly ironic tone. Her June 23, 2003, entry reads:

> I live a pleasurable life, with a busy, rewarding job and a very human hobby after work—making love. I have a wide choice in my sex partners and never want in supply. I do not have to take any responsibility for them, do not have to be emotionally involved, and nor would they cause me any trouble. They are just like my CDs, clicked on to play when I want to listen and shut off when I don't. A man with a stocking fetish calls at midnight—"Are you free tonight?" "No." Turned off the phone and went back to sleep. Woke up at noon to find a text message from a painter. "Why do you turn off your phone? What a bore!" By lunchtime, the stocking man called again. "Free tonight?" "No." "Why, all booked-up?" "Yes." "What time then?" "Maybe in a long time. Didn't I tell you? I hate the repetition" [Muzimei, 2003].

This voracious, pleasure-seeking but emotionally remote approach to sex infuriated some readers who attacked her for being "unfeminine" and "irresponsible" (Li, 2003). Some questioned whether she was really a woman, others worried about her pernicious influence on "masses of poorly educated people and young people who lack rational judgment," and one established psychologist opined that she must be physically abnormal and had too much male hormones in her body (Y. Zhao, 2003). Even Weihui's *Shanghai Baby* pales in comparison, as Coco is never promiscuous but invests intense emotions in her relationships. The supposedly "carnal" affair with the German lover leaves her emotionally battered and torn with guilt toward her Chinese boyfriend. Muzimei, by comparison, is not plagued by Coco's anxiety or moral unease but goes full throttle for physical pleasure in an assured, self-determining, and playful manner. In one blog post she claims to have told a Beijing reporter, who phoned to ask for an interview, that the length of their interview would depend on his sexual performance: the interview would go for the same amount of time as he would last in bed with her (Muzimei, 2003).

It would be simplistic to laud Muzimei simply because she reverses established perceptions of male and female sexuality, or asks for a sort of sexual parity by appropriating male roles. By itself, this would reinforce the normative sexual binaries that privilege masculinity and aggression. Instead, what is noteworthy is that her blogs help to broaden the range of female desires by not limiting them to nurturing, emotionally involved experiences. In this regard, she is also supported by Hooligan Yan, who claims to be a proponent of "pure casual sex" because it is "most pure," and "you do not need to be a hypocrite" (qtd. in Jacobs, 2012, p. 98).

By putting her emotion-free, pleasure-oriented sexuality on display, Muzimei also pushes the sexualized male body into the limelight, treating it as an object or commodity and judging and commenting on its sexual performance accordingly. This unveiling of what she calls the naked "truth" of men in which they are now the object, instead of the subject, of a sexualized gaze proves most discomforting. One entry on June 29, entitled "Afraid to Be Famous," reads:

> Went to a bar last night and talked to the men at the next table. "Would you have sex with me?" "No, I am afraid." "Why?" "You are too famous. I fear fame. Every man who has slept with you ends up miserable." "Nonsense. I won't write about you in my blog." "I don't believe you." ... "I think you have a great body and must be good at sex. To me sex is the fastest way to know each other. It allows us to be intimate and true." "I fear 'true'" [Muzimei, 2003].

Much of the criticism of Muzimei is directed against her seeming victimization of men and violation of their privacy by "outing" them (People.com, n.d.). The "outed" Canton rock singer went into hiding for two months and many of her one-night stands reacted with fury over her disclosure of their real identities. The girlfriend of a man Muzimei mentioned challenged her in a bar fight, not just because she slept with her boyfriend but mainly because the "outing" made him lose face in public (Murongliansheng, 2013). This stress on privacy and the need to cordon off the private and sexual sphere from public prying is interesting; particularly in view of the fact that much postsocialist literary and popular discourse has highlighted the important role of the private and the sexual in resistance to socialist repression. However, many public commentators were discomforted when Muzimei utilized that same humanistic rhetoric to justify recording her private sex life in an act of "ethnographic" self-exploration (*Now News*, 2011). Perhaps this was because *male* privacy was in this case threatened, and it was the male body being sexualized. Most postsocialist literature extolling the liberation of the private and the sexual has used women's sexualized bodies as a trope and symbol, with men always the subject. The sexualized female body has also been widely displayed in advertising and other media. It seems that Muzimei's audience are disturbed because it is now the male sexualized body on display, subject to a woman's "ethnographic," dispassionate and judgmental gaze.

Furthermore, none of the offended commentators seem to be alert to the fact that their own reading of Muzimei's blogs and voyeuristic gaze into her sex life involves complicity in a similar act of invasion of privacy. Blogging by its very nature implies an erosion of traditional boundaries of privacy, ethics and public discourse. It is both a private activity, allowing the author to express and perform themselves in a way they are normally unable to, and also public, with an unknown audience watching this self-presentation and commenting on and participating in it (Ray, 2007). One of the chief attractions of blogs is that they offer voyeuristic pleasure through access to the blogger's personal life while allowing the reader to participate and comment anonymously. Certainly Muzimei willingly solicited this gaze, but the public's reaction suggests the inherently sexist nature of voyeurism whereby girl-watching, however intimate or private, is accepted as legitimate, whereas invasion of male privacy causes discomfort.

Although Muzimei's objectification and outing of men has proved threatening to a masculinized audience, she herself refuses to be seen as a feminist (*Global Times*, 2012). Just like Coco in *Shanghai Baby* who denies feminist affiliations, Muzimei rejects the suggestion that she is writing on behalf of women or that she has a strong "gender consciousness." "[A]nytime I do something, I don't first think that I am a woman" (qtd. in Farrer, 2007, p. 23). If she invokes the postsocialist humanistic rhetoric of liberating the "self" or "human nature" from repression, she sees herself only as a "one-woman liberation movement" (Jacobs, 2012, p. 91), and not as a part of feminist collectivist action. In one of her interviews, Muzimei credits Western commodity culture for increasing tolerance toward "sex, homosexuality, affairs and spouse-swapping" in China (*Singbao*, 2013). This consumerist link is also seen in many of her blogs. One blog, for instance, describes an unusual encounter with a black man in Hong Kong, in which she gives him a skillfully delivered blow job with her fingers and some cream, as if she "has just triumphantly kneaded a huge black noodle" (Muzimei, 2003). Such a portrayal of female sexual confidence is set in a context of consumption and pleasurable thrills brought by shopping, eating and football-watching, as Muzimei goes for one of her shopping sprees to Hong Kong, just like many of her cash-rich compatriots who have brought such retail wealth to Hong Kong and other metropolises around the world. If her sexuality is active and uninhibited, it is obviously couched in consumerist terms of freedom and agency, and linked with a seemingly unlimited spending power.

The huge wave of hostile online responses Muzimei received over her outing of men and "playing with men's bodies" (Li, 2003) points to the greater abuse women may be subject to on the Internet. At the same time, the Internet may allow women a new role in shaping public opinion by providing an active voice to ordinary netizens. In Muzimei's case, it was the netizens' heavy online traffic over Muzimei's blogs that attracted the belated attention of journalists and literary and social critics. Without the netizens there would simply have been no Muzimei phenomenon. The fact that Muzimei and the other women bloggers dominate Chinese sex blogs points to women's rising power in the Internet world and their expanding access to new forms of active sexual expression, as female Chinese netizens have risen from a share of 15 percent of the Chinese Internet in early 1999 to 44 percent by the end of 2011 (CINIC, 2013). As yet the Chinese Internet is still dominated by pornography directed at a male audience (Jacobs, 2012, p. 115). Where gender categories are concerned, a dominant tone of moral conservatism coupled with voyeuristic objectification of women prevails, exacerbated by the anonymity and herd-instinct of the Internet environment. Consider, for example, the response of one "worried parent": "What about my 12-year-old daughter? She is obsessed with Muzimei. She says many of her friends read Muzimei every day and some even worship her. I am really worried. Somebody must do something about such corrupting, decadent people!" (People.com, n.d.). More hostile responses take the form of online vigilantism, with netizens revealing intimate details about Muzimei and the other female sex bloggers and making fun of their looks. Muzimei confessed to being completely unprepared for the uproar, begged reporters and netizens to leave her and her elderly mother alone, and eventually shut down her blogs. This indicates that, despite the celebration of the Chinese Internet by some scholars as the world's largest national group of users (Leibold, 2011, p. 1023) and the most important space for public and civic discourse in China (R. MacKinnon, 2008), the Internet does not by itself lead to greater democracy or a social revolution but is significantly shaped by ideas and discourses in the larger society.

Conclusion

Postsocialist sexual politics in China is a scene of expanding debate about sexuality and acceptable sex practices, increasing participation by the public through new forms of expression, and routine state campaigns and censorship juxtaposed with a simultaneous encouragement of sexual expression via consumer culture. Female sexuality figures crucially in this process, and female "body writing" over the years has been at the center of key controversies involving sexuality, thus taking on a public role that is perhaps not seen with Western women's erotica. The evolution of this writing from the earlier literature by "beauty writers" to the later Internet sex blogs indeed suggests a greater willingness in the Chinese sociocultural scene to explore female sexual desire and more agentic, participatory forms of sexual expression. However, an overly optimistic emphasis on emancipation must still take into account the complicated roles played by the state and the neoliberal consumer culture in forging a distinctly postsocialist Chinese female sexual identity. Chinese female "body writers" do assert a form of sexual agency as rights and what Farrer calls "sexual citizenship" (2007, p. 26), but at the same time they also play into a state-approved discourse seeking to direct such "freed" sexual energies into consumerism.

This is further seen, for instance, in the latest turn in the Muzimei story. Despite her earlier claims that she was just writing for herself and for nothing but the naked truth, in 2011 Muzimei resurfaced under her real name, flaunting her newly slimmed-down look and posting online a semi-nude photo of herself in the process of removing her underwear. Netizens expressed voyeuristic wonder at her "becoming at last beautiful," and rumors went rife about her securing a weight loss product advertising deal (*Now News*, 2011). This commodified turn in Chinese female "body writing" thus risks turning attention away from serious discussions of gender and sexuality and may ultimately help to reinforce patriarchal norms.

Note

1. Katrien Jacobs' research on Chinese Internet pornography reaches a similar conclusion about the paradoxical role of the state, in that the state both denounces pleasure industries while also "cultivating them as an area of capitalist expansion" (2012, p. 11).

Part 2
Interrogating the Erotic

Good Vibrations

Shaken Subjects and the Disintegrative Romance Heroine

NAOMI BOOTH

A number of important critical theorists have, in the later twentieth and early twenty-first centuries, proposed a violent shaking-up of the individual and her sense of self as the precursor to radical communal change. In this essay, I will explore the idea of shaking, shattering states in relation to radical thought, and I will present a number of theories that describe shaken states vibrating with the potential to unsettle wider social relations, disturbing our connections to the controlling discourses of gender, capitalism and anthropocentrism. Alongside these theories, I consider another frequently depicted literary state of shaking: that experienced by the vibrationally overwhelmed romance heroine. The contemporary romance heroine is preceded by a long line of female characters who reverberate with the disturbance of their erotic entanglements: Samuel Richardson's Pamela, for instance, fits violently at one of Mr B.'s early sexual approaches (Richardson, 1740, p. 242); the more stately "felicities of rapid motion" are enjoyed by Jane Austen's Emma while dancing (Austen, 1815, p. 246); Thomas Hardy's sensual Tess, who is "throbbingly alive," trembles repeatedly, her tremulous state tending her speech toward shattered syllables, "ecstasized to fragments" (Hardy, 1891, p. 223); and the palpitating body of Bram Stoker's voluptuous Lucy Westenra shakes and quivers and twists "in wild contortions" as her fiancé drives a stake through her heart (Stoker, 1897, p. 231). More recently, E L James has given us a spectacularly popular romance/erotic series, the *Fifty Shades of Grey* trilogy (2012), whose heroine is repeatedly overwhelmed by a vibrational disturbance that jitters her toward erotic climax.

In what follows, I analyze different depictions of the vibrational disturbance of the subject, proposing that we might read the shaking of the romance heroine in new ways, taking into account the radical potential of shattering states suggested by some critics. I will ask whether different traditions (politically radical/erotically charged) of the vibrationally discombobulated might be felt to resonate with one another. I focus in particular on the *Fifty Shades of Grey* trilogy, asking whether its depiction of vibrational states might disturb current social and sexual relations, or whether the radical potential of shattering subjects risks being recuperated to neoliberal gender norms in popular genre fiction. I read the *Fifty Shades* novels as a textual test of the radical potential of shattering states, when the hope of transformation always risks failure or bathos. If popular erotic fiction frequently describes vibrational disturbance, might conventional romance plotting also play a part in shutting down the energies it depicts?

Good Vibrations: Critical Theory and the Shaking Subject

The critic Leo Bersani has, in his work since the 1960s, explored the ways in which aesthetics and sexuality might unsettle our experience of subjectivity. He is a striking advocate for the necessity of the shaken-up or shattered subject as the precursor to radical communal change. "Self-shattering" is the term Bersani uses to describe an aspirational state of disarray, and he uses this term specifically in relation to the explosive potential of sexual pleasure to disturb the subject's coherence (Bersani, 1986). In his work on psychoanalysis and the body, Bersani rereads Freud's key texts on the development of infantile sexuality, particularly the *Three Essays on the Theory of Sexuality*, to argue that *intensity* is the key to sexual experience. Sexual excitement develops as "a byproduct ... of a large number of processes that occur in the organism, as soon as they reach a certain degree of intensity, and most especially of any relatively powerful emotion, even though it is of a distressing nature" (Bersani, 1986, pp. 37–38). Bersani therefore suggests that an erotic resonance is felt in the body as a result of any intense experience. This intensity is, Bersani tells us, experienced as a sort of shattering of the coherence of the self for the infant. Any intensity will therefore be experienced as sexual pleasure when it is strong enough to shatter a certain stability or equilibrium of the self. Bersani draws here not just on the work of Freud, but on other thinkers who have theorized sexuality as a vibrational disturbance of the subject, in particular Jean Laplanche, who imagines sexual excitement as an effect of *ébranlement*, of perturbation or shattering (cited in Jagose, 2013, p. 14). The gap between the "period of shattering stimuli and the development of resistant or defensive ego structures" (Bersani, 1986, pp. 38–39) is psychically bridged by a strategic masochism, Bersani suggests: we cannily find pleasure in being shattered. It is in this sense that, for Bersani, "sexuality—at least in the mode in which it is constituted—could be thought of as a tautology for masochism" (pp. 38–39). If sexuality is "constituted as a kind of psychic shattering, as a threat to the stability and integrity of the self" (p. 60), Bersani argues, then: "sexuality would be that which is intolerable to the structured self" (p. 38). We are "'shattered' into an ego-shattering sexuality"[1] that is a kind of disintegration of the self rather than its triumph.[2] For Bersani, this shattering of the self, through sex as "self-abolition," opens the way for radical new modes of selfhood and society, and "self-shattering" becomes an essential structural precursor for the radicalisation of the relational and the political field.

Bersani's aspirational claims for a vibrational disturbance of the subject resonate with earlier claims made for convulsion by twentieth-century theorists who are similarly interested in revolutionizing the relationship between the individual, aesthetics and culture. Roland Barthes, for example, exploring the power of *jouissance*, describes a perturbation of the self as the effect of textual bliss. Barthes describes bliss as "the site of a loss, the seam, the cut, the deflation, the dissolve which seizes the subject" (Barthes, 1975, pp. 7, 19); it is a state of discombobulation, rather than comfort: "shock, disturbance, even loss … are proper to ecstasy, to bliss'" (p. 19). Texts and bodies are involved in the production of this blissful/awful disturbance of the self. Barthes distinguishes between texts of pleasure, which come from culture and do not "break with it," producing a "comfortable practice of reading," and texts of bliss, which "impose … a state of loss, the text that discomforts (perhaps to the point of a certain boredom), unsettles the reader's historical, cultural, psychological assumptions, the consistency of his tastes, values, memories, brings to a crisis his relation with language" (p. 14). The reader engaged with texts of bliss experiences a kind of crisis of their own sense of selfhood, enjoying "its collapse, its fall" (p. 21). In this sense, bliss is antithetical to the reassuring comfort of pleasure; it produces a shattered relation to language and to the self, a radical disorganisation: "Texts of bliss. Pleasure in pieces; language in pieces; culture in pieces" (p. 51). The radical charge to this sort of ecstatic disintegration is bound up with a subversion of individual identity; the temporary collapse of selfhood that bliss precipitates through its "shattering force" means that it is "no longer clear whether there is a subject, or what gender it might belong to" (Bennett and Royle, 2009, p. 296). Bliss is an admission of the political in unexpected places: its vibrations "depoliticiz[e] what is apparently political, and ... politiciz[e] what apparently is not" (Barthes, 1975, p. 44).

Bersani and Barthes both, then, make a vibrational disturbance of the subject resonate with the disturbing potentialities of erotic vibration. Other thinkers, however, have sought to more definitely distance the idea of radical disturbance from that of sexual climax. Annamarie Jagose, in her recent monograph *Orgasmology*, has described a current of thinking that takes orgasm as "a convenient figure for quiescent normativity" (Jagose, 2013, p. xiii). She suggests that queer theory, by which she means "those posthumanist and anti-identitarian critical approaches that are energized by thinking against the practices, temporalities, and modes of being through which sexuality has been normatively thought" (p. 1) has tended to take a Foucauldian perspective on orgasm, whereby the body is "battened down" through climax. Foucault, Jagose tells us, "specifically aligns orgasm with normalizing, disciplinary power," and goes as far as to renounce orgasm, or at least the "virile form of pleasure commanded by orgasm in the ejaculatory and masculine sense of the term" (p. 3). Gilles Deleuze, she suggests, is similar in figuring orgasm "in the service of the forces of social control" (p. 3). However, despite his suspicion of climax, Deleuze's thinking returns us to vibrating states as a way to imagine alternative modes of being. In *A Thousand Plateaus* (1980), Deleuze and Félix Guattari develop the notion of the plateau to "express a form ungoverned by standard organizational principles, such as hierarchy, sequence, and totalization, 'a continuous, *self-vibrating* region of intensities whose development avoids any orientation toward a culmination point or external end'" (Jagose, 2013, p. 4, quoting Deleuze and Guattari, 1980, p. 22). Climax, understood as the discharging of desire, is substituted in Deleuze and Guattari's model of the plateau by a continuously vibrating plane of unalloyed intensities.

This might return us to the recurrence of versions of vibration (be they climactic or non-climactic) as the basis for further challenges to how we conceive of the subject. Theodor Adorno, for instance, posits an aesthetic *Erschütterung*, the shaking or shuddering (or, more literally, the "vibration") of the subject, as the possibility for her to think beyond herself, to imagine otherness: "For a few moments the I becomes aware, in real terms, of the possibility of letting self-preservation fall away" (Adorno, 1970, pp. 269, 245). This "aesthetic shudder," then, might disturb the "subject's petrification in his or her own subjectivity" and "can break down the hardening of subjectivity ... allow[ing] the subject to catch ... the slightest glimpse beyond that prison that it [the "I"] itself is ... and so to experience the critical possibility of thinking otherness" (Kaufman, 2002, p. 49).[3] Tremors in subjectivity produced by the aesthetic are theorized here as temporarily suspending the experience of the fortified or sclerotic self.

More recently, the political theorist Jane Bennett has suggested that we rethink our relationship to our environment in order to apprehend "vibrant matter," the term she uses to inaugurate a "new materialism" (Bennett, 2010). "Vibrant" is suggestive of material than can act, or move with energy; according to sense 2 in the *OED*, refers to material that is "moving or quivering rapidly; vibrating." Bennett, then, challenges the habitual distinction between dull, inert matter and vibrant life, suggesting rather that the world might be composed of "vital materiality." In Bennett's account, it is politically and philosophically necessary to extend our sense of what might be capable of vibrancy (of vibration), to non-human, non-sentient bodies. Her "new materialism" depends on our receptivity to the idea of vibrational, forceful states being possible in the very things we have tried to see as passive or inert. She examines the capacity of "things—edibles, commodities, storms, metals—not only to impede or block the will and designs of humans but also to act as quasi agents of forces with trajectories, propensities, or tendencies of their own"; "things" might then have "a vibrant materiality that runs alongside and inside humans" (Bennett, 2010, p. vii). Bennett's vibrancy aims to dissipate the "onto-theological binaries of life/matter, human/animal, will/determination, and organic/inorganic" (p. x). She shakes these binaries apart with a term that pulses with the possibility of vibration; the effects of feeling this vibrational pulse would, she hopes, include a radical reconceptualizing of the human and her place in the vital world, inaugurating a new "ecological sensibility" (p. xi).

Much of Bennett's thinking seems to coincide with the work of the critic-philosopher Timothy Morton, who makes a shaking-apart of the habitual distinction between the human and the non-human, between the living and the inert/dead/inorganic/artificial, a profound precursor to the establishment of an "ecological culture." "The further scholarship investigates life forms (ecology, evolutionary biology and microbiology) the less those forms can be said to have a single, independent and lasting identity," Morton tells us; we need "concepts that ruthlessly denature and de-essentialise: they are called deconstruction" (Morton, 2010, p. 1). Deconstruction has elsewhere been conceived of as a forceful disturbance, a vibrational unsettling of matter: "Roughly speaking, deconstruction is desedimentation: to deconstruct is to shake up and transform" (Bennett and Royle, 2009, p. 320). Bennett and Morton both, then, engage with the idea of a vibratory shaking-up (literal and metaphorical) in order to reconceive and radicalize our notions of the human, as have Adorno, Barthes and Bersani before them.

E L James and Contemporary Erotic Shattering

I propose making use of these vibrationally alert aesthetic and political treatises in order to approach the vibrations of the romance heroine in new ways and to extend the debate around erotic fiction in new directions. Might we glimpse something of the radical shimmer attached by various theorists to various kinds of vibration—to self-shattering, *ébranlement*, *Erschütterung*, *jouissance*, material vibrancy, de-sedimentation—in the catastrophic feminine quaking depicted in contemporary erotic literature? Or do such vibrations resonate at a markedly different frequency in the contemporary romance heroine, connoting a quaking acquiescence rather than a radical discombobulation?

In order to draw out some possible resonances *and/or discords* between radical vibrational theories and popular erotic fiction, I offer a reading of the highly successful series penned by E L James: the *Fifty Shades of Grey* trilogy. James, in her descriptions of the novels' heroine, Anastasia Steele, has authored an extended version of a vibrationally-overwhelmed eroticism. Disequilibrium is essential to Ana's experience of falling in love with Christian Grey from the very first moments of their relationship. When Anastasia Steele first meets the billionaire CEO, she falls head over heels: tripping at the threshold she finds herself "on [her] hands and knees in the doorway to Mr Grey's office" (James, 2012a, p. 7). This is the first of an array of somatic demonstrations that indicate that Ana's body is now out of her control. Ana's first few meetings with Grey are characterized through her errant physical reactions to him: she blushes and flushes, she shivers, she quivers, her heart rate accelerates, she flutteringly blinks, her "eyelids matching [her] heart rate," her legs turn to "Jell-O" (p. 8). "Desperately I scrabble around for my equilibrium," she tells us; however, she is rendered profoundly incapable of physically composing herself. The most extreme examples of this disequilibrium are in her liability to lose physical balance and then consciousness. Her very first experience of desire is articulated in the context of a physical fall: "It all happens so fast—one minute I'm falling, the next I'm in his arms and he's holding me tightly against his chest.... And for the first time in twenty-one years, I want to be kissed" (p. 48).

When Ana's relationship to Grey becomes sexual, she describes her newly-discovered orgasmic potential in terms of a climax of this initiatory disequilibrium, where falling in love becomes falling apart. The terms used to describe her experience of the erotic might seem to resonate with the theoretical terms of vibrational disturbance discussed earlier, in particular the intense, masochistic pleasure that Bersani describes as self-shattering sexuality. As Grey pins Ana down, pulling her hair and violently kissing her, he puts her senses into "disarray" (p. 80); when she first orgasms, she "fall(s) apart in his hands, [her] body convulsing and shattering into a thousand pieces" (p. 116); she "splinter(s) into a million pieces underneath him" (p. 118); she is "coming apart at the seams" (p. 118). The source of Ana's "delicious" pleasure might certainly be seen to reside in the *intensity* of her experience of Grey, and in its somatic manifestations which humiliatingly overwhelm and disorganize her body—blushing, quivering, vomiting, swooning and ecstatic shattering—throughout the novel.

Romance Fiction: Plugged in or Tuned Out?

Perhaps, then, it is the vivid descriptions of sexual convulsion that have made these books reverberate erotically with so many female readers, and we might begin to detect strong resonances with Bersani's descriptions of erotic shattering. However, as a markedly derivative project,[4] there are also louder resonances that *Fifty Shades*' descriptions of physical disarray create: the jellied legs, the blushing, the various palpitations; all of these moments of disequilibrium are clichéd tropes within romance fiction, which create a continuity between *Fifty Shades* and other popular romance novels. We might already, then, be on slightly shaky ground in attempting to read these novels as depicting shaking subjectivity in a radical or progressive sense: these jellifying tropes call backwards toward familiar descriptions of female sexual response in romance fiction, descriptions which often idolize female physical passivity, insufficiency and fragility. Early feminist critics of romance novels have argued that their glamorization of female helplessness has helped to ameliorate and sustain the (patriarchal) status quo rather than challenging it: Tania Modleski, for instance, has likened romance fiction to a tranquilizer, the dose of which must always be increased "in order to alleviate problems aggravated by the drug itself" (Modleski, 2008, p. 57). In Modleski's reading, romance fiction, even when it describes palpitative states, is a political sedative; the duped reading of such fiction becomes one of the problems that feminist thought must address.

However, subsequent feminist critics have suggested that the denigration of genre fiction with a large female readership is itself a reflection of ideological positions that describe women as particularly passive and prone to being duped. Denigrations of the texts large numbers of women enjoy reading might slide inexorably into "contempt for the reader," Radford cautions (1986, p. 14). Perhaps the most influential study to challenge the idea of the passive victimhood of the romance reader is Janice A. Radway's. In her influential "ethnographic" study of a group of U.S. readers of romance fiction, Radway suggests that romance reading practices are far more complex, fraught and *active* than previous scholarship has suggested; romance reading, she argues, is *enabling* for many women as an act that gives them a literal escape from the demands of their domestic obligations, a rare opportunity for leisure time and privacy (Radway, 1984, p. 12). The act of reading novels that repeatedly romanticize *passive* female sexuality is nevertheless construed as an *active* means of negotiating the disappointments of "patriarchal marriage" in Radway's analysis; she argues that "the struggle over romance is itself part of the larger struggle for the right to define and to control female sexuality" (1984, pp. 14, 16). Radway countenances the possibility that romance might, finally, "stitch" women into the fabric of patriarchal culture. However, she also makes the compelling argument that reading romance fiction involves an active struggle when it comes to gender relations, rather than a tranquilized acceptance of the heterosexual, patriarchal status quo.

What seems to be at stake in these different feminist approaches to romance fiction is the potential *activity* of female readers. In Modleski's approach, women might be duped into tranquilized acceptance of certain situations through their consumption of sedated heroines; whereas Radway insists on the activity of female readers, a vivid pulse that beats beneath the consumption of genre fiction as proof of the possibility of struggle. While a full consideration of the contemporary romance genre is beyond the scope of this essay, it seems to me that *Fifty Shades of Grey*, with its prominent depictions of ecstatic, shattered states, is a particularly important text for romance studies. *Fifty Shades*, with its spectacular vibrations, might be read as a narrative charting the ways in which disruptive, active female energy is narratively released and then *dealt with* in romance fiction. We might, therefore, read *Fifty Shades* as a paradigmatic text, a text that might illuminate some of the critical arguments made in respect of the recuperative operation of genre fiction. I'll attempt to demonstrate, in the paragraphs that follow, how Ana's potentially disruptive discombobulation is rebalanced in the *Fifty Shades* novels according to romance clichés of masculine power and financial domination; how her spectacular propensity to shatter makes her especially prone to being pieced back together by the male lead; and how the romance-plot progress of the novels resolves the radical potential of Ana's vibrational disturbance into bathos.

In *Fifty Shades*, Ana's inability to stay balanced on her feet functions as an early warning of a developing symptomatology of female fragility and insufficiency that will narratively necessitate Grey taking control of Ana's body for her *own good*. Grey is there to catch Ana when the ground rushes toward her in her faints; he is there to repeatedly instruct her, "Breathe, Anastasia," when her body fails and her "medulla oblongata has neglected to fire any synapses to make [her breathe]" (James, 2012a, p. 67). The novels seem to suggest that our hapless heroine might actually expire without Grey's timely interventions and instructions regarding basic physical processes, like remaining upright and respiring. Perhaps most remarkable in this regard is Grey's constant insistence that Ana eat. His frequent exhortations and threats in this regard are so numerous that some commentators have suggested the novel's primary erotic charge for weight-embattled contemporary female readers is the fantasy of a masterful man forcing stacks of pancakes upon a woman.[5] Even if *Fifty Shades* were primarily a fantasy of calorific orgy, the necessity of male approbation for such eating would be enough to make one sick to one's stomach. But the fantasy works in an altogether more anorectic direction. The conversations around food are designed to reveal to us that Ana neglects to eat when she is left to her own devices (at one point she is described as ingesting only coffee and cola for five days, then breaking her fast with "a cup of yoghurt") (James, 2012b, p. 7). What Grey suggests through his insistence on directing Ana's eating is her inability to take care of herself, her propensity to self-dereliction, her inherent physical fragility (her "gauntness" [p. 12]) which necessitates him taking all control.

Grey's power over Ana is exercised in increasingly invasive and totalitarian ways as the novels continue. The later novels chart a neo–Pygmalion remaking of Ana according to Grey's turbo-capitalist version of female beauty and civility, which begins with Ana's initiation into the rituals of the female beauty regimen:

> Under [my best friend's] tireless and frankly intrusive instruction, my legs and underarms are shaved to perfection, my eyebrows plucked, and I am

> buffed all over. It has been a most unpleasant experience. But she assures me that this is what all men expect these days [2012a, p. 85].

By the end of the novels Ana has capitulated to the punishing regime of "grooming" that she initially felt was "time consuming, humiliating and painful" (2012a, p. 85), and records the results in a way that would make any TV make-over show producer proud:

> My body is so different these days. It's changed subtly since I've known him.... I've become leaner and fitter, and my hair is glossy and well cut. My nails are manicured, my feet pedicured, my eyebrows threaded and beautifully shaped [James, 2012b, p. 41].

Grey's control of Ana's body is yet more invasively exercised in relation to her fertility. He arranges for a gynecologist to come to his apartment to administer contraception, and despite her initial grumblings ("It's my body"), she accedes to his contraceptive decisions ("Yes, my body is his ... he knows it better than I do") (James, 2012b, p. 168). That both Grey and Ana see her body as his property is emphasized and eroticized everywhere in the novels. He repeatedly touches her intimately, mouthing the claim "Mine," and by the third novel she joyously claims: "You own my body and my soul" (James, 2012c, p. 232). "He is master of my universe," Ana remarks elsewhere, playing on the original title of the online serialization that preceded the publication of *Fifty Shades*, and on the fantasy of masculine omnipotence it perpetuates (James, 2012b, p. 376).[6] When Grey buys the publishing company Ana works for, making him her "boss's boss's boss" (p. 58), Ana becomes his employee as well as his chattel: he insists that she change her professional name once they are married as a matter of brand control: "I'm just looking after my assets.... Some of them need rebranding" (James, 2012c, p. 143).

Shaking feminine states in these novels, then, rather than constituting a sustained, radical interruption of social and sexual relations, are hijacked as the pretext for masculine control and discipline to re-affirm the most conservative gender stereotypes in romance fiction: a hapless heroine is rescued from her own self-dereliction by a masterful man. The *Fifty Shades* novels might therefore trace the bathetic failure of the radical or liberatory charge to self-shattering, when an imputed propensity to shatter and to self-divest is hijacked as the pretext for patriarchal *protection and control* of the romance heroine's fragile body. The novels might therefore be read as a cautionary tale: they are the story of *the failure* of an active struggle to renegotiate patriarchal relations, a struggle which Radway associates with romance; the heroine might convulse violently, but eventually she cedes all control of her body to her partner, and the capitalist context in which he thrives. By the end of the *Fifty Shades* novels we seem to have found ourselves in decidedly Foucauldian territory: Ana's vibrational energies, even in their non-ejaculatory, non-masculine forms, have become the pretext for masculine regulation and control, and Ana's transformation into a super-groomed corporate asset disappoints the hopes voiced by Bersani et al., for a reconceived relationship between the self-shattering individual and her culture/environment.

The "Little Woman": Masochism and Shrinking Subjects

The mitigation of the radical vibrational potential of female subjects might be seen to operate through a long-history of "protection" being used as the pretext for the control of women's bodies. It is useful here to consider some of the arguments that have been made about masochism in relation to female subjectivity, considering claims made for the subversive potential of submission alongside the ways in which an imputed masochism might be used to control and discipline female sexuality. "Romantic, *liberating* and totally addictive" is how the large-type blurb of the *Fifty Shades* novels promotes the trilogy. This cover copy invokes the possibility of emancipation, a possibility that has been much discussed in relation to the novels' depiction of BDSM sexual practices. In recent years, sex-positive feminist critics have celebrated the choice that BDSM promotes in terms of the exploration of female sexual fantasies, *including fantasies of domination*.

A thriving sub-genre of erotic fiction with BDSM content now exists, accompanied by claims about the subversive, emancipatory potential of the sado-masochistic practices depicted therein. The possibility for women to *choose* alternative types of relationship and sexual practice is one basis for claims made about the "liberating" potential of these texts, with masochistic fantasies featuring as part of this suite of sexual choice. Stephanie Wardrop has written about "rape sagas," found even in mainstream erotic fiction, constituting a ritualized s/m dynamic that is enabling for female readers (Wardrop, 1995). Wardrop suggests that women might gain both "control and pleasure" through s/m rituals, which are designed to create a "mutual dependency." In fact, she suggests, "female readers derive a nonmasochistic—even empowering—pleasure from [s/m] texts"; what might appear as passivity in a heroine is felt by the readers of these texts to be "inherent strength." The suggestion that masochistic fantasies produce positive affects and effects in female readers has also been made in relation to *Fifty Shades*. Katie Roiphe, for example, in a cover story for *Newsweek*, suggests that the novels tap into something "liberating about being overcome or overpowered. The thrill here is irrational, untouched by who one is in life, immune to the critical or sensible voice, the fine education, or good job" (Roiphe, 2012). These claims for liberation through masochistic overwhelming must put us in mind again of Bersani's concept of masochistic self-shattering, and his suggestion that sexuality, as an experience of overwhelming intensity, "could be thought of as a tautology for masochism" (Bersani, 1986, pp. 38–39). The "self-abolition" that Bersani aspires to in masochistic sexuality is a liberation from the ego, which is also the freedom to constitute new modes of selfhood and community.

However, the BDSM content of the *Fifty Shades* novels is arguably deployed in the context of a more conventional romance narrative than usually features in less-mainstream, overtly BDSM erotica. In a recent special issue of the journal *Sexualities*, devoted to *Fifty Shades*, the editors suggest that "the novels blend a somewhat conventional romantic narrative with sexual passages that have a BDSM (Bondage, Discipline, Domination, Submission, Sadism, Masochism) flavour. What distinguished the novel series from other forms of erotica or romance novels, however, was their visibility" (Deller et al., 2013, p. 859). The editors focus on the successful "capitalization" on these novels and their enormous mass-market success, while other contributors analyze their supposedly "transgressive" BDSM content in relation to their status as successful commodities. Alex Dymock, for example, argues that the "subversive" content of these books becomes a mechanism for reinforcing both capitalism and heteronormativity, making the effects of the books essentially conservative (Dymock, 2013). And this might return us to some of the contradictions inherent in the claims made for the liberating potential of these novels and their particular brand of masochism. The contradictory coincidence of "liberation" and "addiction" in the *Fifty Shades* blurb, the chiasmatic convergence of freedom and compulsion in the seemingly straight-forward claim, advertises some of the problems of the branding of female "emancipation" in relation to masochism. Liberation and exigency jostle uncomfortably here, reminding us of the complexities of "choice" and "liberation" in the context of consumer capitalism. Margot Weiss highlights the neo-liberal assumptions that underpin some evangelistic approaches to masochism as a sexual *choice* for women:

> I am wary of the claim that embracing our inner sexual desires is a sure path to liberation.... This seems to me a liberal understanding, where our fantasies and desire are private, ours alone to discover and nurture, and detached from a social or political world.... BDSM, like all sexualities, is a product of our social environment, not an age-old, unchanging orientation ... gendered relations of power *structure* our sexual desires—even in consensual BDSM spaces (where sexist assumptions about manly dominance and feminine submission remain depressingly common) [Weiss, 2012].

In the context of the social and political structuring of our desires, it becomes necessary to inflect some of the radical claims for a liberating, "self-shattering" masochism with the bathetic counter-history of the exploitation of woman's imputed, inherent "masochism," an imputation that might serve various vested interests (economic, patriarchal, political and medical).[7] Paula J. Caplan questions the freedom and integrity of such choices and labels, arguing that the term "masochism" has been tendentiously attributed to and taken-up by women in a way that serves dominant interests: "A misogynist society has created a myriad of situations that make women unhappy. And then that same society uses the myth of women's masochism to blame the women themselves for their misery" (Caplan, 1985, p. 9). We might see a similar tendency operating through Ana's adoption of masochism in *Fifty Shades*: the abnegation of choice inherent in Ana's masochism directly serves Grey's desire to be in control; her masochism is not a privately, or individually, constituted sexual preference. What "liberation" might mean for Ana is defined solely by Grey in these novels, and it seems to neatly coincide with what he wants: "Free your mind," he *instructs* Ana, and presumably the rest is meant to follow (James, 2012a, p. 294).

Ana's masochism, as part of her role of submission, has the effect of *diminishing* Ana as a subject rather than expanding her choices or her areas of activity. Numerous exchanges in the novels highlight submission as part of a process of Ana shrinking, both literally and metaphorically. Discussions about Ana's weight, for instance, serve to indicate Ana's tendency toward *smallness*, producing an unsettling, anorectic rendering of female appetite: Ana's propensity to thinness is part of an elision of any female desire independent of heteronormative male instruction. And it is also part of a practice of self-diminution which is simultaneously a journey back toward the smallness of childhood: Grey's admonishments and instructions about eating are noticeably infantilizing and Ana's imputed inability to take care of herself require him to take charge of her eating as the disciplinary father ("So help me God, Anastasia, if you don't eat, I will take you across my knee" [2012a, p. 31]). Ana regularly describes herself as small and childlike in her interactions with Grey ("[He] grabs me before I fall and hoists me into his arms, holding me close to his chest like a child" [p. 61]; "He patiently caresses me as if I'm a small child" [p. 330]; "Why does he always make me feel like an errant child" [James, 2012b, p. 13]). And when Grey fails to kiss her, Ana "sinks" to her knees, "wanting to make myself as small as possible. Perhaps this nonsensical pain will be smaller the smaller I am" (James, 2012a, p. 51).

Ana's desire to make herself smaller makes her masochism appear as part of a process of *self-shrinking*. And this shrinking might be another way in which the romance heroine's masochism distinguishes itself from Bersani's hypothetically radicalized masochism, chiming as it does with a history of discourses that have diminished women. The New York psychoanalyst Natalie Shainess, writing in *Sweet Suffering: Woman as Victim*, makes the remarkable claim that she has never met a "truly expansive woman," whereas she has met many expansive men (Shainess, 1984, p. 243). Ana's liability to shrink might be seen as a capitulation to this sort of depiction of female subjectivity, which spatially diminishes women while mythologizing their tendency toward masochistic self-diminution (the "little woman"; the "shrinking violet"). Erich Fromm's work in *Escape from Freedom* on the question of masochism in connection to the shrinking size of the subject might take us further down this narrowing track. In Fromm's analysis, modern capitalism has freed man from certain historical forms of oppression, but has failed to realize a positive freedom for the individual. The old certainties (religion, community and a connection to the natural world) that once conferred a sense of belonging and security have been stripped away, but there has been no successful establishment of a modern, connected society to replace them. Man therefore "necessarily feels his insignificance and smallness in comparison with the universe and all others who are not 'he'" (Fromm, 1941, p. 20). In the face of mechanization, digitalization, atomic threat and population explosion, man feels himself to be "a particle of dust" and is "overcome by his individual insignificance." Masochism, Fromm suggests, is a pathological attempt to remedy this, by which the individual strives to overcome his alienation by fusing himself with somebody or something bigger in the world outside himself, renouncing his own alienated freedom and finding pleasure in his subjection. For Fromm, this is an ultimately futile strategy, which fails to challenge the underlying structures of capitalist alienation and which finds its most heinous expression in the willing submission to Fascism. The masochist, Fromm suggests, already feeling small, makes himself yet tinier.

In *Fifty Shades*, the "somebody" bigger with whom the disappearing Ana can be seen to masochistically "fuse," is, of course Christian Grey, the billionaire giant-among-men. Apart from Ana's descriptions of herself as small in comparison to him, the imputation of him as "Daddy" to her as "Baby," there are other ways in which Grey looms from the text, in particular through the physical spaces he owns and occupies, from his "huge twenty-storey office building," with its "enormous—and frankly intimidating" dimensions, to the capacious suites of the hotels he inhabits, to his home, where the main room is "enormous," making it more like a "mission statement" than a domestic space (James, 2012a, pp. 4, 94). Even his shower is "oversized" (James, 2012b, p. 469). And when Grey takes Ana to see a home that he is intending to buy for the two of them, "The Big House," its proportions are "palatial," "enormous: twelve thousand square feet on six acres of land" (James, 2012c, pp. 423–26). Grey's immoderate occupancy of physical space is inextricably linked to the exorbitance of his wealth: "Anastasia, I earn roughly one hundred thousand dollars an hour," he immodestly tells her (2012b, p. 109), the statement's gratuity underscored by the fact that the size of his buildings has already done the talking for him: "This is seriously rich," Ana has remarked, seeing his monstrous apartment for the first time (James, 2012a, p. 423).

In these enormous spaces, and in their lateral positions, significant distortions of scale are allowed to take place. Grey is always at the top, in the penthouse, the perspectival position from which the people below are rendered tiny: "Life in the clouds sure feels unreal. A fantasy—a castle in the air, adrift from the ground," Ana remarks (James, 2012a, p. 369). And then, looking down on the people below them: "[Grey is] too beautiful for the little people below; too beautiful for me" (p. 370). E L James draws here on the tropes of masculine size and elevation through money that are familiar to the point of exhaustion in romantic films and TV series marketed to women in recent decades: the big, powerful, rich man, typified in the moniker "Mr. Big," and then just "Big," in contrast to the female protagonist as "Kid," in the *Sex and the City* series, for example (Star, 1998–2004); or the melancholy pent-house-dwelling millionaire looking down on the untroubled, quotidian little people, typified by Edward Lewis in *Pretty Woman* (Marshall, 1990). Unlike the more ambivalent and likeable Lewis, however, Grey never experiences vertigo in his penthouse. He is utterly delighted by his position, his great ascendancy and the diminution of those around him, who are "dwarfed by [his apartment's] sheer size" (James, 2012b, p. 453). One thinks here of Mike Leigh's film *Career Girls*, in which the new affluence of one of the main characters is marked by her viewing an apartment in the sky: "I suppose on a clear day, you can almost see the class struggle from here," she quips, revealing the fantasy of social ascendancy such an elevated city residence connotes, and the tensions it effectively euphemizes through the distortions of scale (Leigh, 1997). For Ana's exalted, enormous Grey, the "class struggle" would be a distant, indecipherable skirmish below, the barely perceptible concern of the "little people." And E L James invites women to shrink into this romanticized ideal.

Shattering the Cult of Female Fragility

"Christian is still treating me like I'm made of glass," Ana tells the reader toward the end of the trilogy; "He still won't let me go to work" (James, 2012c, p. 528). Female vulnerability to the loss of physical integrity—exemplified repeatedly in these novels through Ana's disintegrative orgasms, her propensity to faint, her physical diminution, and her vulnerability to sexual assault[8]—is not here the precursor to radical change; instead, it becomes the justification for the exercise of phallocentric financial power to protect the female body. The exclusivity of the heterosexual couple and family unit is only bolstered through Ana's vibrational self-shattering, as is Grey's vision of her as permanently endangered, liable to shatter like glass. If Ana's shattering into sexuality has the potential for new forms of self, relation and society along the lines proposed by Bersani, if her broken pieces might form part of a fantastic new communal mosaic, these moments of possibility are also the ones that Grey might, and does, seize to impose his conservative version of gender relations upon Ana.

Fifty Shades spectacularly demonstrates the importance of vibratory states, of vivid, active discombobulation, to depictions of female sexuality in contemporary erotic/romance fiction. I have sought to suggest that these moments of vibratory potential might chime with the good vibrations envisioned by so many critical theorists as possible points of sexual and political departure. However, *Fifty Shades* also demonstrates how, even in supposedly subversive romance fiction, this potential might be commuted by gender-specific notions of physical vulnerability into new narratives of feminine capitulation. Any radical potential to the vibrational disturbance Ana experiences as the erotic is, in the *Fifty Shades* narrative, bathetically voided through the remaking of a female subject in accordance with the slavish specifications of contemporary commodity fetishism. The struggle that critics such as Radway detect in the romance genre, the active female energy associated with it, always risks recuperation. *Fifty*

Shades gives us a highly romanticized version of the recuperation of erotic energy into traditional heterosexual marriage. The potential chaos of Ana's vibrational pleasure is regulated according to Grey's essentially conservative, super-consumerist ethos: her disruptive physical energy is contained through normative romance patterns, so that by the end of the novels the heroine is married to a physically and financially dominant man she vicariously exercises his colossal spending power, and she has allowed him to take absolute control of her body.[9] *Fifty Shades* might therefore be read as a cautionary tale about the *recuperation* of potentially subversive female energies. But reading *Fifty Shades* alongside radical theoretical accounts of shaken states might also help us to focus on moments of vibration as brief, vulnerable pockets of possibility. This might, in turn, help us to think about ways in which ecstatic disruption might be sustained in and through depictions of vivid, vibrant states, and about the ways in which female subjects might more successfully struggle against the commutation of their energies. Let's celebrate the shaking-off of tired old fantasies of female physical vulnerability, rather than the romance of recuperation.

Notes

1. Bersani, describing in Laplanchian terms his work in the *Freudian Body* (Bersani, 2000, p. 108).
2. "The self which the sexual shatters provides the basis in which sexuality is associated with power" (Bersani, 1987 [2010], p. 25).
3. I am indebted here to Timothy Morton, who presents these ideas together (Morton, 2007, p. 168).
4. The novels began life as *Twilight* fanfiction; they therefore borrow heavily from the teen vampire romance series, and more generally from popular romance fiction (Deller et al., 2013, p. 863).
5. Victoria Coren's description is worth quoting at length:

> [W]hat kind of a hussy says openly that she'd like a stack of pancakes and syrup? As if she cared not a fig for social rules of weight and waistline? The unabashed satisfier of calorie cravings: she is today's outlier, outsider and outcast.
>
> If a masterful stranger instructs us to eat pancakes, however, we're not sluts at all. Not our fault! Just following orders! Dear oh dear, *another* big mouthful? Must I really? That, I posit, is the erotic charge of *Fifty Shades Of Grey* [Coren, 2012].

6. The *Fifty Shades* novels appeared in an earlier serialised version online as *Master of the Universe*. There are resonances here with the financial power as the delusion of omnipotence as described by Thomas Wolfe in his *Bonfire of the Vanities* (1987) in which a Wall Street financial trader thinks of himself as "Master of the Universe."
7. Feminist anxiety over the contentious medical application of the term "masochism" in relation to women was made evident when feminist psychiatrists and psychologists in the United States lobbied against the creation of the diagnostic category "Masochistic Personality Disorder" by the American Psychiatric Association, on the grounds that it would be applied pejoratively, and near-exclusively, to female patients (Leo, 2005).

8. Ana is presented as being increasingly subject to unwanted sexual advances as the novels progress: from her friend, her boss, and strangers.

9. I do not refer just to the orchestration of Ana's sexual pleasure here, but to the more totalitarian way in which Grey controls her eating, her beauty and exercise regimen, and, by the end of the novels, how she will give birth.

On Not Reading *Fifty Shades*

Feminism and the Fantasy of Romantic Immunity

TANYA SERISIER

Writing in July 2012, *Guardian* columnist Alexis Petridis (2012) quipped that it was time for him to "pay heed to the recently passed law that demands every newspaper columnist in Britain must write something about the *Fifty Shades of Grey* series." An indication of the validity of Petridis' law can be found through a simple search of the "Factiva" news database of English-language news outlets. The search reveals that in the year following publication of the *Fifty Shades* trilogy in 2012 there were 11,297 articles which mentioned the books.[1] As a point of comparison, the figure for the two years after publication of Dan Brown's (2003) literary blockbuster, *The Da Vinci Code*, shows just over half as many mentions, in 6,632 articles.

It is this cultural response, rather than the books themselves, that is the subject of this chapter. While this response is significant for the sheer volume of commentary produced, my interest here is in the content of this commentary, specifically marked similarities that appear throughout discussions of the text. This essay is, therefore, not intended as a general survey or cataloguing of these review articles, or a claim that there was no examples of media coverage that did not conform to this pattern. Instead, in it I attempt to think through some of the key tropes that I observed arising again and again. The analysis is based on surveying articles that appeared in large metropolitan newspapers, and current affairs and political magazines (both online and print) in Australia, the United Kingdom and the

United States. This was in order to reduce the number of articles and to look for trends and patterns among influential news outlets.

The most immediately striking feature of these reviews is the way in which commentators describe the activity of reading, or more precisely, "not reading" *Fifty Shades*. Petridis (2012), quoted above, uses the verb "skimmed" to refer to his reading of the book. This word reoccurs throughout these articles, joined by synonyms such as "flicked," "skipped" and even "stopped," and some who wrote commentary without reading the book at all (for example Crampton, 2012; Galanes, 2012; Groskop, 2012; Flood, 2012b). While it may be mandatory to write about *Fifty Shades*, there appears to be an equally compelling taboo against reading the books, at least for these reviewers. This lack of reading, however, does not prevent reviewers from having come to very decisive opinions on the books which is that they are not only bad, but bad for a number of different reasons. Almost unanimously, commentators agree the books are badly written, the prose is, amongst other things, "execrable," "cringe worthy," "repetitive" and "irritating" (Washington Post, 2012; Butler, 2012; Nick, 2012; Dowd, 2012). One reviewer estimated that bad reviews in print and online would outnumber good by twenty to one, an estimate that I would agree with (Groskop, 2012). Perhaps more surprisingly, there is a similar level of consensus that the books are bad erotica and even worse depictions of sadomasochism. Jaded, perhaps disappointed, reviewers claim that the books are merely "comfort reading posing as porn" or that, despite their reputation, most of the sex scenes are actually "vanilla" and even "boring bog standard" (Marrin, 2013; Roiphe, 2012; Arnold, 2012). Further, the books demonstrate the characters', and by extension the author's gaucheness, whether through poor taste in music and film or celebration of conspicuous consumption (Petridis, 2012; O'Hagan, 2012). Finally, and the criticism of most significance here, the books are heavily criticized for their gender politics—the depictions of the heroine, hero and their relationship are seen to be anti-feminist, stereotyped, regressive and, depending on the reviewer, borderline or actually abusive. On the basis of these articles, the only conclusion to be drawn is that the *Fifty Shades* trilogy could only appeal to someone with no literary discernment, no sexual sophistication, no cultural capital, and terrible gender politics.

Given that these criticisms are made almost entirely on the basis of a very limited reading of the books, the skipping, skimming and stopping mentioned above, the dismissal or condemnation of the books is generally carried out quite quickly. Almost without exception, these articles, even those purported to be reviews, are about the cultural phenomenon of the books and related topics, such as the etiquette of reading erotica on public transport or the importance of sexual experimentation in marriages and other long-term heterosexual relationships (O'Connor, 2012; Godson, 2012). Most broaden this focus to take the opportunity to reflect on what the popularity of the books tells us about contemporary gender relations and female sexuality. And it is precisely the popularity of the books that is the key issue here. What the reviewers are interested in most of all is what the popularity of the books tells us about the many women who have not only read the books but recommended them to others, given the early lack of marketing efforts and reliance on word-of-mouth sales. To put it another way, the depiction of all that is wrong with the books easily slides into a quest to ascertain what precisely is wrong with their readers.

This connects to the final element of this archive that is particularly noteworthy. There is a shared presumption among many, if not all, of the reviewers that these books are not only bad in and of themselves but they are bad for us. When it comes to these books, it seems, reviewers take a similar position to Theodor Adorno (2005, p. 25), agreeing that reading can only make us "stupider and worse." In this way, the not-reading practiced by the reviewers becomes a mark of their cultural integrity and their determination to resist the corrupting influence of the books. It also means that the reviews function as acts of public service. The reviewers have sullied themselves by contact with these books only so that their readership don't have to even repeat their experience of "skimming," "skipping" and "stopping," with some even offering tips of better choices in erotica for "those who who don't want to suffer through three big, fat books of this" (Cremen, 2012). This again leaves us with questions about those readers who actually enjoy the book, a group who nearly all columnists presume to be separate from their own audience. These strange readers almost invariably become objects of bemusement or concern and occasionally hostility. But a common practice involves "worrying" about the books' effects, which, it seems, go beyond the threat of becoming stupider and worse. Instead, columnists' worries range from the slightly tongue-in-cheek fear that women will gain "unrealistic" expectations regarding their sex life to fears that they will internalize unhealthy models of relationships, unable to distinguish between consensual sadomasochism and domestic abuse (Crampton, 2012; Flood, 2012a).

The response to *Fifty Shades* is highly gendered and reflects a long-standing cultural tendency whereby women's interests and pastimes are labelled as less worthwhile than men's pursuits (Modleski, 2008, p.xvii). But the sheer volume of commentary, the vociferous denunciations and the element of worry go beyond trivialization. The other fact that means this commentary cannot be dismissed simply as patriarchal media institutions devaluing women is that the majority of the articles and reviews are written by women and a sizable proportion are located in sections of the paper specifically marketed toward female readers, such as the "Daily Life" section of the *Sydney Morning Herald* and *Age* websites in Australia. Further, the criticisms and worries are linked, by both male and female authors, to a set of "feminist" concerns; the books are deemed harmful in large part because they are seen to be sexist. These responses bring to mind Tania Modleski's (2008, p. 4) comments regarding the responses of feminist and female critics to romance novels in the early 1980s. These responses, she states, tend to fall into three types: "dismissiveness; hostility—tending unfortunately to be aimed at the consumers of narratives; or, most frequently, a flippant kind of mockery." She argues that while such "discomfort" may be justified it also manifests a defensiveness that has not been "felt through":

> Whereas the old heroines have to protect themselves against the seductions of the hero, feminist critics seem to be strenuously disassociating themselves from the seductiveness of feminine texts. And whereas the heroine of romance turns against her own better self, the part of her which feels anger at men, the critic turns against her own "worse" self, the part of her which has not yet been "liberated" from shameful fantasies.

This kind of attitude toward romance "seems to betray a kind of self-mockery, a fear that someone will think badly of the writer for even touching on the subject, however gingerly."

In what follows I argue that many feminist reviews of *Fifty Shades* are marked by just this kind of "anti-romantic fantasy" that mirrors the fantasy dynamics of romance reading. This fantasy is marked by a slippage between the text and women who read it, with feminist commentators seeking not only to assert their immunity from the romantic fantasy but also their distance from those women who find themselves subject to it. This relationship is characterized not only by distance but by a form of "worrying" based on the insistence that female readers are endangered by, and require rescue from, the text. This "anti-romantic" fantasy is not only illuminating about the differing relationships women have with the romance genre but also helps to consider the location of feminism within popular culture and its relationship to women's consumption of that culture. In what follows, I do not wish to deny that feminist responses to romances remain vexed for very good reasons. I am, however, interested in thinking about potentially more productive feminist practices of reading and engaging with romance than those that are evident here.

Reading and Not Reading: Romantic Fantasy and Female Subjectivity

The popularity of *Fifty Shades*, with its endless repeat orgasms, limitless wealth, and all-powerful yet supremely vulnerable hero, is hard to read as anything other than almost a limit-case of romantic fantasy. To say, however, that romance fiction is fantasy is not to dismiss its cultural import or to suggest it is inherently harmful. Reactionary myths about feminine sexuality and subjectivity are not unique to romance literature or movies. What is unique about these texts is that they reverse a widespread cultural practice where women's preoccupation with romance is taken for granted but situated in the background or the margins of the real story of men's action. Romances are thus deeply ambivalent; by insisting on the significance of the heroine's experience romance performs an important centering of feminine subjectivity even while it reinforces the relegation of women to the private sphere of love and sex (Radway, 1991). Fantasy, as Jacqueline Rose (1998) reminds us, is a more complex process than simple wish fulfilment. Rather, it is a precondition of social and psychological life in a society where reality is difficult, complex and marked by dissonance between our socially-constructed expectations and reality. The multiple dilemmas and uncertainties faced by Anastasia in *Fifty Shades*, her conflict between desiring and fearing Christian and the troubled relationship between sexuality and violence and consent and violation that exists between them, speaks to the experiences and fears of many heterosexual women.

Elizabeth Cowie (1997) similarly suggests that fantasies are useful as coping mechanisms that operate within society as we experience it. In fantasy, we 'stage' our desires in a way that allows us to imagine, look at, and at times enact elements of them without the danger of real-life consequences. The result of such a fantasy staging can be that it allows us to exclude particular scenarios as models for action after viewing or enacting them in our head. Playing out fantasies, imaginatively or through cultural consumption, can draw attention to their undesirability as much as it can draw one into them. In this way, romance allows us to imaginatively explore the fantasy of male dominance and female submission that is embedded in our culture, and assist us in navigating social, romantic and sexual domains structured through this dynamic. Tania Modleski (2008, p. 35), following Roland Barthes, describes this process as "inoculation": a small dose of acknowledged evil allows one to cope with intractable social problems while also protecting against generalized subversion.

Romance novels like *Fifty Shades* acknowledge the dangers of heterosexuality, such as violence and the possibility that the male partner is incapable of fulfilling women's emotional needs. This acknowledgment, coupled with their successful resolution, serves to make these dangers bearable and to allow women to develop strategies for dealing with them. But what these fantasies do not do is enable us to challenge the existence of these unequal dynamics, meaning that while they are not necessarily harmful they are decidedly not emancipatory.

In contrast, the promise of emancipation, of changing the nature of heterosexual dynamics rather than simply successfully navigating them, is what is offered by feminism. However, as noted above, this emancipatory promise produces its own particular relationship to romance, the 'anti-romantic' fantasy introduced above. In contrast to the inoculation of the romantic fantasy, this is a fantasy of immunity, of being untouched by romantic archetypes and tropes. This is the fantasy that the emancipatory potential of feminism has already been fulfilled, at least in the individual herself and it is a fantasy that deeply marks contemporary feminist cultural criticism.

This fantasy can be seen, I suggest, in the almost ritualistic disavowal of any attraction to the text found in the feminist and feminist-inflected reviews. The fact that such a claim can only be made in the context of "not reading" the book, however, suggests that this fantasy of immunity is fraught with anxiety, that reviewers do not really believe they have been so lucky as to escape completely the romantic fantasies which saturate popular culture. Further evidence of the fragility of these claims is found in the alternate means reviewers use to buttress their assertions of immunity. As noted above, reviewers, with a few exceptions, do not solely object to the sexism of the books. Rather, this criticism is often tied to claims to superior levels of cultural discernment and sexual sophistication. *Fifty Shades* is criticized for being neither "real" literature nor "real" erotica and reviewers are at pains to make clear they are familiar with both. A surprising number of reviews compare the text to Austen, the Brontes, *Tess of the D'Urbervilles*, and even *La Nouvelle Heloise* by Rousseau, which function as examples of the kind of romantic literature that the reviewer does take pleasure in (Kelly, 2012; Birmingham, 2012; Petri, 2012). It is worth noting that as Anastasia is a literature student, some of these authors and texts are referred to in the books, with Christian even buying Anastasia a first edition of *Tess of the D'Urbervilles* as part of their courtship (James, 2012a). So, it is not that the reviewers have arbitrarily mentioned them. However, most references to these texts are undertaken in a way that derides Anastasia's, and by extension E L James' use, and understanding of them, which provides a variant on the argument that I am making (Kelly, 2012). Just as these reviewers find pleasure in "real" literature they also are clear that they are not opposed to the attractions of erotica per se. Here, knowledge of "real" S and M practices performs the same function as knowledge of "real" literature. The text not only falls short when measured against literary masterpieces, it is also frequently castigated for its "vanilla" sex scenes and lack of real knowledge about sadomasochism (Dowd, 2012).

Immunity to the text is thus obtained through various combinations of feminist consciousness, literary taste and sexual cosmopolitanism, problematically conflating feminist politics with middle-class distinction and the products of high culture. The particular inference that the high culture texts referenced above offer a progressive or feminist model for exploring the role of romance in contemporary women's lives is difficult to sustain. In a review for the Australian "Daily Life" website, for instance, Alecia Simmonds (2012) references Rousseau, Austen and the Brontes to make the claim that "romance has the potential to explore the relationship between power and intimacy." She follows this by noting that contemporary society has "collectively ignored" this potential by "relegating romantic fiction to the trivial," leaving it in the hands of authors such as E L James (Simmonds, 2012). While *La Nouvelle Heloise* is undoubtedly an interesting cultural artefact, and a "better book" than *Fifty Shades*, it is difficult to argue that it undertakes a more in-depth exploration of the relationship between power and intimacy. Indeed, for its many faults, connections between power and intimacy are central to almost all of the *Fifty Shades* plot developments—Christian's wealth, the dominant/submissive relationship it constructs and the conflict and negotiation between Christian and Anastasia around control, work, marriage and pregnancy, all significant sites of intimacy and power in contemporary women's lives.

The "we" who have "trivialized" romantic fiction and "ignored" its potential, is not, it transpires, a universal "we." It is a "we" composed of those who, like Simmonds, are committed non-readers of the text, a "we" that read "good" books and a "we" that includes neither the authors nor the readers of contemporary romantic fiction. As Ann Snitow (1979) argues, it is either mistaken or disingenuous to claim that our "society" trivializes romance. In fact, it is the bastions of "high" culture, "serious" literature and social commentary that tend to either ignore the topic or treat it with irony or contempt, as when *Guardian* columnist Suzanne

Moore (2012) dismisses romance as merely a "tired old fantasy" that "keeps women in their place." In contrast to this dismissal, romance continues to be a primary category of the female imagination, central to many women's lives, and a part of female consciousness that has remained largely untouched by the women's movement. Romantic novels such as *Fifty Shades* similarly "eschew irony; they take love straight" (Snitow, 1979, p. 160). It is precisely the refusal to relegate romance to the trivial that becomes one of the points of difference between readers of romance and feminist non-readers and critics.

The recourse in these reviews to high culture and cultural capital speaks, I suggest, to the anxiety of authors writing from a feminist perspective in a postfeminist era, which is both deeply indebted to and highly suspicious of feminist politics (McRobbie, 2004). As demonstrated by responses to *Fifty Shades*, feminism is neither silenced nor powerless in contemporary culture, but it does occupy a precarious position. Feminism, like romance, is highly vulnerable to dismissal and denigration, as evidenced by a small but noteworthy group of articles in my selection which used the popularity of *Fifty Shades* to denounce feminism as anachronistic and opposed to pleasure (for example, Albrechtsen, 2012). Linking feminism to education, good taste and sophistication helps to buttress its position, particularly within papers of record that cater to a predominantly middle-class readership that has similar investments in cultural capital. The flip side, of course, is that it risks making feminism the exclusive domain of the discerning middle-classes, ironically making the position of feminism and feminists more precarious by alienating large numbers of women and confirming accusations frequently levelled by anti-feminists.

Asexual Mommies and Vulnerable Girls: The Readers of Fifty Shades

The vast majority of discussions of *Fifty Shades* were as or more concerned with the readers of the text than with the books themselves. As noted above, the assertion of immunity from the text was often inextricable from claims of cultural superiority to its readers. To claim immunity from romance involves aggressively differentiating oneself from the large numbers of women who display no such immunity. This distancing and denigration was repeatedly achieved through dividing readers into two categories: "mommies," shorthand for married, suburban women without paid employment, and very young women or teenage girls. These two groups were almost universally depicted as the primary readers of the text, despite the lack of any evidence that they consumed the book in larger numbers than any other categories of women.

References to the book as "mommy porn" demonstrate the slippage between critiques of the book and denigration of its readers. The term gains its effect from its presumed oxymoronic character, the absurdity of linking its two elements. The connection with "'mommies," routinely depicted as both asexual and unsexy, is most commonly used to demonstrate that to the extent the book is pornographic it is second-rate and has no transgressive elements. As one reviewer concludes in relation to BDSM: "What were once transgressive sexual practices have become standard mumsy desires" (Simmonds, 2012). This phrase, from an avowedly feminist reviewer, could not be clearer about the connotations of the term mommy porn. The association with "mommies" relegates the book, like mothers themselves, to a domain outside of eroticism. To completely dispel the specter of "mumsy desire," however, many reviews go one step further. Upon elaboration it becomes clear that "mommy porn," like "food porn," refers to the deflection of sexual desire into other areas. In the numerous reviews that ponder the appeal of *Fifty Shades* to mommies, the conclusions reached are that mommies fantasize about, amongst other things, shopping, brand name products, cuddles and, above all, cleanliness (Williams, 2012; O'Hagan, 2012). The following excerpt is typical in this respect:

> When Anastasia walks into Christian Grey's beautifully kitted out dungeon room it smells faintly of lemon, polished leather and wood. It's clean, waxed, cared for and warm, hardware and full-size cross notwithstanding [Krupka, 2012].

It is undoubtable that many women are overworked and find their almost universally disproportionate share of housework onerous. It is also undoubtable that wealth, luxury and freedom from housework are important components of the fantasy world created by *Fifty Shades* and the romance genre more broadly. However, to make the "full-size cross" in the book merely a distraction is to attempt to erase the fact that without it no fantasy exists at all.

If the association with "mommies" is used to confirm the book's banality, it is the other category of imagined readers, girls and very young women, who give substance to the idea that the book is harmful and that its readers require rescuing. Here, reviewers draw on resonant cultural tropes of worrying about the sexual activities and the sexualization of girls and young women more broadly (Attwood, 2006). Ironically, such a move positions readers as possessing the same traits—naivety, dependence and sexual inexperience—that many reviewers find problematic in the depiction of Anastasia, the text's heroine. Further, using the figure of the young, naïve girl as an archetypal reader works to infantilize readers more broadly, enabling reviewers to presume that the text's readers lack the ability to read critically or outside the viewpoint of Anastasia. This is despite the fact that the text itself frequently positions the reader as knowing more than Anastasia, as in a scene where she and Christian watch a fireworks display under the strict surveillance of Christian's bodyguard. At this point in the text, the couple are being stalked by an ex-lover of Christian's who is known to be armed. When Christian comments that the fireworks display must have "taken ten years off" the life of the bodyguard, Anastasia asks if the bodyguard is scared of fireworks. Here, in a move Radway argues is typical of the genre and the pleasure it offers its readers, we are invited, with Christian, to partake in amused tolerance of Anastasia's innocence (James, 2012b).

Such a relationship to the text is rarely countenanced in reviews which identify readers entirely with the heroine and insist that they are likely to attempt to emulate her story. The following passage, taken from feminist author and columnist Gail Dines (2012), illustrates this tendency:

> I meet many women who started out like our heroine, only to end up, a few years later, not in luxury homes, but running for their lives to a battered women's shelter with a couple of equally terrified kids in tow. No happy ending here, either.

When the fictional story of the heroine is equated with the actual future of her readers, the ending of the book becomes a cruel deceit rather than a fantasy. A similar move is made by the director of a UK women's shelter who is quoted by *The Guardian* in an article about a protest the shelter organized against the book. She states that the book is not a romance but "really is about a domestic violence perpetrator, taking someone who is less powerful, inexperienced, not entirely confident about the area of life she is being led into, and then spinning her a yarn. Then he starts doing absolutely horrific sexual things to her." The story, she says, has a "subliminal message," which "is the classic narrative of domestic violence—'that you can heal this broken man, that if you just love him enough and take his shit enough, he will get better.'" In fact, a real life Anastasia would be "physically traumatized and potentially dead." The article concludes with the director's warning: "You have to walk away from the Christian Greys of this world" (Flood, 2012a).

The analysis in these reviews relies on a set of conflations that deny Anastasia, and by extension her readers, the possibility of sexual pleasure or sexual agency. This is evident in the description of the consensual and, largely, mutually pleasurable BDSM in the book as "absolutely horrific sexual things" that are "done to" Anastasia by Christian. This construction erases Anastasia's consent and pleasure, both of which are demonstrated at length in the text. It also mirrors the text's own tendency to construct an equivalence between consensual sexual practices that involve physical pain and, for instance, Christian's controlling and violent response to Anastasia sunbathing topless, which is to bite and bruise her breasts to prevent her from doing so again (James, 2012c). Failing to acknowledge the legitimacy of either Anastasia's or the reader's pleasure in BDSM ironically obscures the ways in which the text excuses or romanticizes these instances of abusive and controlling behavior rather than highlighting why they are troubling or disturbing. Reviewers committed to the practices of "not reading" are incapable of making these distinctions, instead constructing a hypothetical morality tale of the consequences of consumption of the text for an imaginary "typical reader." This attitude not only presumes that readers lack the interpretive abilities to distinguish between fiction and reality but also easily slips into hostility, blaming readers for their own projected victimization, or for contributing to others' victimization. This can be seen when *Independent* columnist Yasmin Alibhai-Brown (2013), after making similar claims to the two articles above, asserts that the popularity of *Fifty Shades* demonstrates that the women who read it "have completely capitulated to the forces of darkness." In another review, she brings together the two common categories of imagined readers, asking rhetorically: "Will all the mumsy fans of the book want their daughters to learn that?" (Alibhai-Brown, 2012).

In "The Desire to be Punished," Wendy Brown (2001) uses Freud's "'A child is being beaten'" to explore the often complex relationship between feminist activists and women's suffering. Brown argues that feminists may require suffering in order to legitimate their identity and speaking position. In other words, if women are not suffering then feminists have no basis on which to make political claims or demand to be heard. On the other hand, feminist struggles work to ameliorate that suffering and most people, feminists included, would rather avoid than experience injury themselves. As a result of these competing desires, suggests Brown, feminists may locate this necessary suffering outside of oneself, in women whom one can claim to speak on behalf of, in this case, the imaginary readers. This is done through rhetorical gestures which, according to Brown, work to generalize specific instances of suffering, and erase boundaries between stories of victimization and violence, and between the reader of these stories and the one who speaks about them. We see this in the slippage between feminist readings of Anastasia and Christian's relationship as abuse and the projection of that abuse onto the reader whose future becomes one of injury, poverty and possibly even death, and who becomes a victim of the text as much as the male violence it presages.

The displacement of suffering produces a degree of sadistic gratification, witnessed here in both the production of elaborate narratives of projected suffering and suggestions that readers have, at least in part, brought their suffering upon themselves. But the displacement, and its accompanying gratification, also produces guilt that the subject must seek to expiate. The guilt disrupts identification with the one onto whom the violence is projected. As this identification is essential for the feminist speaking position, this disruption creates a new round of anxieties about the affirmation of identity and the legitimacy of one's speech. In other words, the differentiation of themselves from the text's readers leads both to gratification and guilt on the part of the reviewer, but also disrupts her attempts to speak as and on behalf of women victimized by the text and its romantic narrative.

The result of all this, writes Brown (2001, p. 55), is "a surplus of scenes of suffering." Ultimately, this dynamic results in political paralysis; the subject is attached to suffering and also to the cause of its suffering, but displaces its anger elsewhere. To continue to claim the speaking position of feminist critic of popular culture, the critic requires popular culture to retain its sexism and particularly its harmful romantic mythologies. The point of hostility thus becomes the text which draws these myths out into the light rather than the myths themselves, leaving the feminist peculiarly attached to and dependent upon the romantic fantasies she disavows and condemns. This means that while she heaps scorn upon the readers of *Fifty Shades* she herself requires the perpetuation of the preconditions that create that narrative, meaning that she is singularly incapable of taking Modleski's (2008) urging to turn her fury from the text itself to the social world that enables it. Neither can she insert her politics into the gap between the fantasy of the text and the lived reality of women's lives because she is invested in eliding that gap. A successful feminist intervention in romance culture cannot ignore that gap and, indeed, must use it to find points of commonality with the reader of romance.

Romance and Feminist Reading

Responses to *Fifty Shades* tell us as much about the relationship between feminism and popular culture as they do about the politics of romance fiction. Indeed, the broad consensus that feminism and romance reading are mutually exclusive suggests a strong, albeit negative, relationship between the two. This conviction was shared by those who offered their identification with feminism as reason in itself for not reading the books and those who proclaimed feminist discomfort with the books to be yet more evidence that feminists are out of touch wowsers determined to ruin everyone else's good time (Galanes, 2012; Albrechtsen, 2012). The significance of this is that all parties in these debates appear to agree that feminism, whether as a perspective or a source of identification, plays a significant role in contemporary culture and in debates over women's cultural practices.

For this reason, feminist readings, particularly of women's writing and reading practices, matter. In this concluding section, I look at what responses to *Fifty Shades* tell us about feminist readings of popular culture, arguing that we need feminist reading practices that are critical, but also engaged with and sympathetic to the complexities of gender and sexuality in contemporary culture. This, I think, is different to reading "as a feminist," a practice based on enacting a particular political role or identity that too easily falls into the traps outlined in the preceding sections: those of cultural elitism, a desire for immunity from contemporary cultural norms and attitudes of dismissal, and worrying and hostility toward those seen as "non-feminists."

Similarly to romance, feminism is a site of intense affective attachment and identification. The identity of a "good feminist subject" is, at least within certain milieus, as desirable as more conventional aspirations to be a "good feminine subject." In the case of *Fifty Shades*, the good feminist is the woman who has conquered her "unliberated" desires and is immune to backward romantic fantasies. Like its feminine counterpart, however, such an identity is always aspirational, constituted through the anti-romantic fantasy identified above. This fantasy must be enacted through the disavowal of patriarchal sexuality, popular culture texts that represent it and the women who find pleasure in these texts. At its worst this fantasy produces a vision of sexuality that is purely utopian in that it has no grounding in or connection to contemporary culture and the desires that inhabit it. Without the resources of a utopian feminist movement to draw on, such a vision can seem to be simply opposed to sexuality, resulting in the stereotype of the "anti-sex" feminist. It is particularly ill-equipped to speak to the complexities and contradictions of women's heterosexual experiences and the romantic fantasies that arise from them. It also harbors a tendency to reify divisions between good feminists and other unenlightened women, a tendency which too easily slides into a form of cultural elitism which positions feminism as a project of middle-class distinction rather than women's emancipation.

As Jacqueline Rose (1998) argues, we need a language in which we can talk about women's oppression and at the same time discuss the complicated elements of women's fantasy lives. Currently, romances such as *Fifty Shades* are, for better or worse, one of the major tools we possess to do this and, for this reason, feminist engagement with the text is important. So what might this engagement look like? According to Modleski (2008), it must be open to the pleasures that women receive and the multiple meanings that they draw from even compromised and complicated cultural texts. This does not mean, as some critics suggest, refusing to criticize texts that women enjoy. Acknowledging women's pleasures does not restrict feminist analysis to documenting and celebrating them. Rather the place for feminism is perhaps to engage these fantasies through the gap they expose between what is and what ought to be, or at least what is and what women desire. It is this gap that potentially provides the space to begin to articulate truly utopian visions of women's (hetero)sexuality.

A second necessary ingredient for engagement is acknowledgement of our own attachments, conflicts and ambivalences with these texts and the romantic fantasies they articulate. We also, as feminists, need to recognize that this is bound up with our relationship to the idea of feminism or being a feminist, particularly in the postfeminist era in which we live. Feminist readings of these texts, and of women's reading practices, require reflexivity regarding the positive and negative affects of romantic fantasy. While I have not explored them here, the dismay, disappointment and disgust that many women feel when reading these fantasies can also provide points of critical engagement, and for many readers, these responses may alternate with more pleasurable emotions at different points in the text. Reading with a cognizance of these responses, and with the openness to the possibility that at least some of our anger may be directed at our own attraction to fantasies that we believe to be bad and bad for us, allows for points of engagement between "feminists" and readers of romance fiction.

In relation to the text itself, it is important to remember that both resistant and sympathetic reading practices can offer important critical tools, but that both require actual reading of the text. Immunity bolstered by non-reading represents a dead end, not only in terms of the text itself but for understanding its appeal and what its popularity might tell us about contemporary gender and sexual relations. We need to recognize that claims that the text is unrelentingly patriarchal are themselves ideological, based less on engagement with the text than with what it is seen to represent. As any close reader of Sade's *Justine* (2012) or Andrea Dworkin's *Mercy* (1990) can attest, it takes a great deal of literary skill to construct a novel that maintains a singular ideological focus on the victimization of women. E L James does not possess the skill, or probably the desire, to do this in a series that is over 1500 pages long. Rather than ideological singularity this is a text that is in fact marked by contradiction, ambivalence and even incoherence, and it is this that allows it to fulfil its ambivalent function as fantasy. There is, in other words, no unitary meaning to be found in the text. What this means is that detractors of the text, and also its far less numerous defenders, must ignore scenes that do not fit their over-arching interpretation. For instance, reviewers make claims such as that Anastasia "never has to think about the consequences of her actions" and that "she grows even more passive throughout the trilogy" (Simmonds, 2012). On the first point, in fact, many other reviewers complain that when the book is not documenting endless scenes of throbbing loins and pounding orgasms it is chronicling Anastasia's endless internal dialogues between her "subconscious" and her "inner goddess" regarding the likely consequences of her actions. The third book in the trilogy also documents one of the most well-known consequences of frequent heterosexual intercourse, an unplanned pregnancy (James, 2012c). And while Anastasia does display intense passivity at times, to reduce her character to this ignores her frequent displays of agency: leaving the relationship, maintaining her professional life over Christian's objections and, in the concluding moments of the trilogy, rescuing Christian's sister from an armed kidnapper while heavily pregnant (James, 2012a; 2012b; 2012c). This is not to say that Anastasia deserves emulation or admiration but, rather, to note that she does both think and act, and it requires an ideological refusal to read in order to claim otherwise.

Writing about the response to pornography of radical feminist writers such as Catherine MacKinnon, Wendy Brown (1995) notes that the desire to condemn male power can, inadvertently, depict it as more coherent and less vulnerable than it actually is. Rather than seeing, as MacKinnon does, the ubiquity of misogynist pornography as evidence of the strength of patriarchal power, Brown argues it makes more sense to see it as a sign of weakness. If gendered power structures were solid and stable there would be little need for their continual, almost hysterical reassertion. Similarly, in reading *Fifty Shades* purely as a text that depicts unrelenting male violence, and even has the power to transfer that violence into the lives of its readers, we make a stronger case for masculine dominance and inviolability than that found in the text itself. Pointing to the ways this power is compromised and undermined in the text, as in life, refuses to grant it absolute authority and dominion although, again, such a reading does not require us to simplistically celebrate the text as transgressive or empowering. An example can be found in Christian's emotional dependence on Anastasia. At one point, when he fears she will leave him for the second time, he literally prostrates himself before her, adopting a position of extreme submission (James, 2012b). Reading this dependence as purely empowering is to engage a fantasy that ignores the emotional labor that is demanded of women to foster that dependence in men and the ways in which that labor is generally neither valued nor returned. Refusing to acknowledge the dependence, however, is a refusal to acknowledge that Anastasia has power at all in the relationship, or to recognize the ways in which women may establish and exercise power in their intimate relationships more broadly. Finally, this is a fantasy where the happy ending produces the relationship that Anastasia, not Christian, has desired from the outset (James, 2012c). Their happiness is produced through adopting her vision of the world, not his, and again, this is a point that requires acknowledgment.

The responses to *Fifty Shades* demonstrate that we still need feminist readings of romance, and of women's attachments to it, that can analyze both the perils and the pleasures of women's entertainment. The restricted terms of debate around the trilogy suggest that such a perspective is lacking, at least in the domain of "quality" journalism and commentary. What is particularly concerning is that currently feminism, as a political perspective, appears to be foreclosing rather than opening up possibilities for discussions, and particularly for discussions that could include readers and fans of the books. Rectifying this is important, not only in order to produce a more sophisticated public dialogue around gender, sexuality and popular culture that does not position women as cultural dupes in need of rescue but also to avoid feminism becoming more closely tied to a politics of cultural elitism than of collective emancipation.

Note

1. Throughout I will use *Fifty Shades* to refer to the trilogy as a whole which is my main focus of concern and which, for convenience, I discuss as a single text comprised of three volumes. The three novels are *Fifty Shades of Grey, Fifty Shades Darker*, and *Fifty Shades Freed* (James, 2012a; 2012b; 2012c).

Selling Gay Sex to Women

The Romance of M/M and M/M/F Romantica

Carole Veldman-Genz

Over the last 20 years approximately, late modern Western cultures have increasingly opened up new market spaces for a dizzying proliferation of sexualized or eroticized commodities for women, including trendy sex toys, sexy lingerie and erotic media. As Feona Attwood explains, businesses increasingly target women "as sexual consumers" and "women's consumption of sexual commodities is regarded as a huge growth area" (Attwood, 2005, p. 392). The trade on female hedonism is typical of the ways late twentieth and early twenty-first century capitalist societies have been affected by the widely diagnosed sexualization of culture, variedly termed the "rise of raunch" (Levy, 2005), the process of "pornographication" (McNair, 1996) or the spread of a "pornosphere" into everyday life (McNair, 2002). As Adrienne Evans et al., (2010) point out, "[w]omen's participation in the sexualization of culture can be located within a context of shifts in gender relations, including the rise of women in paid employment, postfeminist rhetoric and a culture dominated by consumerism and neo-liberal sensibilities" (Evans et al., 2010, p. 125).

Against the backdrop of this more heavily sexualized culture—accompanied by more permissive sexual attitudes and a diversity of sexual identities and practices—this article tracks down the commercialization of female sexuality and physical pleasure to one specific media form that has proven particularly responsive to shifting social conceptions of sexuality and that has keenly imagined and addressed the sexually liberated and adventurous female consumer. My focus is on a particular strand of erotic romance fiction for women published by market leader Ellora's Cave under the copyrighted term romantica. While the term "romantica" is sometimes used by journalists or reviewers to describe a broader range of erotic romance fiction, this essay is a study of the fiction published as romantica by Ellora's Cave. In this context, the term romantica has come to describe a particular generic extension of the category "erotic romance." A crossbreed of romance and erotica, romantica mostly, though not exclusively, comprises electronically published short stories, novellas and novels. It incorporates sexual content that is more explicit and risqué than that of the "classic" erotic romance of the 1970s and 1980s[1]; for example, anal intercourse, BDSM elements,[2] voyeurism, and group sex. It also potentially revises some of the narrative traditions of the older category by allowing a greater diversity of romantic configurations beyond the standard monogamous, heterosexual couple. Though the bulk of romantica is still dedicated to a committed relationship between one man and one woman, Ellora's Cave also sells romantica that focuses on other romantic constellations: gay, lesbian, ménage and polyamorous. In other words, romantica combines a romance-driven plot—one in which the development of a central love story must culminate in a happily-ever-after ending—with romantic constellations that may go beyond coupledom and hetero-normativity and with erotica elements such as plentiful and graphic sexual scenes and sexually explicit language. I focus specifically on Ellora's Cave romantica because Ellora's Cave has spearheaded the growth in popularity of digital erotic romances and their ever-expanding romantica portfolio is a near-perfect testament to the ongoing generic revisions to the category "erotic romance" that e-publishing has afforded.

I hope to provide both a broad and precise focus when theorizing the sexual in romantica: broad in the sense that my discussion attempts to highlight the corporate practices and technologies of women's erotic writing, and precise in that I am keen to consider the generic and textual specificities of the material at hand. To put it another way, my examination entails a reflection on a cultural phenomenon as much as a meditation on a subgenre with more fine-grained analysis of individual romantica texts. I am interested in the ways romantica has opened up the category "erotic romance" to new structures and plotlines that capture the pluralistic sexual landscape characteristic of Western postmodernity and how it has claimed positions of authority for myriad sexual subjectivities in the process. In romantica, the nature of the love story is permanently altered to allow for the articulation of sexual relations that are not necessarily heteronormative, of "illicit" or formerly non-romantic identities and structures: gay/bisexual men or the romantic polyamorous threesome, for example.

My case study centers on male-male (m/m) and male-male-female ménage (m/m/f)[3] romantica, not only because they are popular subcategories, but also because they point markedly to the contradictions and conflicts in current thought on sexuality, gender, corporeality, pleasure and agency. So far, little attention has been paid to the ways in which the homoerotic male-male encounter in women's popular erotic fiction triggers female sensuality and elicits female pleasure. In its precise aim, this article investigates male homo- and bisexuality as fantasy tropes for women. Is male-male eroticism for straight women what "girl-on-girl" eroticism is said to be for straight men? How can the male homoerotic encounter engender a quintessentially *romantic* reading experience? In its broader aim, this article asks how the commodified fetishization of male bodies addresses straight women as active sexual consumers in the emerging market of digital publishing, and what these texts tell us about the construction and commercialization of female sexualities.

The "Big O" for Women Is Big Business: The Marketing and Technologies of Romantica

With the phenomenal blockbuster success of E L James' *Fifty Shades* trilogy and Sylvia Day's bestselling *Crossfire* series, it is evident that there is great demand for sexual writing for women and that explicit female erotic fiction has, by now, been firmly established in the mainstream.[4] The mainstreaming of sexual writing for women has made sexually explicit female consumption easily accessible and acceptable; yet it is debatable how fast and seamlessly this grand-scale assimilation into the mainstream portfolio would have progressed had it not been for early experimentation with lead users[5] in niche markets establishing financial viability. Founded in 2000, romantica publisher Ellora's Cave (EC), has been one of the pioneers of digitalized erotic writing for women, exploiting the then-untapped electronic marketplace and paving the way for the mainstream. Initially conceived as an e-publisher, Ellora's Cave has grown exponentially from a small niche publisher to become the self-proclaimed "first and foremost publisher of erotic romance," a "multi-million-dollar publishing empire" selling 250,000 books per month (Ellora's Cave, 2015).[6] As Associated Press commented in 2006, "[i]t's hard to ignore sales figures like [Ellora's Cave's].... Mainstream publishers have taken notice" (Associated Press, 2006).

Innovations in technology, in particular the e-book format, have been instrumental in advancing female erotic fiction as they have facilitated production by cutting printing/storage/marketing/distribution costs, shortening turnaround times and providing easy, cheap and discrete access to sexually explicit material. The medium of the Internet has proven a fertile hub for productive and consumptive experimentation, bringing together pleasure-seeking female consumers and niche e-commerce businesses in synergetic interdependency. It is beyond the scope of this essay to explain in detail the complex processes which determine the formation of female consumers' sexual tastes and the reasons why they have used digital technologies to perform identity work including sexual exploration—I leave this to business analysts and media anthropologists. I am equally aware that the interrelations between consumer demands and media output are far from straightforward and direct, caught up in the circular flow of supply and demand and entailing a "complex apparatus which is interposed between cultural creators and consumers" (Peterson, 1978, p. 295). Here, I am interested in the materializations of conceptions of sex in an emerging market and the technological formats that have facilitated them. EC's core business is in e-book publishing, although by now they have expanded into print publishing and even own their own printing press. As EC publisher Raelene Gorlinsky explains:

> It was very difficult selling erotic romance through the chains; they were wary of what they put on their shelves. So, going digital made a lot of sense when it came to selling, not having to worry about printing and distribution. For readers, they could buy the books anonymously, quickly and inexpensively [qtd. in Greenfield, 2011].

The limited financial exposure of e-publishing and the "up-for-it" attitude of their target audience have triggered publishers such as Ellora's Cave[7] to experiment freely within the loose confines of erotic romance, gauging market trends and branching out where sales figures lead them. Gorlinsky adds that "[p]retty much everything we've done [is] listening to readers who say, 'why aren't there stories about...' And we give it to them. That's the advice I'd give to any publisher of any size: Find a way to figure out what the readers want and profitably give it to them" (qtd. in Greenfield, 2011).

The Ellora's Cave publishing model is fuelled by consumer-driven experimentation and this, in turn, has engendered an umbrella category of "romantica" that comprises a promiscuous intermixing of lines, formats and themes. Ellora's Cave caters to an array of nuanced fetishes, kinks and fantasy tropes, including lines such as the multicultural/interracial "Fusion," the BDSM "Taboo," the fetish line "Kink" and the line "Sophisticate" (featuring older women and younger men), and themes such as "Female Female," "Rubenesque" (featuring overweight heroines), "Ménage or More" and "Male Male." The ever-expanding nature of the romantica product line is testament to the fact that the genre boundaries of erotic romance are driven by consumer demands, shaped by sales figures and continuously pushed outward; they are not fixed but constantly in motion, sites of revision rather than immutable inscription. A form continuously in flux, romantica traces shifts in constructions of sexuality, in characterization and plotlines as well as market trends and degrees of sexual explicitness. As Gorlinsky explains, "as erotic romance has become popular, readers have gotten acclimated to it.... And they've become jaded. Things that were shocking five years ago—anal sex, ménage à trois—have now become vanilla" (qtd. in Robbins, 2008, p. 30). So, as readers have become more familiar with explicit sexual writing for women, EC has continuously been upping the ante as far as sexual content is concerned. This also means that there has been an ongoing progression to include a greater diversity of ever more risqué sexual repertoires and more adventurous, not necessarily dyadic or heterosexual, romantic constellations.

As I have argued elsewhere, marginalized groups previously unheard of in mainstream romances are afforded representation in romantica. "Here, bigger women and women with wrinkles have sexual identity and subjecthood.... The sexually desiring and desirable woman of romantica may be older, fatter, blacker, and more hedonistic than anyone else in romance" (Veldman-Genz, 2012, p. 117). Similarly, the focus on homo/bisexual men as erotic spectacles in m/m and m/m/f romantica bears witness to an emerging anti-hetero-normative market trend within women's erotic fiction. Elaborating on the "newest frontier in erotica," Berkley Heat editor Cindy Hwang observes that "more and more authors [explore] committed, polygamous relationships, usually between two men and one woman" (qtd. in Robbins, 2010). Kara Wuest at Cleis Press similarly points out that "interest in gay erotica among heterosexual female readers was once a bit of an industry secret.... Perhaps now it's become more generally known that many women read gay erotica because they enjoy the eroticization of the masculine form, regardless of orientation" (qtd. in Robbins, 2008, p. 32).

The next section will focus exclusively on the representational praxes of male-male eroticism in individual romantica texts. At this stage and from a contextual perspective, suffice to say that in the absence of a predefined and established discourse of active female desire, romantica has filled a gap in the market and in the wider realm of cultural imagination by providing a safe platform for the articulation of a broad array of sexual repertoires. EC stories problematize who and what should count as desirable and romantic and carve out a fictional space for narratives about a multiplicity of sexual sensibilities. The proliferation of EC themes and lines exemplifies the publisher's entrenchment in what Joseph Bristow terms "diverse eroticisms" and it clearly marks the intersectionality between sex, age, race, gender, corporeality, sexual orientation and pleasure (Bristow, 2011, p. 197). By its very nature, this nexus of converging discourses must speak of and to previously neglected sexual sensibilities and in this, it inherently carries emancipatory impulses. It is tempting to believe that such articulations allow us to "posit possibilities beyond the norm or, indeed, a different future for the norm itself" (Butler, 2004, p. 28). Yet it is equally important to remember two things: first, despite the multiplicity of sexual subjectivities portrayed in romantica and despite the diverse positionings for pleasure on offer, romantica still addresses readers through the discourse of romance and its plotlines remain driven by the strictures of romantic conventions; and, second, one should not be lured into confusing a politics of multiplicity with market trends and marketing strategies.

In what follows, I want to elaborate on the marketing that has helped sell EC products. If one believes the publisher's marketing strategies, romantica envisions an autonomous female sexuality. The EC website plays up to women's entitlement to sexual pleasure, proudly proclaiming that "[a]t Ellora's Cave, we believe women's sexuality, in all its various forms, is legitimate, positive and beautiful" (Ellora's Cave, 2013). There is, of course, nothing new about promoting the female body as a key site of femininity and coding it as sexually receptive and ruled by instinct—those are age-old practices that have dominated our visual and textual landscape for centuries. Nor is there anything inherently progressive about celebrating women lusting after one or two men. Indeed, most romantica novels do not transcend the heterosexual presumption for women; here, the phallus remains the prime signifier of female desire and female sexual enjoyment remains mostly fixed on men. Rather than in content, the difference lies in the branding of romantica: now sexually rapacious femininity is available for reading as a pronouncement of female power, and female sexual enjoyment is publicized as an emblem of independence. EC books are sold on the premise that sex is one of the main delineations of female freedom, and the EC corporate image depends on maintaining the idea of a female-directed fantasy space directly inspired by reader fantasies where women are free enough to make sexual choices on their own terms. The private consumption of sexually explicit material is marketed as a liberating and empowering experience that gratifies diverse sexual fantasies and positions female consumers as active, hedonistic "sensation-seekers" in pursuit of their own pleasures (Bauman, 1999, p. 23). As Esther Sonnet rightly says when discussing Virgin Books' now discontinued Black Lace erotica imprint, "what this most lucidly signifies is how adept capitalist commodity markets have become at appropriating the language of freedom and the political project of feminism to market products" (Sonnet, 1999, p. 176).

I do not want to rule out romantica's potential for democratizing sexual discourse, nor do I want to downplay the complexity of the "mobile and transient subjectivities" invoked in romantica "which cannot be subsumed by the uni-dimensional power structure of *gender-defined* heterosexuality" (Sonnet, 1999, p. 183). However conflicted romantica may be, here is one way in which active female sexuality can be imagined and materialized in culture. Romantica clearly embraces female sexuality, yet it remains a category fuelled by escapist fantasy and recreational consumption, not politics. EC characters' pursuits of erotic fulfillment and romantica's emphatic prioritization of sexual pleasure thus resonate with an ethic of acceptance that foregrounds "pleasure over the *politics* of pleasure" (Waters, 2007, p. 258). The category's negotiations with sexual subjectivities are clearly embedded within the confines of consumerism and romance. For EC, as for most businesses, it is not only about innovating the market but offering innovative products that sell. So, the consumption of EC products needs to be understood not only in relation to notions of sexual democratization, pleasure and liberalism, but also to the ways these intersect with commodification, consumer culture, economics, emerging technologies and the discourse of romance. To take any of these parameters out of the analysis would mean missing what is distinctive about these consumption opportunities that allow women to experience themselves as active sexual consumers. We are thus dealing with a complexly inter-woven mesh of privately held fantasies, visions of sexual empowerment, cultural discourses, sales-driven market forces, mass explorations of new technological advancements and commodity choices available in consumer culture.

I would shy away from imputing a progressive politics of multiplicity to romantica. Women's engagement with romantica is fraught with contradiction, ambiguity and conflict. The technological infrastructure that has bolstered the rise of erotic romance is a case in point. On the one hand, electronic publishing and the e-book format have been instrumental in the mainstreaming of erotic fiction for women and providing a much-needed platform for the articulation of female sexual desire. On the other hand, and rather ironically, they have wrested back sexuality into the realm of the secretive and hidden. Displaying no telltale, brandishing cover, e-reading devices have made reading romantica anonymous, discrete and intensely private. As Brenda Knight, associate publisher at Cleis Press, points out, Kindles, iPads and Nooks are "the ultimate brown paper wrapper" (Rosman, 2012). While the personal is undeniably a crucial site for women's empowerment, these "under-the-hood" articulations of sexual liberation are conflicted to the core. At worst, women's engagement in romantica is a hidden, guilty secret that is most profitably sold to them as a diluted form of female sexual empowerment; at best, it can be a grass-roots review of hegemonic notions of gender and sexuality. This potential alone should be reason enough not to underestimate romantica or write it off entirely. As Marilyn Corsianos notes, "if images of more diverse sexualities and sexual performances were as much a part of many people's consciousness as are the mainstream sexual images, and if these were all perceived as possible 'choices' for people, then the opportunity for sexual agency could become possible" (Corsianos, 2007, p. 863).

"Normal female interest in men bonking": The Case of M/M/F and M/M Romantica

The above quotation is taken from Shoshanna Green, Henry Jenkins and Cynthia Jenkins' (1998) well-known discussion of slash fiction, slash being defined as fan-generated erotic literature that centers on the relationship between two or more same-sex (usually male) characters appropriated from the realm of popular television. It hardly needs demonstrating that there are insistent analogies between m/m/f or m/m romantica and other popular-culture products addressing women and focusing on the homoerotic male-male encounter. Indeed, if one were to look a little further afield, one would find a variety of media examples targeting women and dedicated to the eroticization/romanticization of male homosexuality; for example, slash fiction, Japanese Boys' Love *shonen-ai* and *yaoi* manga[8] or mainstream blockbusters such as *Brokeback Mountain* (2005)—a movie which, according to Michael Jensen, 'straight women' took to "like bar flies to over-salted peanuts" (qtd. in Nayar, 2011, p. 236). Ellora's Cave CEO Patty Marks even credits the latter movie with mainstreaming male-male romanticism and popularizing the "Male Male" subcategory at EC, claiming that the "Male Male" category exploded in the erotic romance industry after the movie "Brokeback Mountain" came out. The movie portrayed the angst and emotional relationship that women love and it didn't hurt that the actors were hot and extremely popular. I think that piqued more curiosity to read the books and helped to enable us to give ourselves permission to enjoy it [qtd. in Clark-Flory, 2012].

There are, of course, great disparities between the above articulations of male homosexuality in terms of format, production, consumption, cultural context and audience reception. Japanese Boys' Love manga, for instance, is not understood as catering to risqué erotic sensibilities as "Japan has a long tradition of aestheticizing certain male homoerotic relationships as representative of a 'beautiful and pure form of romance'" (Wood, 2006, p. 395). Similarly, slash, unlike romantica, still has a distinctly subcultural allure and is seemingly detached from sales-driven commodification; it is a fan-based rather than commercial practice. Despite these differences, many critical points made about slash, Boys' Love manga or movies such as *Brokeback Mountain* also ring true for romantica; so does Marni Stanley's claim that

> slash and *yaoi* [and I would argue, by extension, m/m and m/m/f romantica] interrupt the dominant narratives of manga, television, and even pornography [and romance] by giving females a chance to play with boys and the male body in ways that male authors/artists have traditionally assumed to be their right to manipulate and play with the female body. ... [I]t is the male body that is on display. And here it has been rendered poseable, penetrable, and subject to disruptions that serve to queer the dominant narratives in playful and irreverent ways.... A whole new toy box has been opened by these genres for female artists, writers, and readers [Stanley, 2008, p. 107].

Like slash and Boys' Love manga, romantica—particularly m/m and m/m/f romantica—positions the male body as an object of erotic desire and female contemplation. It is eroticized in the same ways the female body has been objectified for centuries, both textually—in the graphic depictions of gay sex and the sexy male body—as well as visually. Romantica covers typically feature scantily clad, pinup-style men who are obviously constituted as objects of desire. Predictably young, slim and muscular, the cover models exhibit a range of visual representation as limited and heavily standardized as that of their female counterparts in male-directed pornographic imagery. Romantica texts also appropriate male bodies and male sexual activity for reader gratification. Much of the textual vocabulary of romantica is reserved for the depiction of male sexiness. The following descriptions from Sedonia Guillone's m/m romantica *Barely Undercover* (2007) and Katie Allen's m/m/f novel *One-Two Punch* (2008) are typical:

> The show had just started and Damien writhed and slunk his way on. Of course, all the guys up there had been hot, but Kaz had gotten an instant hard-on watching Damien. Something about the guy, his sleek, muscular body, the delicious trail of chestnut hair down the center of his tight abs, that perfect ass and ... well ... killer green eyes had made Kaz an instant love slave [Guillone, 2007, location 67].

> [T]his man was ... unworldly. His skin was the color of creamed coffee and his slanting cheekbones narrowed his eyes, which were shadowed by the longest lashes, so thick and dark that Beth noticed them from fifteen feet away. His full lips had a sulky twist that just made him that much hotter. [Allen, 2008, p. 93].

Romantica's men are "incredibly sexy" (Kersten, 2008, p. 56), "drop-dead hot" (Guillone, 2007, location 125) and "any woman's wet dream" (Bast, 2006, p. 15). These representations of male bodies are clearly marked and marketed as erotic and arousing—again, an unmistakable gender reversal of male-directed pornography. EC covers and romantica's textual descriptions of the sexy male body reverse the trend of men as consumers of female objects of desire. Here, men are objectified spectacles of contemplation and consumption; they are "both idealized and debased, the object[s] of erotic obsession" (Waugh, 1995, p. 326). The visual and textual vocabularies highlighted above stipulate the existence of a desiring gaze fetishizing male bodies and writing them over into highly eroticized pin-ups. One must presume that the consumer wielding this gaze is heterosexual and female if one considers the overall narrative focus and targeted readership of romantica.[9] This, in turn, anticipates the possibility of active female desire triggered by the act of looking or reading about the sexualized male body.

If the eroticized depiction of one man is enough to prompt readerly pleasure in romantica, the prospect of two men entangled in romantic and erotic interaction in m/m and m/m/f romantica seems to amplify the female readers' enjoyment in the eroticization of the male form. "[T]here's a huge number of straight women who want to read gay erotic romance," says the founder of ManLoveRomance Press Laura Baumbach, "Why not? They like men. One man is good, two are exciting together" (qtd. in Robbins, 2008, p. 32). While I believe that m/m and m/m/f romantica cannot be fully understood without attending to its mainly heterosexual female readership, I do not want to speculate on the reasons underlying women's investment in homo/bisexual men as erotic tropes. My focus moves away from *why* women would construct homoerotic fantasies and concentrates on *how* these same-sex relationships are written in m/m and m/m/f romantica. Here, male-male sexual interaction is positioned as integral to a heroine's—and, by extension, a female reader's—quest for erotic titillation. In Samantha Kane's m/m/f novel *At Love's Command* (2007), the heroine Sophie is "shocked by the intensity of the desire that swept through her as she watched the two men kiss. It was the most arousing thing she had ever seen" (Kane, 2007, p. 160). In Rachel Bo's *Double Jeopardy* (2004), the "visual stimulation of watching" two men make love drives the heroine "to a fever pitch" (Bo, 2004, p. 80). In Katie Allen's *One-Two Punch* (2008), heroine Beth is "enthralled by the two masculine bodies locked together in a desperate, almost violent embrace.... Just watching was enough to send Beth over the edge of orgasm" (Allen, 2008, p. 220). Similarly, in Kele Moon's BDSM novel *Beyond Eden* (2010), heroine Eve finds out that she is a "hardcore voyeur," who can "climax right there at the thought of seeing [two men] together" (Moon, 2010, pp. 263, 223). As the above extracts exemplify, gay eroticism is clearly marked as a voyeuristic experience for the female spectator, both reader and heroine; it prompts a kind of auto-erotic pleasure that is controlled by the gendered gaze of the onlooker and all the more gratifying because it involves participants 'other-than-me.'

M/m and m/m/f romantica co-opt male homosexuality into straight women's economy of desire, thereby challenging the monopoly of heterosexual masculinity as exclusively desirable. Male homo- and bisexuality are thus positioned as potential triggers for female heterosexual desire; they are anti-hetero-normative additions or extensions to what women should deem erotic or romantic. I would argue that m/m and m/m/f romantica appropriate male homo/bisexuality by invoking a logic of homonormativity predicated on discourses of romance, consumerism and integration. This is in line with what Marlon B. Ross points out when describing contemporary black gay romance novels: "In the homonorm, queer love follows a heteroromance script, the only difference being that the queer person has an additional obligation of 'coming out'" (2013, p. 669). Romantica's engagement with homoeroticism is as much an indication of the ways in which queer content has been inserted into popular culture, as it is an attempt to rescript gay tales onto a female-directed plane of hetero-romance. These practices open up a female "queer space" in which 'things happen that challenge the way gendered and sexual identities and practices are defined and policed into rigid categories" (Lothian et al., 2007, p. 109); at the same time, they are a means of disciplining homoerotic physicality and framing queerness within the female-directed and romance-driven discourse of romantica. As Christopher Pullen argues, "such female-oriented framing essentially stimulates the romance of desire, more than focuses on the action of sexuality. This may reveal new scope in examining sexual diversity, despite allusions to the compression of homosexual identity within the heterosexual frame" (Pullen, 2010, p. 137). In my opinion, romantica's appropriation of gay content largely forecloses the radical, deconstructive or subversive implications that the articulations of variant sexual subjectivities might otherwise have had; yet the trade-off involved in pairing these articulations with tried, tested (and marketable) hetero-normative romance conventions has also facilitated the mainstreaming of said articulations and the engagement with a wider audience.

All romantica texts continue to function within a highly circumscribed set of generic parameters that preserve these texts as romances. These parameters dictate the main characters' exclusive emotional commitment to each other and a narrative closure in a happily-ever-after ending; moving beyond these romantic parameters also entails moving beyond the realm of romantica. At EC, any storyline that does not adhere to the prescribed romantic strictures is relegated to other imprints such as the "no strings attached" "Exotica" imprint which "focuses on a heroine's sexual adventures or journey, rather than on the development of a committed relationship" (Ellora's Cave, 2014) or the recently launched "EC for Men" imprint which focuses on "men's needs, desires and fantasies" of "hot sex and great storytelling, but without the emotional attachment and commitment of traditional romance novels" (Ellora's Cave, 2013).[10] EC classifies content and splits it into separate imprints based on the narrative focus of the plotlines: in Exotica and EC for Men, for example, these revolve around the sexual adventures of women or men; in romantica, they concentrate on the development of erotically charged and emotionally exclusive romantic relationships. This reinforces the notion that fictions about sex and fictions about romance belong in different categories. While these categories are not exclusively bound to one sex—after all, Exotica centers on non-romantic sexual writing for women—there are still lingering echoes here of the old cliché that women want romance and men want sex. This leaves me with a number of questions: how is the all-male sexual encounter envisaged in romantica? And how can gay eroticism be assimilated into the feminocentric discourse of romance?

The rereading of gay content in romantica often results in the depiction of "feminized" or romanticized gay sex. In m/m and m/m/f romantica, readers are invited to endorse the emotional and sexual intimacy between male characters, and male-male sex is often scripted in terms of both nurture and sexual adventure. Thus even a BDSM novel such as Kele Moon's

Beyond Eden (2010) stresses the nurturing and loving bond underlying the hardcore sexual encounters between pain-fetishist Paul and his master, Danny: "Trust radiated off [Paul], mixing easily with desire, because he knew Danny would never take advantage of him, never use his desire to be punished and hurt to do more than turn him on.... [Danny] wanted to tell Paul he loved him and he could be sweet and gentle.... He wanted to kiss and nuzzle him, to whisper endearments" (Moon, 2010, pp. 46, 50). Gay sex in romantica is often intimacy-driven, the focus being on foreplay and extra-genital erogenous zones as much as penetration. Here are examples from Shayla Kersten's m/m novella *Past Lies* (2008) and Samantha Kane's m/m/f novel *The Courage to Love* (2006):

> Soft lips nibbled on his earlobe. The scratch of slight stubble against his face was a sharp reminder of what he was doing, but he couldn't stop now. Shivers of need raced down Paul's spine.... Hot kisses trailed down his neck. A warm mouth sucked at his nipple. Teeth tugged at the hardening nub. A shudder of helpless desire raced through him.... He needed to touch, to taste. Randy's lips fascinated him. Soft surrounded by the harsh grate of stubble. Lean muscles, a flat chest.... Paul licked a path down Randy's neck. Each moan and gasp from the other man increased Paul's excitement [Kersten, 2008, pp. 24–34].

> [Jason] kissed him, his lips soft against Tony's. The kiss was more searing for its tenderness, and Tony's mouth opened on a sigh. Jason licked into his mouth, rubbing against his tongue and encouraging Tony to do the same. The kiss quickly escalated, and Tony wrapped his arms around Jason, reveling in the hard feel of him, the taste of him, the sheer joy of having him like this [Kane, 2006, p. 131].

Framed by a female gaze, these are intimate and romantic erotic encounters in which gay men excite by virtue of their caring and nurturing abilities as much as their virility and hyper-masculinity.

This gender-blending of "masculine" and "feminine" traits is an indication of how the gay/bisexual male body has been offered up for heterosexual female reading in romantica and how gay sex has been romanticized and made "female-friendly" in these texts. Though fully active sexual beings, these EC heroes do not necessarily act out gay/bisexual experience but enact a homoerotic desire safe and familiar enough to be sold to a female mass audience. So, is gay eroticism in romantica what "girl-on-girl" eroticism is said to be for straight men? Is it a purely self-gratifying and voyeuristic female experience entailing feminized and domesticated male sex objects entirely controlled and manipulated by a female onlooker? I would argue that it is not as simple as that. More is at stake in romantica than a straightforward "traffic in men."[11] A lot of texts take great care to afford male characters a semblance of agency and to position them outside the realm of "to-be-looked-at-ness."[12] It is common practice in m/m romantica to switch between the points of view of the two male protagonists, and m/m/f romantica frequently switches among all three as the protagonists kiss, seduce, penetrate, are penetrated, engage in sex acts or watch others engage in these acts. This character-hopping allows for multiple, coexisting, cross-gender identifications: the alleged female reader can thus identify with either of the male or female protagonists, all of which can simultaneously function as agents of spectatorial identification and objects of spectatorial desire. The complexity of identifications and desire in these erotic constellations creates constantly shifting intersections of formerly dichotomous pairings: active/passive, subject/object, voyeur/exhibitionist, male/female and heterosexual/homosexual.

Romantica has proven particularly flexible in opening the genre of romance to new characters, structures and plotlines. It offers a forum for the articulation of non-standard romantic identities and structures, for example, the gay or bisexual man as romantic hero and the threesome as ideal romantic constellation. Ménage has traditionally been perceived as opposed to cultural expectations of marriage, a step toward hedonistic sexual anarchy rather than happily-ever-after closure; yet, the romantica ménage is constructed as a committed and sexually exclusive structure. In Katie Allen's *One-Two Punch* (2008), heroine Beth gets to live "every woman's dream" as she and her lovers Harry and Ky "fit together—[like] perfectly matched [Lego] pieces" (Allen, 2008, pp. 232, 217). In Rachel Bo's contemporary novel *Double Jeopardy* (2004), the triad functions as the only structure allowing complete romantic expression. The "long-term, permanent relationship" binding protagonists Sutter, Joshua and Kendall is legitimized in a semi-religious ceremony in which the two men become Kendall's "husbands" (Bo, 2004, pp. 60, 117). Bo's novel revises received notions of wedlock and positions three-way love as an authentically romantic, if not universally accepted, alternative to dyadic couple-dom: "We have to be true to ourselves," Kendall states, "[T]here are people now who don't approve of the three of us. But there are quite a few who do. They understand that we don't choose who to love. Love chooses us" (Bo, 2004, pp. 123, 145). In Samantha Kane's *The Courage to Love* (2006), only the ménage provides romantic closure. As heroine Katherine explains to her husbands Anthony and Jason, "I need to be surrounded by love, mine for you, yours for me, and yours for each other. It makes me feel safe, complete" (Kane, 2006, p. 203).

As we have seen, coding the homo/bisexual man romantic has considerable implications in terms of narrative focus and characterization and it illustrates the homo-normative appropriation of gay content for a mainstream audience. The homo/bisexual romantica hero has been made safe enough to function in accordance with hetero-normative romance conventions such as the happily-ever-after ending or the insistence on sexual exclusivity and monogamy. Indeed, m/m and m/m/f romantica frequently feature male heroes who are fervently monogamous, sexually inexperienced or even virginal. Against prevailing notions of gay sex as promiscuous and disease-ridden, male-male sexual interaction in romantica is often presented as distinctly committed and sexually exclusive. In Sedonia Guillone's *Barely Undercover* (2007), "hopeless romantic" Damien feels "lucky to have hit the romance jackpot on the first round" as his lover Kaz is "his first guy. And only guy," "the love of his life" (Guillone, 2007, locations 147, 920, 147, 297). Similarly, Katie Allen's protagonist Ky in *One-Two Punch* (2008) is a "closet romantic" and "the only man [Harry] had ever wanted" (Allen, 2008, pp. 220, 106). In Carol Lynne's m/m/f romantica *Necklace of Shame* (2008), Callum is "the only man [Brody has] ever been with, the only man [he has] ever wanted" (Lynne, 2008, location 529). In Angela Claire's m/m romantica *Male Bonding* (2013), protagonist Mark is "the gay version of an old maid" and his love interest Jamie has only slept with men with whom he thought "there might be some possibility of a relationship" (Claire, 2013, location 175, 285). In Shayla Kersten's m/m novel *Past Lies* (2008), Randy initiates small-town lawyer Paul into the delights of gay sex. As Paul discovers "sex with the right gender," he feels like "a teenager all over again" (Kersten, 2008, p. 128). This is a story of sexual exploration and liberation, not promiscuity: "Maybe it was the newness of gay sex, maybe it was a lifetime of repression, but Paul had embraced sex with Randy like a duck took to water" (Kersten, 2008, p. 113).

The use of the virginal homo/bisexual hero in romantica goes against Laura Vivanco and Kyra Kramer's claim that "[v]irginal heroes do not exist in [romance]" (Vivanco and Kramer, 2010). This is the gender-reversed appropriation of a well-established, comfortably known and reactionary romance trope since "for most of the genre's history ... the romance novel heroine was depicted as a virgin" (Regis, 2007, p. 35). More importantly, depicting homosexual or bisexual men as inherently committed, monogamous, sexually inexperienced or even virginal lends an additional air of innocence and lovability that makes them available for reading as romantic heroes. Here the use of well-known romantic staples (the virgin; sexual exclusivity; monogamy) familiarizes and standardizes the otherwise "alien" gay sexual content, turning it into a romantic scenario for the female readership. This is yet another way in which the figure of the gay/bisexual man has been appropriated within romantica.

Conclusion

The points I have made here should have provided insight into the contextual and textual mechanics underlying m/m and m/m/f romantica. I hope to have shown that the most profound tenet of romance—the belief that love conquers all—remains intact in romantica, irrespective of shifts in characterization and plotlines. At the same time, genre boundaries are continuously pushed outward in romantica. This category accommodates an ever-increasing and diverse array of sexual identities, performances and repertoires; appropriates them for a female readership; and codes them romantic. M/m and m/m/f romantica novels have afforded representation to formerly non-romantic identities (the bi/homosexual man) and structures (the ménage; the homoerotic dyad) and made them desirable. They have made additions to women's socio-sexual economies of desire and provided much-needed articulations for underrepresented sexual sensibilities. My analysis has also shown that there has been no easy assimilation of progressive values with the narratives of romantica. The cultural politics of romantica are deeply conflicted, tainted by consumerism, romance conventions and mass-market commercialization. Yet, in the absence of an established definition of female desire, we must acknowledge these commercial constructions of sexuality as attempts to formulate, imagine and materialize active female desire.

Notes

1. In *The Romance Revolution: Erotic Novels for Women and the Quest for a New Sexual Identity* (1987), Carol Thurston focuses on erotic heterosexual romances for women as revolutionary expressions of female desire, "the first large and autonomous body of sexual writing by women addressed to the feminine experience" (Thurston, 1987, p. 10). According to Thurston, the category "erotic romance" came into prominence in the 1970s with the emergence of erotic historicals or "bodice rippers." Thurston also explains that during the 1980s, contemporary erotic romances featuring older and more sexually experienced heroines became popular. It is worth noticing that Thurston only explores erotic romances featuring heterosexual couples.
2. BDSM combines elements of the following non-standard sexual practices: Bondage and Discipline (BD), Dominance and Submission (DS), and Sadism and Masochism (SM).
3. M/m/f refers to a type of romantica featuring two men and one woman in which there is sexual interaction between the two men as well as between each man and the

woman. In contrast, m/f/m novels feature sexual interaction between each man and the woman, but do not feature homoerotic elements.

4. Early niche print publishers of erotic romances include Red Sage Publishing, which released its first erotic anthology in 1995 and now mainly focuses on e-publishing, and the Virgin Books imprint Black Lace which opened in 1993 and was discontinued in 2010. Major publishing houses such as Kensington, Harlequin, Avon and Penguin now publish erotic writing for women. Kensington began to release erotic anthologies in 1999 and its Aphrodisia imprint was launched in 2006; Berkley Heat was launched in 2003; Avon Red was launched in 2006; Harlequin Spice was launched in 2006.

5. The term "lead users" refers to users who are ahead of the majority of the market on market trends and who also have incentives to innovate.

6. Sales figures based on Lulgjuraj (2013).

7. Sarah Frantz offers a useful chronology of early digital erotic romance publishers apart from Ellora's Cave: Mundania Press, which opened its erotic romance imprint Phaze in 2004; Amber Quill Press, which opened in 2002; Torquere Books, started in 2003; Loose Id, started in 2004, and Samhain Publishing, started in 2005 (Frantz, 2012, pp. 58–59).

8. Boys' Love manga presents romantic narratives that visually depict homoerotic love between male protagonists. By and large, these comics are created by and for women, with *shonen-ai* manga being a more suggestive and extensive bildungsroman type and *yaoi* manga being more pornographically explicit and having a relatively undeveloped plot (McLelland, 2000).

9. I do not wish to rule out the possibility of heterosexual male, gay or lesbian romantica readers. It seems logical, for example, that subcategories such as m/m romantica could claim the interest and identification of a gay readership. Yet, since these subcategories remain cushioned and are marketed within the overall category of romantica, I focus on romantica's targeted (female, heterosexual) readership.

10. It is important to point out that while EC provides its readership with the option to explore non-romantic sexual writing for women, their romantica imprint is, by far, the most extensive and profitable. I would argue that smaller imprints such as Exotica or EC for Men allow EC to test the waters and the financial viability of other niche publishing areas.

11. I use the phrase "traffic in men" as a tongue-in-cheek reversal of Gayle Rubin's much-discussed notion of "traffic in women." According to Rubin, patriarchal heterosexuality can best be discussed in terms of a traffic in women. Women function as an exchangeable property for the primary purpose of cementing male bonds. The giving and receiving of women by men, especially through marriage, is a way of organizing and maintaining a sex-gender system in a society where women are systematically oppressed (Rubin, 1975).

12. In her seminal "Visual Pleasure and Narrative Cinema" (1975), Laura Mulvey investigates the objectification of women in Hollywood film, arguing that women are framed and subject to a controlling and scopophilic male gaze. The male spectator functions as the sculptor of a passive and objectified femininity. The "determining male gaze projects its fantasy onto the female figure, which is styled accordingly.... The man ... emerges as the representative of power ... as the bearer of the look" (Mulvey, 1989, pp. 19–20).

Permissible Transgressions

Feminized Same-Sex Practice as Middle-Class Fantasy

Jude Elund

This essay discusses the positioning of erotic and romantic fiction in relation to female sexuality, particularly same-sex practices and desires. Focusing on the representation of lesbianism in mainstream erotic fiction, the essay principally investigates the idea of experimenting with one's sexual orientation as an aspect of the cultural shift toward embracing sex practices that depart from the norm. In mainstream erotic fiction, I will suggest, female-female sexuality is primarily represented in the context of, indeed, as an element of, heterosexual, white, middle-class fantasy. The sudden popularity and visibility of the *Fifty Shades* trilogy in 2012 heralded a proliferation of popular fiction texts featuring erotically "subversive" subject matter, including same-sex practices, in the neo-liberal marketplace. One particular novel, *Till Human Voices Wake Us* by Patti Davis, serves as a key text for analysis. A self-published novel about an upper-class American woman who falls in love with her sister-in-law after the death of her child, *Till Human Voices Wake Us* appears to have little claim to either "literary" or "erotic" merit and would probably be completely unknown except for the fact that Davis happens to be the daughter of Ronald Reagan. However, an analysis of this novel and its discursive context will provide some insight into the uncertain position of same-sex desire in relation to mainstream women's erotic fiction.

The ensuing discussion views Davis' text through both a postfeminist and queer theory lens, identifying the tensions that exist between mainstream heterosexual female fantasy and lesbian/queer identification.

Although a relatively obscure text, it is a particularly useful one in investigating contemporary understandings of gender and sexuality because of its particular positioning within the marketplace, its romantic and erotic content, and its representation of middle-class femininity. The protagonists are representative of American nouveau-riche society and so display sexual agency fitting of this class. The novel can also be viewed as an extension of the *Fifty Shades* phenomenon insofar as its narrative follows a woman who reluctantly experiments with her sexuality.

In order to unpack the ideological work of Davis' novel, the discussion follows three key areas of investigation. The first looks at lesbianism as eroticism in terms of the mass-media framing of female same-sex practice, as well as the issues that arise in relation to authorship, authenticity and intentionality. The second area explores the idea of sexual fluidity as a middle-class aspiration. Of particular interest here is the cultural shift toward a certain acceptance of queer and/or non-normative practices, as well as niche marketing in relation to sexual fluidity. Thirdly, the essay investigates the notion of heterosexual female experimentation and persistent femininity.

Lesbianism as Eroticism

The 2000s saw an increase in the generic forms of erotic and romance fiction. Rosalind Gill and Elena Herdieckerhoff (2007) attribute the increase in romantic fiction to 1990s cultural phenomena such as the novel *Bridget Jones's Diary* (1996) and the TV series *Sex and the City* (1998–2004), both of which represented women as un-ashamedly sex-positive. The proliferation in erotic fiction, however, can be partly attributed to this cultural shift, but also to the development of Internet technologies and changes in the ways fiction is consumed. The networked communications that the Internet has fostered enable individuals of specific tastes and niche communities to communicate across the globe. The coalescing of these consumer nodes despite geographical distance has not only allowed marketers to directly target consumers with niche products, but has also allowed for dialogic communication between producers and consumers. A key phenomenon associated with this development is fan culture, which has had a specific impact on the content of fiction. In short, two-way communication has allowed for consumers to direct feedback to producers, allowing for content to be tailored in a way which ensures a captive audience. This, in turn, has allowed producers to alter their content and move it away from safer storylines and character representations. Rosalind Hanmer (2013) describes the interaction that occurred between fans of the TV show *Xena: Warrior Princess* (1995–2001) and the show's writers, which influenced the content and narrative direction of the show in addition to forging a lesbian/bi/queer female fan-fic community. Furthermore, networked technologies and improved electronic distribution mean that novels are able to be self-published, dispensing with the gatekeepers of traditional publishing. With the advent of e-books, tablets and e-readers, consumers are able to download risqué material that they would previously need to seek out in person, running the risk of being "found out." Internet technologies allow for just about anybody in Western society to consume romance and erotic fiction of any particular bent without this risk.

Lesbian fiction, including lesbian romance and lesbian erotica, has become a small but niche genre in contemporary popular fiction, often featuring a relatively uniform selection of plots and narrative devices. The genre tends to feature women in high-powered and/or exciting positions within society (there is a particular over-representation of doctors), and the texts tend to follow a formulaic narrative whereby

> Girl A meets Girl B and thinks she's cocky/reckless/mysterious/looking very Shane today. An often work-related situation forces the girls to spend every waking moment together, and Girl A realizes that there's more to Girl B than nice arms and a smokin' hot swagger. However! Despite their sexual tension, Girl A keeps Girl B at arm's length as she undergoes a brief but intense struggle to overcome her deep dark secret and/or crippling emotional baggage. The tide changes when a confusing figure from either girl's past shows up and/or a tragic accident forces Girl A to consider life without Girl B in it. They say "I love you" and have "earth-shattering" sex. The End [Crystal, 2011].

Crystal, the author of this article on the popular culture site *Jezebel*, implies that she herself is a straight woman. Her commentary makes mention of the access now granted to many individuals through e-books who would not normally feel comfortable viewing the lesbian sections of traditional bookstores: "I did something that I admit, shamefully, I've never done in a bookstore: I perused titles in the 'lesbian' category" (Crystal, 2011). The angle that she takes, coupled with the responses to the article from other apparently straight women, raises the possibility of an emerging community of straight female readers of lesbian erotica. This seeking out of non-heterosexual texts is arguably a queer development in the consumption of contemporary fiction; however, it is questionable how queer the content of these texts is. Gill and Herdiekerhoff (2007) argue that for a text to be queer means

> not simply replacing heterosexual protagonists with homosexual ones, but, more fundamentally questioning the very binaries on which conventional romance depends (male/female, gay/straight, virgin/whore, etc.) as well as the premise of fixed stable identity, and the idea that a declaration of monogamy represents narrative closure [p. 492].

Without the disruption of critical boundaries in relation to gender and sexual practices, such texts cannot be said to be queer texts on the basis of their content. However, what they do sometimes represent is a notion of sexual experimentation which in many ways queers the cultural norm of monogamous heterosex, given a heteronormative readership.

These questions about what makes a lesbian love story, or the reading of it, queer or subversive are pertinent to a critical analysis of Patti Davis' *Till Human Voices Wake Us*. Although sometimes positioned as a piece of "LGB fiction," the novel sits rather uncertainly between identity and genre categories, especially in comparison to the lesbian erotic romance novels which Crystal includes on her list discussed above. Davis identifies herself as a heterosexual woman, and the novel does not appear to be written primarily, and certainly not exclusively, for a lesbian audience. If anything, it appears to be written primarily for an audience of straight women as evidenced by the marketing of the book. Potentially, then, there is something "queer" about this text in that it appears to disrupt the solidity of identity and sexual orientation. However, the framing of this text requires some critical scrutiny—especially the ways in which lesbianism is made to signify the erotic. The attachment of the label erotic fiction to the novel is curious given that the narrative reads primarily as an emotional love story with a small number of sexual and erotic elements throughout. The novel is written in the format of a romance between Isabelle and Iris, described as being a "lesbian love story" (Monaco, 2013) as well as "a romantic story" that does not feature explicit sex scenes despite the adult content (Dean, 2013). Yet, upon release the novel was framed as "the new 50 Shades of Grey" by celebrity reporter and commentator, Perez Hilton (Hilton, 2013), and other reviews framed it as an addition to the proliferation in "mommy-porn" (Poladian, 2013) since the *Fifty Shades* phenomenon. However, for a book marketed to a mainstream female audience (through Amazon and some mainstream, mainly celebrity, news sites), it is unsurprising that a novel with lesbian content is defined as risqué and ultimately discussed in relation to its erotic content. To publicize the novel, Davis was interviewed by *People* and *More* magazines, which both have strong heterosexual female readerships and feature articles on celebrity, style and relationships, and *Neworld Review*, which mainly features articles on books, other literature and theatre. All three can be considered to have middle-class audiences. In her interview with *People* magazine, Davis comments that the novel is

> a saga about wealthy L.A. sisters-in-law who fall in love, leave their comfort zones to begin a lesbian partnership and cause a society scandal.... This isn't a book about sexual orientation; it's a book about being human [Powell, 2013].

In marketing the novel, then, Davis seems to have made an effort to position it primarily as a romantic fantasy for an audience of white, middle-class, heterosexual women. The novel's representation of lesbian experience thus functions to reinforce an idea of female-female sexual experimentation as aspirational for white, middle-class women.

By claiming the label 'erotic fiction' and emphasizing its female authorship, Davis' novel is able to invoke the idea that erotic fiction written by women for women automatically and necessarily expresses a feminist and progressive liberatory impulse. That is, the framing of the novel taps into the kind of rhetoric about "postfeminism" and women's erotic writing that Esther Sonnet identifies in her analysis of the marketing around Virgin Books' Black Lace range. Sonnet argues that this rhetoric about "erotic fiction by women for women" implies a somewhat regressive and unsophisticated emphasis on authorial intentionality and correspondingly a move away from a consideration of the significance of ideology and social power structures:

> Whilst most contemporary theories of reading have long dispensed with such intentionalism, it is interesting to see the use to which an essentialist 'female authenticity' is put here: the connection between female authorship, authorial intention, the kind of specifically "feminine" sexual fantasies produced and the meanings of those fantasies for the readership assumes that there is an untroubled passage of meaning and understanding between women simply by the fact of being women [1999, p. 175].

As Sonnet suggests, it is highly problematic to assume that female sexuality, as if it were some homogenous phenomenon, is empowering in all its forms if, and only if, it is shown or discussed from the perspective of a female author. Classifying a text such as Davis' novel as "women's erotic fiction" grants it an aura of authenticity and progressiveness, deflecting attention away from any consideration of the conditions in which the representation comes into being, or whether the sexual practices are depicted in such a way as to offer any genuine critique of patriarchal or heteronormative culture.

However, texts and their representations need to be considered in light of the contexts and conditions in which they come into being. Representations of femaleness or homosexuality aren't exempt from critique simply because an author identifies as female or gay. Among other things, the author's economic and social conditions must be taken into account. Rosalind Gill and Laura Harvey illuminate the tensions in relation to identification in their argument about "post-feminist" representations of female sexuality:

> A new binary opposition that has emerged in the last decade among feminist scholars attempting to make sense of a Western postfeminist landscape relates to whether the proliferation of representations of women as desirable and sexually agentic represents a real and positive change in depictions of female sexuality, or whether, by contrast, it is merely a postfeminist repackaging of feminist ideas in a way that renders them depoliticized and presses them into the service of patriarchal consumer capitalism [2011, p. 54].

It is worthwhile applying these questions to the recent establishment of a niche "lesbian erotic romance" market, in particular texts like Davis' novel. In this context, female sexual fluidity and experimentation is seen as acceptable only when framed by commodity culture and hyper-femininity, and reified through heterosexual understandings of female relationality and desire. Ultimately, the marketing of sex as a fashionable commodity, a means of consumer identification, tends to reinforce dominant values and moralities around gender and sexuality.

Mainstream romance and erotic fiction are neither written nor marketed for women of non-normative sexualities. Instead, the readership is often assumed to be homogenously straight, white and middle-class—this is evident both in the marketing of texts and their representations of women. The treatment of female same-sex practices as risqué in *Till Human Voices Wake Us* means that it is placed outside of the (mainstream) romance fiction genre, in the category of erotica with other "deviant" practices such as BDSM. As Feona Attwood discusses, the recent emergence of a market in sexual commodities for women has generated a certain dollar value on "subversive" sexual practices. She analyzes:

> the emergence of a form of "porn-chic" in which the traditionally despised genre conventions of porn are reinterpreted as stylish and sophisticated. Texts displaying these characteristics tend to be shocking even while they remain within the mainstream; indeed they gain their charge precisely by the disturbance of boundaries between acceptable and unacceptable sexual style and content [2005, p. 397].

In the context of this new market for sexual commodities, "the erotic" is increasingly being defined in relation to the boundary between normative and non-normative sexuality. In mainstream erotic fiction, promiscuity, non-monogamy, group sex, BDSM and same-sex practices are often used as shorthand for the erotic. In other words, "the erotic" is taken to be that which is outside of the normative, monogamous, heterosexual coupling that is the aspirational model of adult sexual relations. However, these representations of non-normativity are not necessarily subversive in relation to patriarchy; in many, if not all, cases they are contextualized in relation to normative, heterosexual male desire.

Sexual Fluidity as Middle-Class Aspiration

The apparent acceptance of women experimenting with different modes of sexual experience indicates that as a society we have reached a stage where (some) women are granted sexual agency. This agency is not afforded to all women, with those who fall below a certain economic status unable to participate in different modalities of identity and sexual practice. Moreover, the identities and practices offered are ideologically founded on a patriarchal economic system that privileges some forms of exchange value over others. That women are seen to actively take charge of their own sexuality, sexual expression and desire appears to fulfil the post-feminist aspirations as discussed by Gill and Harvey:

> From one perspective, recent representations of women—from the humorous "sex bombs" of bra advertising to the stars of "alt porn" sites ...—constitute a clear break with representations from the past in which women were passive and objectified, now showing them as active, desiring and "taking charge" sexually in a way that clearly reflects feminism's aspirations for female sexual self-determination [2011, p. 54].

However, these commonplace expressions and representations cannot be either brought into existence or understood outside of the economic, cultural and ideological system in which we live—one in which economic and hetero-masculine power are deeply integrated. It is therefore highly problematic to read such representations as constructed primarily through female agency.

Economic agency also allows for what can be labelled "sexual tourism": the experimentation with different modalities of sexuality in order to allow for a liminoid experience. In playing with and "trying on" non-normative identities, the individual participates in practices that suspend social norms, even if momentarily, giving that individual power over their place in society as well as presenting them with experiences that transcend the everyday. Gail Mason and Gary Lo have studied the sexual tourism phenomenon in relation to heterosexual people visiting the Sydney Mardi Gras. They found that a surprising number of people visiting the parade did not necessarily support LGB rights, but rather appeared to be present for liminoid experiences, such as encountering something different and strange. Mason and Lo remark that "[s]pectatorship (as opposed to participation) allows the sexual tourist to momentarily immerse him/herself in this strange sexual culture but to do so from a dispassionate distance that demands neither commitment nor support" (2009, p. 115). The reading of a novel or viewing something on a screen can have a similar effect to the spectatorship that Mason and Lo witnessed at Mardi Gras, in that the audience is at a safe distance from the subject matter presented.

It is important to acknowledge that this "sexual tourism" does indicate a limited queering of mainstream culture, in that such engagement disrupts, even if momentarily, the normative structuring of gender and sexuality and, perhaps more importantly, how the reader or viewer relates their identity to different modes of gender and sexuality. While these texts and representations aren't necessarily queer in their content, the shift toward sexual fluidity, and the associated idea that sexual experimentation is not only acceptable but desirable, is queer insofar as it subverts normative sexual conduct. However, momentary subversion and/or transgression do not contribute to the destabilizing of normative practices when viewed as an extension of economic agency. Alex Dymock explains this connection in relation to the notion of carnival and stylized excess:

> [T]ransgression is understood as an inert form of sexual license, an empty carnival of imagined excess whose aim is to create "exemplary consumers of commodities" (Hester, 2013). Stallybrass and White, reading transgression in relation to Bakhtin's theory of carnival, argue that it is a deliberate and controlled mechanism under which we are permitted to experience an exhilarating if short-lived sense of freedom while hierarchies of social power are ultimately preserved and unmoved [2013, p. 881].

When reading fiction such as Davis' novel which offers some form of sexual tourism to its audience, the liminoid experience is mediated by the author. Authors such as Davis who write from privileged positions (educated and middle-class) thereby reinforce the hegemonic position of class. As the daughter of ex-president Ronald Reagan, Davis is representative of the aspirational political and creative classes of the American elite. Attitudes toward sex, and what may be considered progressive practices, are subsumed within this aspirational model. Sexual experimentation is positioned as a mass commodified product—it is another aspect of identity that can be sold to us.

Davis' novel reflects and normalizes an elite view of the world. When the main character, Isabelle, leaves her wealthy marriage to pursue the relationship with her sister-in-law Iris, Isabelle does not seem capable of living her new life in the absence of affluence. Indeed, it is entirely because of this affluence that she and Iris are able to live a life outside of the normative. This is neo-liberal ideology at work and is a key driver to how we, as a society, understand and engage with difference: if the market allows it then it must be at least somewhat legitimate and/or permissible. It is unlikely that the relationship between Isabelle and Iris would be sustainable were the money and relative life-comfort not there. Isabelle has no job and Iris works at a women's shelter, yet they are able to support a life on the beach in Malibu, take Isabelle's step-daughter Marjorie to expensive schooling and ballet and afford the very best out-of-hospital care for Isabelle's dying mother. Indeed, much of Isabelle's life is afforded to her emotional whims, something that would be a luxury for many. Her life is aspirational; through her marriage to Thomas she becomes part of the American aristocracy of old money, and subsequently her divorce positions her as part of the American nouveau riche. While these two categories have different significations in relation to identity, culture and symbolism, both reflect the aspirational model of capitalism in the U.S. whereby affluent individuals may behave in ways that are not available to the lower classes and the poor.

Representations of same-sex desire have become pervasive in consumer culture: gay and homo-erotic representations and identifications have become an extension of middle- and upper-class affectations. Sexual and gender diversity are marketable; they illustrate an apparent social consciousness while striving for an edginess that conservative hetero-culture cannot embody. Naomi Klein argues that these representations have become a strong selling point for marketers, whereby marketing has "seized upon multiculturalism and gender-bending in the same ways that it has seized upon youth culture in general—not just as a market niche but as a source of new carnivalesque imagery" (2000). This means, for example, that homosexuality and sexual fluidity become more visible and socially accepted, but only a certain sanitized version of homosexuality and/or sexual fluidity that is suitable for the mainstream market. This is reflected in the version of lesbian identity which is visible in the marketing of lesbian erotica through mainstream outlets such as Amazon. In looking at the top entries for the search "lesbian erotic fiction" on Amazon.com, the majority of titles feature conventionally "feminine" women. The covers of these titles mainly feature one or more women in lingerie with highly stylized femme makeup and hair, reinforcing heteronormative assumptions of female same-sex sexuality. Similarly, a search for "lesbian romantic fiction" on Amazon.com generates a list which also features very femme women albeit with slightly more clothes on. It is not hard to see how these books could be popular with mass audiences given their unproblematic representations of women. While it is difficult to ascertain the gender and sexual orientation of the readers of these books, a lot can be learned from the reviews boards. Many of the comments boards featured male names as well as female names and many of the comments (for example, "I bought this for my husband/wife") disclosed that the reader was in a heterosexual relationship (Amazon Results Page, 2015).

Feona Attwood argues that sexual identity and sexual practices have become part of the postmodern construction of identity that is activated through the marketplace. She notes that there "is an emphasis on the individual as the creator of her own significance, status and experience, and on the need to make these culturally visible and meaningful through the manipulation of appropriate consumer goods" (2005, p. 401). While it can be argued that experimentation in relation to gender and sexual fluidity are in general positive, there remain questions about the extent to which these artifices are dependent on the capitalist market and circumscribed by heterosexual male desire. This is part of a broader issue in third-wave feminism and post-feminism: the individual is positioned as the primary site of meaning and identification, even in the acknowledgement that the deciphering of meaning is done through the various vestiges of patriarchal power. The question asked by Attwood is a poignant one: "Does sexual consumerism ultimately work to reposition women as passive objects of the male gaze or does it—can it—provide the tools women need to fashion something new?" (2005, p. 401). It is a question that needs greater unpacking in view of cultural trends in relation to female sexuality and consumerism, one that has previously been broached by Esther Sonnet in her discussion of female sexuality, liberalism and pornography (1999). It is not enough to assume that the new sex practices, products and experimentation are symbolic of an undeterred sex positivism that will benefit women and society as a whole. There are greater forces at work than just the individual and their personal expression, and so it is important to question the recurring symbolism, representations and statements that become commonplace in this transition toward newer expressions of female sexuality.

Heterosexual Female Experimentation and Persistent Femininity

Experimenting with one's sexuality and sexual fluidity is something afforded primarily to females within society, generally those of a higher social and economic status. Experimentation is most often limited to females because of the prevailing view of gay male sexuality as effeminate and emasculating. Gay male sexuality and homoeroticism is troubling to a culture that values masculinity in males, a culture which is, therefore, in straight men's best interests to maintain. Female homosexuality, conversely, is seen as generally unthreatening to the established order, even of coupledom and domesticity, as it can be reified through male heterosexual desire. Female-to-female sexual experimentation is often unproblematically conceived within heterosexual parameters due to its associations with visual pornographic texts aimed at men, in which hyper-feminine actors perform for the purposes of male arousal. Indeed, this sort of experimentation for women is often seen as a normal part of youth, as indicated through the character of Isabelle in Davis' novel:

> Once when I was eighteen, I drank too many beers with a girlfriend in her house when her parents were gone. Laughing and drunk, we thought it would be fun to try making out, just as an experiment—to see where it might lead [2013, p. 47].

The absence of a male figure here does not make the passage an indication of Isabelle's later female-female relationship, but is rather constituted as a normative part of young female experimentation, and is something that is read very differently to male-male experimentation at the same age. Same-sex female experimentation can be understood as a primer for practices that may later be expected as part of heterosex. This type of sexual performativity, according to Megan Yost and Lauren McCarthy (2012), is now common amongst women at college parties in the U.S. They cite one study that found "roughly half the heterosexual women in one dormitory reported having kissed or fondled other women at parties, and their most-often stated reason was to get attention from men" (p. 8), adding as part of their study that the women they interviewed did not view kissing as a sexual behavior that defined their own sexuality (p. 20). This latter study group described same-sex kissing by women as "normal," even though the "majority felt sexually objectified or exploited." In a similar study investigating female-female kissing at a U.S. college, Lannutti and Denes found that around half of their female participants had kissed another woman and that both "men and women perceived a woman who kissed a woman to be more promiscuous than a woman who kissed a man" (2012, p. 49). This latter point is poignant when framing same-sex behaviors, particularly when they are contextualized within the heterosexual discourse of college. Even in the absence of male onlookers, same-sex attraction and practices are conceived through these parameters of acceptance and desire for many women. With respect to Davis' novel, Isabelle and Iris are not principally engaging in sexual activity for a male onlooker within the text (and it can be assumed that the majority of Davis' readers are not male either), yet their gender normativity as well as their sexual interactions as written by Davis are premised upon these prevailing assumptions about female-female sexual interaction within a heterosexual context.

This behavior has been described by Breanne Fahs (2009) as "compulsory bisexuality" whereby young women are expected to be "up for" same-sex behaviors, often at the behest of men. She states that women "may engage in same-sex sexual behavior, but this often occurs in the presence of men, with men's approval, and for men's sexual arousal," adding that women "are classically heterosexual even while performing as bisexual" (p. 445). Within the novel this foundation of heterosexuality is often represented through the depictions of sexual interactions that are premised on a very heterosexual understanding of female-female sex. Firstly, it is firmly established that both Isabelle and Iris are typically feminine in their appearance as well as their actions. Upon deciding to pursue Iris physically, Isabelle narrates,

> Early on, I felt I could never get naked enough with Iris. There are many versions of nakedness. Emotional, psychological, spiritual ... skin is only one of them. But skin is an important one, not to be discounted or trivialized. So with that in mind, I walked into a beauty salon one afternoon and asked for a Brazilian bikini wax, although I asked for a slightly modified version. How much more naked can you get than that? At least on the skin-deep level. You're being turned nubile again, smooth and silky as a newcomer [Davis, 2013, p. 37].

That Isabelle's behavior represents it as appropriate for women to be waxed and beautified prior to a new sexual encounter points to the internalization of the male gaze in positioning the female body, in all of its superficialities, as premised on sign value as a precursor to exchange value.

These allusions to beauty and femininity persist throughout the novel, and are often specific to sexual interaction. Iris returns Isabelle's beauty efforts by getting herself waxed similarly, as well as her attention to eradicating "defects" from her body such as the ritualistic removing of a nipple hair from one of her breasts:

> She does this for me, I think—her lover. For my mouth, my tongue. Looking for it, noticing how long it takes to grow back and how many days pass before it's removed again is my secret in the dark [Davis, 2013, p. 126].

Further to the highly feminized appearance of Isabelle and Iris are the types of sexual activity they engage in, being focused predominantly on very tepid sex acts, often referred to as vanilla sexual practice. This serves a double purpose: it confirms commonsense understandings of lesbian sexual behavior and also invites the reader to view Isabelle and Iris as normatively and unproblematically feminine. There are also allusions to what Barbara Creed (1995) has termed "the narcissistic lesbian body" here—both women are highly feminine and get waxed similarly, which suggests the idea that their love is an extension of love for themselves. The idea of the narcissistic lesbian is also affirmed through the focus of fashion and conspicuous consumption. Feona Attwood suggests that female homosexuality as an extension of homosociality may be easier to read in this context, so that rather than "performing for a male gaze, self-fashioning may provide women with a culturally approved way of producing themselves for themselves" (2005). Here, female-female sexuality in its feminized representations can be read as an extension of commodification practices through which female sexuality is performed as an extension of femininity.

The attraction and subsequent relationship between Isabelle and Iris is premised chiefly on emotional attraction and compatibility rather than sexual or physical attraction. One of the major failings of Isabelle and her husband Thomas' relationship, his inability to engage with Isabelle on an emotional and compassionate level, is constantly reiterated. When Thomas and Isabelle's marriage breaks down in the aftermath of their son's death, Iris and Isabelle's relationship grows mainly as a result of Isabelle's emotional needs. Physical attraction and sexual desire appear as extensions of emotional connection, and are highly feminized as a result. Romance built from friendship forms part of the mythic view of female-female attraction and lesbianism as primarily romantic friendship which exists until a suitable male figure is able to take the place of the incorrectly desired female partner. This archaic notion was commonly accepted throughout the nineteenth and twentieth centuries prior to the introduction of the neologism of "lesbian" in reference to identity as well as same-sex practices (Vicinus, 1992). However, this notion persists through to contemporary notions of same-sex attracted women just needing to find the right man. This substitution is implied in Iris' confession to Isabelle:

> "I found myself wishing the other day that you were a man. It would just remove one of our huge complications, you know? It was just a weird thought" [Davis, 2013, p. 78].

That the only penetrative sex Isabelle experiences is with Thomas is a case in point. Sex between Isabelle and Iris is written as emotional and spiritual, or what Esther Newton describes as "pure and ennobling" (1984, p. 561) in her description of nineteenth century romantic friendships. This notion is also represented in some early twentieth century novels, such as *Mrs. Dalloway*'s Clarissa and her affections for Sally: "The strange thing, on looking back, was the purity, the integrity, of her feeling for Sally. It was not like one's feeling for a man" (Woolf, 2012). Similarly, Iris and Isabelle's sexual interactions are premised on an essentialized feminine love and intrinsic knowingness:

> As two women making love, Iris and I are citizens of a new country, yet strangely it's as if we've come home. We laugh about it sometimes, rising from the tangle of our bodies, our faces flushed and damp with each other's scents. Neither of us knew how to do this—make love with another woman—but some kind of knowing took over ... takes over ... every time [Davis, 2013, p. 37].

There is a particularly second-wave feminist symbolism at work here of the female-identified female that posits the female body and femininity as natural and spiritual, in intimate knowledge of itself. Conversely, Isabelle recalls sex with Thomas as physical and perfunctory:

> As I moved downward from the bars of his ribcage to the pulse point on his stomach he woke up, startled. It sounded like words were about to come from his mouth but he gasped instead as I took him in my mouth and went to work. I was efficient, deliberate, and when he had what I wanted I straddled him and plunged him into me. This was not love-making, this was fucking—fierce and ruthless, with only conquest as a goal [Davis, 2013, p. 54].

The binary opposition constructed here between female-female attraction and heterosexuality reproduces archaic, normative assumptions about heterosexuality and lesbianism. In doing so, it confirms a universalist idea of women as essentially and naturally more emotional and spiritual than men, downplaying the significance of the differences between women produced by class, race and sexuality.

Given the essentializing of gender along with the heteronormative portrayals of the characters, it is surprising that the novel has been promoted by selected LGB media such as *The Advocate* (Broverman, 2013) and *Gay Star News* (Hernandez, 2013) amongst others. In particular, it is the overt descriptions of female masculinity and the mythic mannish lesbian (Newton, 1984) that are most challenging in viewing the text as gender-positive. In stark contrast to the acceptable, feminized same-sex female attraction as represented in the relationship of Isabelle and Iris, lesbian sexuality as a historical archetype is positioned as both different and undesirable. This undesirability is premised upon an incongruence of gende: a deviant departure from the aspirational identities embodied by the two main female characters. Borne out in Isabelle's fear of same-sex attraction as she begins to contemplate her feelings for Iris, she recalls a time from her past:

> Madge and Hazel turned out to be two fiftyish lesbians with men's haircuts, men's clothes, and packs of cigarettes in their breast pockets. They slapped my father on the back and then led out four over-ridden, sad horses. Madge was going to be our trail boss. For an hour, we plodded along, coughed up dust, listened to my father and Madge talk about gambling and the track and God knows what else. I didn't care how Madge and Hazel chose to live their lives, I just wanted the day to be over, which is why I didn't even know the memory of those women was still in me.
>
> But apparently it was, because in my dream, I was Madge—or at least a reasonable facsimile of her. Same Elvis-style haircut, same manly clothes ... and I was standing on a dusty piece of land looking at the back of a blonde woman as she rode away from me on a slow, worn-down horse. I never saw the woman's face in my dream, but I understood her to be Iris [Davis, 2013, p. 56].

Isabelle's aversion to gender non-normativity is profound in this section of the narrative. That not only Isabelle herself but also the horses are miserable in the company of Madge and Hazel is irrefutable. As explained by Esther Newton (1984, pp. 566–67), the mythic mannish lesbian was a term introduced by Richard von Krafft-Ebing as a means of pathologizing lesbianism, whereby the most masculine was the most deviant. In furthering this position, Havelock Ellis simplified Krafft-Ebing's scale to not only attach masculinity to deviance, but also to classify types of relationship within the model. The first and least deviant were "passionate friendships" and the most deviant were modelled as a replicate of heterosexual relationships where the most masculine partner was seen as the invert. The relationship between Isabelle and Iris could safely fall under the category of passionate friendship within this model, comfortably distanced from the trope that persists within our contemporary culture of the deviant, masculine lesbian.

The binary model still permeates contemporary notions of acceptable queer identity where often it is assumed, by mainstream society as well as some sections of the queer community, that a highly masculine female wants to be a man and may be in some sort of pre-transsexual gender crisis. In addition, it is often assumed that any female with masculine behaviors is either a lesbian, wanting to be a man, or both. Judith Halberstam illuminates the complexities of identity for masculinized females in the last fifty years, arguing that lesbian sexual identity became privileged over an ambiguous gender identity to the point where gender fluidity and notions of inversion became demonized:

> As the notion of lesbianism gathered strength, so the masculine woman became a paradoxical figure within lesbian communities; she was representative of those communities as the "butch," but she was also ultimately rejected as an anachronistic reminder of the rejected discourse of inversion. Indeed, to this day, many contemporary lesbian communities signal their modernity by denying the stereotype of the mannish lesbian [1998, p. 96].

It is possible that this disdain for female masculinity has roots in the gender wars prompted by the initial movements of feminism in the 1970s where men, and associated masculine behavior, were heavily criticized (particularly in the radical feminism of Andrea Dworkin and Catharine MacKinnon) and seen as inferior to women and "the feminine." In more recent history, and as a response to the radical feminist movement's rejection of men and male behavior, the non-feminized female was made an object of ridicule by both men and those women who wanted to distance themselves from radical feminism. Indeed, in an arguably post-feminist world that supposedly permits a fluid range of gender identities, the subject position of the masculine female remains problematic, marginalized and delegitimized as an actual and proper identity.

Moreover, the friendship and collegiality over gambling between Madge and Isabelle's father adds to the binary positioning of the lesbians as bad and undesirable in contrast with the present-day Isabelle in all of her good and aspirational qualities. There is a highly regulated binary throughout the text between the masculine and the feminine, with nearly all of the male and masculine characters (who are both under-represented and under-characterized) written as uncaring, inconsiderate and cold. Isabelle feels disappointment in her father as well as Thomas, and positions them reductively as displaying a masculine/male condition of being unfeeling and incapable of love. In contrast, the female characters are given generous characterization, are universally written as good and often speak for themselves through dialogue. Iris, for example, works at a local women's shelter; Isabelle's mother is shown to be very spiritual and has an almost martyr-like quality in her reactions to and memories of Isabelle's dead-beat dad; Marjorie is written as a quiet and precocious child who likes ballet and has a barely-suppressed dislike for her father; and Isabelle herself is an emotionally complex woman who cares deeply for her family and others. The only male characters given any real positive regard and depth within the text are Harlan and Bruce, the gay neighbors to Isabelle and Iris in Malibu. However, they are stereotypically both very good-looking and emotionally astute. Ultimately, the novel is written with such a strict binary of masculine/male-bad to feminine/female-good, emphasized in such reflections as "[m]ale egos are so fragile" (Davis, 2013, p. 222), that even given the "risqué" subject matter of female homo-relationality, the text feels retrograde and reductive. As with essentialist strands of second-wave radical feminism Davis' novel helps to maintain a normative and homogenizing understanding of "male" and "female."

Conclusion

The appearance of popular lesbian erotic fiction in the erotic romance market initially appears to be formulating a progressive dialogue about female same-sex sexuality. However, on closer inspection, many such texts undermine the diversity of LGB and non-normative individuals and reinforce a narrow conceptualization of gender. *Till Human Voices Wake Us* is one such example—the text is essentially a safe, upper-middle-class and heteronormative conceptualization of same-sex female attraction that reinforces the heterosexual matrix through fiercely entrenched gender norms. In doing so it advances a neo-liberal, heteronormative representation of female sexuality within what appears to be a subversive and progressive narrative. Esther Sonnet's description of the 1990s Black Lace range of erotic novels: "in many ways curiously old-fashioned in attempting to stabilize and even naturalize the connection between gender and sexuality" (1999, p. 183), is applicable to Davis' novel. The popular marketing of "lesbian fiction," apparently partly directed at heterosexual women, needs to be treated with caution insofar as such texts present lesbianism or bisexuality as a form of sexual tourism, whereby a heteronormative version of same-sex experimentation is offered as the most acceptable fantasy. In such texts, homosexual liaisons are enacted within strictly defined parameters of acceptability, such as the maintenance of gender normativity and that of strict femininity regulation.

Part 3
Uses of the Erotic

The Politics of Slash on the High Seas

Colonial Romance and Revolutionary Solidarity in Pirates *Fan Fiction*

Anne Kustritz

Controversy over women's erotic literature often intersects with cultural taboos about female sexuality. Although less well known than romance novels or feminist porn, slash fan fiction—amateur, female-produced, same-sex erotica using pre-published characters—has frequently become embroiled in similar debates over the social meaning of romantic fiction and women's sexual imagination. The pendulum has swung back and forth and back again in the academic consensus on slash's political value over the 40 years since its inception in its current form. Thus, mirroring analysis of romance novels, erotica, and pornography, slash has been at times called anti-female and stridently feminist, radically liberatory and conservative, both queer and heteronormative. This incoherence partly results from a homogenizing impulse to make a single political judgment of the entire practice. In addition, such dueling political pronouncements indicate an inability to navigate cultural objects that simultaneously resist some forms of political domination while ideologically shoring up and reinforcing others, including not only sex/gender hierarchies, but also race, class, and geopolitics. Thus, what the field currently needs is an analytical lens of smaller and more specific scope to cope with the ideological complexities across slash genres and even within individual narratives.

Consequently, this chapter attempts to chart the specific layers of literary and social history within which individual slash stories create political meanings. In this respect, several slash novels drawn from the *Pirates of the Caribbean* franchise pairing Commodore James Norrington with Captain Jack Sparrow exemplify the multiple ideological maneuvers at work in slash practices, while still retaining room for slash's political utility. Because the source films elide the political ramifications of their own highly loaded premise, they also create a structural narrative gap that fan writers eagerly fill. By staging numerous thought experiments in how the archetypal pirate and pirate hunter, poised at opposite ends of the colonial hierarchy, might use sex and romance to bridge a vast socio-political divide, slash authors collectively analyze contemporary modes of remembering and representing colonial exploitation, and the tricky rhetorical overlaps between sexual and political bodies. Some of these dreams paint imperial landscapes with the brush of romantic nostalgia, as feminized Jack is domesticated into social and political compliance. Yet, others imagine a much more radical and overtly political version of the *Pirates* storyworld, as Jack seduces Norrington out of the false consciousness of privilege, toward recognition of their shared humanity, and the potential for revolutionary sexual, personal, and political self-determinaton. They thus demonstrate slash spaces' ability to sustain dialogue between multiple political narratives, including some that challenge readers to grapple with transformative versions of erotic, economic, and geopolitical exchange.

Ideological Analysis in Fan Studies

Academic assessments of slash's political meaning often follow larger theoretical waves and fashions in media studies and feminist theory. As an interdisciplinary subfield, fan studies has only just begun to create its own independent corpus and identity; fan works, communities, and practices have previously only surfaced in academic debate when useful to illustrate other principles. Thus many references to fans reinforced Frankfurt School-inspired analyses of popular culture as mass deception with the fan as the figure of passive consumerism *par excellence* (Adorno and Horkheimer, 1972; Lewis, 1992). In the '80s and '90s fans represented Birmingham School-style popular culture analysis, in which consumers became active makers rather than passive receivers of meaning, and scholars emphasized the cultural hierarchies that devalue media associated with oppressed groups and classes (Hall, 1981). Because slash involves female fans asserting power over the mass media, it attested to audiences' ability to use media to talk back to capitalist, sexist, and heterocentric forms of political oppression (Jenkins, 1992). Although it remained contentious whether to label slash as romance, erotica, or pornography, as a form of often explicitly sexual writing produced by women, for women, slash was also celebrated as a space for the production and circulation of uniquely female sexual representation and fantasy (Lamb and Veith, 1986; Penley, 1991; Russ, 1985).

However, in the late '90s and early 2000s two developments began to turn the tide of academic opinion in another direction. First, many scholars critiqued Birmingham School analyses of popular culture on the grounds that if subversion can be found everywhere the meaning of "subversion" becomes too diffuse to retain significance, and in addition most studies of the subversive meanings and pleasures that audiences find and create through popular culture remain only at the semiotic and psychological level, never leading to actual change in either mainstream structures of representation or material conditions. On the other hand, the cultural position of fans had also changed. Instead of a limit case or narrow subculture, the industry's marketing strategies increasingly centralized fan communities, while fan behaviors once considered isolated and extreme formed a common part of mainstream interactions with media, now termed a "participatory culture" (Jenkins, 2006). The industry's tacit approval of and even reliance on fan communities often appears to dull the potentially subversive edge of a once fringe phenomena (Felschow, 2010; van Dijck, 2009; Ward, 2009).

Thus some current scholarly works about slash can be read as a reaction against the phase wherein slash was recuperated as politically subversive. Many of these caution that slash stories often reproduce the same homophobic, racist, sexist structures prevalent in mainstream media and thereby should not be seen as truly subversive of anything (Hunting, 2012; Jones, 2002; Scodari, 2003). However, the ideological heterogeneity of fan fiction narratives, and the multiple vectors of oppression that regulate social hierarchies, are frequently underemphasized. As a result, sweeping statements that slash is or is not politically radical overlook the many different types of storytelling within slash, and the possibility that even a single story often subverts some forms of regressive stereotype while reproducing and reinforcing others; for example, offering a radically queer vision of sexual variation yet including caricatured characters of color. Nor do ideological analyses of fan fiction's content often keep in mind the very interpretative diversity of reception that produces fan fiction's proliferation. Just as the multiple storylines in fan fiction show that audiences find many pleasures, investments, and meanings in popular culture, so too may the audiences of fan fiction texts construct multiple readings of slash from numerous political and pleasurable points of view. Therefore, making political pronouncements about all of fan culture or about an entire sector or genre of fan writing invokes an insurmountable incoherency as their heterogeneity in content and readership defies any straightforward political valuation.

Romantic Conquest and Boys' Adventures

While the *Pirates of the Caribbean* films provide a winking, postmodern pastiche that reawakens the romantic allure of pirate adventures, largely drained of political context, slash fan fiction produces an array of thought experiments in how alternate arrangements of colonial bodies and passions might remake the world. From its inception, slash fan fiction routinely played upon characters that embody political, historical, and social oppositions, making the dynamics of their relationship a negotiation of both their individual psychologies and the larger mythological structures they represent; rearranging their physical bodies thus often implies and requires a concomitant rearrangement of the body politic. In the original slash pairing from *Star Trek*, Kirk stood at the apex of most social hierarchies, while his embrace of Spock often became a statement about the social incorporation of out-groups. As part human and part-alien, Spock embodied an alterity that could metaphorically stand in for an almost endless array of social difference, and scholars have read him as a representative of Jewish or other racialized identities, autism or other non-neuro-normative states, a communist, an immigrant, a woman, and a symbol of queer subversion of categories including bi-racial and bi-sexual (Coppa, 2008). Each individual slash interpretation of their relationship emphasized different aspects of Spock's alien heritage, and created its own larger political implications depending on how the author bridged the social divides that Kirk and Spock embodied. Many of the commonly slashed couples who followed also represented political mythologies, and the spiritual, social, and physical union of these characters in slash stories often requires authors to also engage and resolve the opposing social and political forces and histories they symbolize, or even to use these characters to overtly comment upon social structures. However, every individual story does so in its own way, creating an enormous range of thought experiments on the interpersonal negotiation of micro- and macro-political mythologies.

To analyze the ideological value of individual slash stories, one must consider the way in which they revise many layers of cultural mythology, including genre and period-specific contexts. Although slash narratives most often involve either mixed genres or genre transposition, in many cases the romance plot carries significant symbolic weight, and in the case of *Pirates of the Caribbean* it is specifically the colonial adventure-romance. While the romance genre obviously and overtly deals with the construction of sexuality, gender, and relationships, it also often contains larger-scale political mythology. On the one hand, romance repeatedly becomes a metaphor for understanding historical eras and conflicts, while on the other hand the romance between individual characters also often stands in for a larger story about the fruitful or dissonant union between the groups, ideals, or historical forces that the two potential lovers represent. In her landmark 1972 article "Is Female to Male as Nature is to Culture" and her follow-up article "So, Is Female to Male as Nature Is to Culture?" (1996), anthropologist Sherry Ortner proposes that these basic semiotic connections became the foundations upon which many more complex mythologies depend. At this level, the gendered structures of heterosexual romance as the opposition between nature and culture underlies many, if not all, of the most common Western narratives. This resonates throughout literature as well as political rhetoric, as individual historical events may also be figured within the romantic tangle between nature and civilization. Perhaps the most famous of these may be the framing of the colonial encounter as a romance, both in common political as well as literary descriptions of non–Western countries as feminized, wild, and untamed, requiring the benevolent control and discipline provided by masculinized Western governments, but also as embodied by the memory of specific historical figures' colonial romances, represented both benevolently, as in the Pocahontas story, and more darkly, as in La Malinche (Candelaria, 1980; Davis, 2007; McClintock, 1995; Pratt, 1993; Stoler, 2002).

These hybrid political-romantic forms are not limited to heterosexual narratives, and also draw upon structural legacies in the representation of homosocial and homoerotic bonds between men, particularly though not exclusively within the context of imperial fiction. Eve Sedgwick argued that throughout the Western canon the heterosexual romance form uses the exchange of women to suture relationships between men (1985). For Sedgwick, romantic rivalries establish equality among men who recognize each other as worthy opponents. So superfluous are actual women to this formula that they may be replaced with any feminized object around which rivals prove their mettle and triangulate their desires. In the Age of Sail, ships easily serve this purpose, as do territories and nations, which are so often female embodied as Mother India, Lady Liberty, Britannia, and so on. Sedgwick's work thus reads triangulated relationships between rival men as potentially homoerotic, and consequently also exposes homoerotic undercurrents within the political and literary figuration of colonial romance, wherein men test each other's worth against the rhetorically feminized forces of nature and native people.

In addition to the symbolic centrality of triangulated homoerotic desire, Leslie Fiedler argues that passionate interracial bonds between men form the bedrock of the particularly American literary tradition of colonial romantic adventure (1948). Examining *The Adventures of Huckleberry Finn*, *The Last of the Mohicans*, and *Moby Dick*, Fiedler draws attention to the chaste, boyish love between pairs of white men and men of color in these classics, made possible by the supposed freedom from restraint and responsibility in "uncivilized" colonial spaces. Fiedler recounts the surprising intimacies frequently afforded to such pairs, as Huck and Jim float down the Mississippi lying side by side, and Ishmael reflects, "thus, then, in our hearts' honeymoon, lay I and Queequeg—a cozy loving pair" (p. 666). Fiedler notes that it is not only the absence of women that enables this archetypal attraction to emerge, as is often said of men living in homosocial spaces such as sailors and prisoners. Rather, he argues that it is the anarchic space of boyhood, superimposed upon the sea as well as frontier and colonial landscapes, that grants the license to love those whom racial, economic, and hetero-patriarchal orders will later require to be set aside in adulthood. Although he does not explore the homoerotic undercurrents of the premise, in "Imperial Boyhood" Bradley Deane (2011) likewise formulates a close tie between romantic imperial adventures of both the political and literary sort with boyishness. He argues that late Victorian British literature shifted from imagining the colonies as a testing ground that turns boys into men, toward a locus of endless childish play with no rules and no *teleos*, to mirror the political shift to conservative colonial policies that idealized Empire in and of itself, beyond a "liberal civilizing mission." Thus, in combining these theoretical threads, the colonial landscape of the political and literary imagination becomes laced with numerous alluring transitional objects that white boys might use to become men both through sex and combat, or where "lost boys" might choose to remain forever, drawn inexorably to the anarchic freedoms and forbidden love objects deemed impossible in the imperial center. Notably, none of these scenarios consider colonialism from the perspective of colonized or enslaved people, nor do they consider the human cost of treating colonies as a white boy's playground.

Turning specifically to *Pirates of the Caribbean*, the relationship between Captain Jack Sparrow and Commodore James Norrington, known by the portmanteau "Sparrington," offers numerous points of potential political symbolism for fan authors to exploit. Although a total of three films in the *Pirates* franchise featured both Jack and Norrington, slash writing for the couple took off after the first film, but slowed considerably after the second, perhaps because the second film retread many of the storylines already thoroughly explored by fan fiction when Norrington lost his naval post and temporarily joined Jack's crew, then spent the third movie doing very little apart from brooding and (spoilers!) dying tragically. However, the first film provided ample fodder for slash expansion by establishing a kind of equality between Jack and Norrington through their rivalry as the greatest pirate in the Caribbean and the greatest pirate hunter. Most Sparrington slash begins by forcing the pair into closer proximity than generally allowed by their opposing mythological significance and social position, and then differs in how authors deal with the aftermath of that proximity. As predicted by Ortner, the oppositions overtly set by their characterizations in the film identify epic conflicts between order and chaos, honor and trickery, social convention and self-determination, duty and adventure, stoicism and emotionality, and planning and improvisation, most of which depend on the underlying division between culture and nature, masculinity and femininity. Thus, while they overtly represent a series of mythological oppositions in the film, they also accept each other as worthy opponents, a mutual recognition that sets the stage for slashers' homoerotic expansion of their story.

Yet, these form only the overt structures of the film in which, as explained by the director's DVD commentary, in any other story Norrington might just as easily have been the hero and protagonist (Verbinski, 2003). The almost generic way in which Jack stands for freedom and Norrington for duty echoes Thomas Frank's argument that popular culture reproduces the stylistics of politics without its content, insofar as the film represses the historical specificity of colonialism upon which its own premise depends (1997). In the model of the apolitical boy's adventure narrative Deane (2011) describes, the films therein include characters of color, but do not mention slavery, mention Spanish slaughter of natives but depict native people only as animalistic cannibals who cannot be reasoned or sympathized with, and show British troops only protecting innocent villagers from supernatural rather than human threats, ignoring their involvement in the brutality of conquest. Historically speaking, pirate ships utilized a democratic form of decision-making, and included many groups that received little social recognition or were actively oppressed, including run-away slaves, mixed-race people, independent women, and wash-outs or deserters from the navy (Mackie, 2005). In contrast, a high-ranking officer like Norrington sat at the top of an intersecting series of race, class, and gender hierarchies, and engaged in constant active and passive forms of violence in the perpetuation of slavery and colonialism. Yet, while Norrington plays the antagonist to Jack, the films rarely politicize that choice. They instead position the audience to identify with Jack largely because he is whimsical, drives the plot, and represents a loose version of "freedom" easily inhabited from any given political perspective. The films, with their blockbuster, mass market construction, excised the more overtly political version of the story, which they delegated to official transmedia extensions with smaller niche audiences, like the novelizations and online game. These narrative elements include Jack's back story as the liberator of slaves aboard a ship he captained for the East India Trading Company, a vital piece of framing that could dramatically politicize his conflict with the company and colonial government in the films.

Therefore, remembering that Norrington represents an occupying colonial force adds another level of symbolism to the film, also incorporating the characters' opposition around the historically contextual issues of equality versus hierarchy, stealth versus violence, freedom versus slavery, democracy versus aristocracy, survival versus conquest, and theft from the rich versus theft from native people. The relationship between Jack and Norrington is thus stratified by systems of class and race, information brought to reception of the films by only some audience members, but familiar to many fan writers who often include copious historical footnotes as well as detailed nautical terminology. For example, the footnotes on *Caribbean Cartography* by Cupiscent (2004) acknowledge that for the purposes of the plot the author changed the precise sort of map of Santa Catalina that Norrington could have been expected to possess, indicating both an expectation that readers would recognize the error, and that this slight historical discrepancy matters. While some authors certainly approach the pairing as a madcap affair between a laced-up goody-goody and a free-spirit, others use the relationship to engage directly with the films' suppressed political stakes and to explore the political and philosophical positions that the characters represent.

Interpersonal and Political Utopias: Defining Love and Freedom in Sparrington Slash

Thus to bridge both the micro-politics of interpersonal relationships, and the macro-politics of race, gender, heteronormativity, colonialism, class, and geopolitics, fan authors generally either adapt the lovers to fit each other's social status and values, or narrate a path whereby they may meet somewhere in-between. Each of these outcomes pose vastly different commentaries on memory of the colonial past, and on contemporary neo-colonial sexual and racial politics. Three basic approaches will be discussed here: first, stories that replay and intensify the colonial romance of racial and economic domination in deriving a happy ending from Jack's capitulation to the social structure via his abandonment of piracy and sexual surrender as Norrington's feminized partner; second, tragic stories in which the colonial structure remains intact as an insurmountable barrier between the lovers due to their polarized political and social identities; and third, stories in which revolution or disruption of the colonial order becomes intrinsic to the positive resolution of the romance narrative, generally by requiring Norrington's recognition and renunciation of the violence of his own social position before he can have his happily ever after in political and sexual solidarity with Jack. Together, these narratives demonstrate both the range of slash authors' and readers' political engagement, and the method by which erotic narratives about *Pirates* characters can offer deeply resonant political thought experiments, mirroring critiques of the political body via the physical bodies of characters who represent opposing social positions and forces. By tying critiques of the colonial past into the happy resolution of a romance plot, or even merely reflecting upon colonialism's complexities in a more thorough manner than generally acceptable in adventure-romance literature, such stories disrupt readers' ability to engage with colonialism and its attendant injustices on a surface-level as consequence-free play. Instead they require reflection upon the ethical and moral dimensions of global geopolitics, both in the specificities of slavery, race, and Western exploitation during the age of sail, and, by proxy, also in the way that colonialism's legacies still shape racial and global hierarchies of the contemporary neo-colonial world.

In the first instance, stories wherein Norrington's honorable behavior tames and domesticates Jack play upon the romantic structure of feminine surrender under a strong masculine influence. In many of these narratives Jack's love for Norrington leads him to give up piracy to live within the law, sometimes even on land, change his appearance, and conform to the dictates of respectability. As a romantic narrative, this subgenre's allure lies in sacrifice's testament to the strength of the character's love. Therefore, such story structures can offer strong emotional rewards to some readers, and purely in terms of testimony to strong romantic feelings, Jack giving up his ship, the Black Pearl, mirrors narratives in which Norrington gives up his status and values to be with Jack. However, at the macro-political level, the mythological meaning attached to completely absorbing Jack's outlaw protest of the colonial order into Norrington's devotion to King and country mutes any consideration of the injustice of the social structure Norrington represents, and offers an assimilationist approach to social and sexual politics. Therefore, like other popular types of fan activities that romanticize life in the British Navy, sometimes found in fan fiction about so-called 'Men on Ships' fandoms like *Master and Commander* or *Horatio Hornblower* as well as *Pirates of the Caribbean* stories focused solely on the films' naval characters, this mode of Sparrington slash tends to smooth over memory of colonial violence and exploitation for contemporary (neo-colonial) audiences with a thick layer of heroism, honor, and nostalgia.

A second popular subgenre of tragic romance addresses many of the interpersonal, micro-political problematics of the sacrifice narrative, but in doing so also presents Jack and Norrington as archetypal symbols of binary forces that can never, and perhaps should never, be resolved or bridged, again leaving the colonial structure intact. On a psychological level, these stories critique gendered sexual surrender by questioning love's radical destruction of the self in favor of oneness with the other, to instead invest in a definition of the film's central value—freedom—as remaining true to the self above all else. Such stories closely follow Sedgwick's formulation wherein the emotional climax rests upon rivals' mutual acknowledgement of each other's talent, honor, and social value. Yet, this very mutual recognition may make their relationship impossible, as only by denying the other's humanity could they continue to enjoy their deadly game of cat and mouse wherein either pirate or pirate hunter must ultimately meet an ignominious end on the gallows or the plank. Deane (2011) outlines this formula when he argues that many romantic colonial adventure novels present the colonies as a space of endless boyhood play, removed from any moral or political concerns. However, by confronting Jack and Norrington with their mutual humanity, and forcing Norrington in particular to live among a class of people he had categorically consigned to death, many Sparrington authors take the fun out of the game. Suddenly, imperial play has consequences. Yet, in refusing to let love conquer all, those consequences remain personal rather than political, and such narratives end with Jack and Norrington heartbroken, but continuing to serve their archetypal political purposes with the same colonial order intact, although privately destabilized by rogue emotion.

Moonverse, a series of short stories totaling 67,110 words by firesignwriter (2003–04), makes the dilemma especially plain, as Norrington reflects upon how it would feel to order Jack's dead body displayed at the fort after his hanging, an act he would never have questioned before their growing intimacy. In his horror, he begs Jack,

> "So give her [The Black Pearl] up.... Buy new clothes. Get a bloody haircut. You don't have to be Captain Jack Sparrow.... It's just a ship, Jack."
> The pirate's face went hard, rebuking. "You know better."

Norrington has indeed learned better, because in the end neither character can demand that the other give up their vocation or their values, and both must retreat from the field of battle as they can neither surrender nor hold back should the moment of strangely bitter victory arrive. With a grimly cynical outlook on the system he has no wish to escape yet also no longer believes is just, Norrington explains simply that the affair could not continue, "Because we're death to each other." They cannot have each other without changing their fundamental selves, and still survive.

Thus, in another example, the novella-length *Caribbean Cartography* series by Cupiscent (2004) begins as a mutual sacrifice narrative, in which love is ultimately sacrificed to avoid undermining either the oppressive social order or the autonomy of the self. In the beginning of the series, Jack acquires a Letter of Marque to become a privateer, and accepts a mission from the admiralty, thus leaving piracy and its attendant radical self-determination behind in order to remain close to Norrington. Their cooperation in colonial warfare against the Spanish brings Norrington the notoriety and promotion he's always craved just at the moment that his desires find a new object in his relationship with Jack. Orders that he return home to join the admiralty in England should serve as the ultimate form of winning in the boyhood game of empire, as they offer a prestigious return to the "civilized" center and with it full adult power to direct the lives of others on a global scale. Yet Norrington no longer has the heart for the game, as his heart is engaged elsewhere, and winning now means leaving Jack. To escape the strictures imposed by his own success Norrington fakes his death, deserts the navy, and joins Jack's crew aboard *The Black Pearl*. Although the lovers at first appear happy together and Norrington willingly joins in a raid, Jack realizes that he is not compensation enough for Norrington's lost place in the world.

Thereafter Jack realizes that piracy will never constitute freedom for Norrington, because it conflicts with his core characteristic: duty. Telling Norrington that he must return to Port Royal and accept his promotion and its attendant return to London, Jack explains that their relationship is doomed because "you'll hate yourself for it." Jack makes a brief mention of England laying only an ocean away, possibly a promise of a reunion to come, but both lovers acknowledge the finality and inevitably of their parting in the end, with Jack at last requesting, "Make us proud. Marry a good woman. Name your first son Jack." His parting words summon an image of future privileged domesticity and echo Fiedler and Deane's developmental narrative wherein the bad objects of boyhood colonial desire will be put aside in adulthood and displaced upon socially acceptable markers of racial, economic, and heterosexual privilege. In the end, removal from one's place in the social order constitutes the greatest tragedy in *Caribbean Cartography* as it also involves the loss of self, a sacrifice that plays out very differently on the interpersonal and macro-political register, refusing swooning self-sacrifice at the hands of a masterful romantic hero but simultaneously requiring the continuation of an unjust social order because that system constructs cherished individual identities. "The Nature of Freedom" from the novel-length, 101,157-word *The Sparrington Arc* series by Stowaway (2003) echoes this lesson as Jack explains to Norrington why they cannot be together: "You see, love, it's not where we are, it's who we are."

As a sub-type of this narrative form, some Sparrington authors resolve the deadlock with closeting, which allows this usually tragic genre to achieve a melancholy sort of half-happy ending. This narrative structure proposes that after Norrington and Jack understand and value their respective roles in cushioning the extremes of both colonial and criminal brutality, they hide their on-going affair so that they can continue to exploit their positions of power and influence to a newly enlarged political purpose. In such cases, due to the value Norrington places on protecting the weak, Jack may even accept a Letter of Marque and actively turn against other pirates, while the Black Pearl acts as a refuge for those society mistreats, casts out, exploits, and enslaves, as was indeed the case for many historical pirate ships. Seeing that Jack and many among his crew are not inherently evil and instead making the best of their position within an overall unjust system, Norrington, likewise, increasingly grants mercy and clemency to nonviolent offenses, uses naval resources to protect civilians and free slaves, and attempts to funnel vulnerable people toward Jack's crew rather than the workhouse or gallows. Through loving and understanding each other both come to see the social order as oppressive; yet by closeting their relationship and maintaining their existing privileged positions, they attempt to "subvert from within," saving those they can in a strategy of piecemeal appeasement rather than attempting wholesale revolution, a personal but distinctly not political solution.

For example, the *Things Nautical* series, a novel-length 80,603 word collection by Tarn (2004), mirrors the closeting of sexual preference with the closeting of revolutionary politics. Utilizing an overtly political frame to confront readers with the repressed violence of Western wealth, *Things Nautical* defines freedom directly in opposition to the practice of plantation slavery. When Jack is taken captive in revenge for freeing a rival pirate's human cargo, Norrington uses the resources and legal license of his naval position to free his lover and murder those who tortured and held Jack captive. They then help the remaining slaves find safety on the crew of The Black Pearl and return to their lives as Commodore and privateer, an outcome only possible because of Norrington's position in society and Jack's position of notoriety among criminals. Their sexual connection drives their desire to make these risky political compromises—each colluding with the enemy while refusing to fully commit to overturning the status quo—while also underscoring the precariousness of their situation. Although naval law punished sodomy itself with death, in many Sparrington narratives it becomes a hybrid social-sexual crime as the supposed physical deviance of the act is far eclipsed by the social deviance inherent in a Commodore sleeping with a pirate. The story thereby concludes with a farcical court drama that nearly culminates in Jack and Norrington discovered *in flagrante* by a naval lieutenant, a moment played for laughs in the story which nevertheless threatens to undermine the delicate secret that holds the story's political, sexual, and inter-personal compromises in place. Thus the closeting sub-type of the stories that treat colonial structures as an irresolvable obstacle manage to eke out a happy ending for Jack and Norrington by rigidly bifurcating their lives: pirate and pirate hunter by day, secret spies, lovers, and revolutionaries by night. Their affair thereby manages to both call memory of the romance of colonialism into question by emphasizing the brutality of human trafficking and the danger of their relationship, while also making colonialism's full-scale disruption seem impossible, in favor of privatized and thus apolitical compromise and appeasement.

However, still other stories culminate in Norrington recognizing the immorality of the social system the navy enforces and as a result joining

Jack to become a pirate or privateer, rarely as a sacrifice, but most often as a response to Norrington's growing awareness of his lack of freedom and compromised moral position. As freedom becomes an empty cipher in the *Pirates* films (since they rarely specify freedom to or from precisely what), Sparrington authors constantly return to the theme, but define it variously. Frequently, the freedom Jack represents and Norrington longs for parallels nature itself, mapping their relationship onto Ortner's basic feminine/masculine opposition between nature and civilization. Jack becomes a stand-in for natural forces and his moods and movements mirror the tempestuous sea, devotion to which unites the two lovers. In "Trust and Honor," part of Stowaway's *Sparrington Arc* (2004), Norrington makes his decision to be with Jack permanently, leaving his social position behind, while watching the flight of a hawk, an effect also emphasized by the family resemblance between "hawk" and "sparrow":

> The bird turned this way and that; presenting first its dark back and then its pale, streaked under parts and russet tail to his view. The effortless, graceful flight caught at his heart. He wondered how it felt to be so free; no responsibility, no duty—only the wind and sky; and wings to take one wherever one wished to go. Envy, he thought.

In such tales, nature itself calls to Norrington through Jack, especially in his attraction to Jack's body, an ironic transposition of labels branding same-sex desire as unnatural. This formulation may remain at the level of apolitical symbolism, retaining the films' vague championing of freedom as an open and abstract cipher, but the nature/civilization metaphor may also become the vehicle for more overtly political narratives about the unnatural inhumanity of cultural systems, especially capital accumulation.

Thus, as in the *Things Nautical* series, many authors more concretely define freedom against explicitly political forms of oppression including slavery, impressment, class status, hetero-patriarchy, and nationalism, explicitly weaving these themes into readers' experience of the *Pirates* franchise and memory of the colonial period. *Pirate Vindaloo* by Hippediva and Elessil (2005), an epic novel of 182,318 words or approximately 729 pages at the standard of 250 words per page, requires that Jack and Norrington consider each other's perspectives and shared humanity in a concrete, quotidian manner as their impressment into a pirate crew bound for Bombay compels their cooperation over the course of several months, and consistently challenges their ability to empathize and work together across racial and class difference. At first only mutually assured destruction ensures their accord, as the pirate crew will kill them both if their identities are discovered. Yet, a startling intimacy quickly develops when the crew's attempted rape of Jack prompts Norrington to spontaneously claim they are mates, engaged in the quasi-married state of matelotage within which same-sex pirate pairs historically pledged themselves to a long term sexual and civil partnership (Burg, 1983). Surprised by the extent of the crew's respect for their relationship, Norrington demands an explanation for why matelotage seems to "make this sin more respectable." Jack responds,

> All of us, we're just gallows-fodder to the rest of the world. So we take care of our own. ... did ya know that, accordin' to th' Code, if ya lose an eye, a leg or an arm, you get a certain amount o' coin to compensate ya? We aren't bound by the laws that keep fine folk in order so we make our own. Matelots is one of 'em. We know it happens shipboard an' see no reason why it shouldn't be treated fair.

Through Jack's explanation that matelotage encompasses more than merely the act of sodomy, but rather a commitment to share everything that lasts even beyond death, the authors resituate the film's positioning of Norrington as a symbol of order and integrity, by instead making visible a form of law and justice among pirates that surpasses dominant society. The authors thereby expose the dehumanizing social system that informs Norrington's assumptions, which ideologically strips the lower classes of all humanity and morality.

As in *Things Nautical*, in *Pirate Vindaloo* the sexual relationship between Jack and Norrington becomes a prism through which both characters see each other and the world more clearly, and which holds the political transformations within the story in place. They first have sex after two incidents that unseat Norrington's class-based understanding of status and comportment—first a flogging that permanently marks his skin in a manner unacceptable for officers, closely followed by his realization that most of the crew engage in sexual activity and self-pleasure in the open bunk room. Stumbling upon Jack pleasuring himself, Norrington at first demands, "Can't you do that when you're alone?" to which Jack responds, "And just when d'ya think anyone gets a chance t'be alone shipboard? ... Bloody officer." Norrington's initial disgust gives way to a startled realization that the privacy necessary for sexual respectability that he always took for granted is a luxury completely beyond the means of many. The scars on his own back and the ache of his own libido undermine his carefully cultivated separation from those he had deemed beneath him. That revelation allows him to see Jack's growing affection in a new light, and open himself to the interdependence and sexual connection their matelot status already implied. The authors thus ideologically open a privileged body, made rhetorically impenetrable through the workings of dominant masculinity, racial privilege, class mobility, and heterosexuality, and inscribe on his skin and within his heart an indelible reminder of the pernicious lie of his natural separateness and superiority.

The status of outlaw and sodomite are thereafter entwined, as Norrington seems to stumble into each at first unaware, then only slowly becomes politically radicalized as he understands that they need not entail the moral dissolution he had assumed. Eventually, he even questions how people come to be pirates, allowing the authors to ventriloquize a debate between the agency of the individual and the accident of birth, through Jack and Norrington. At first Jack takes this as a hypothetical, and the two argue about Thomas Hobbes and John Locke, debating the merits of a law that does more to protect the powerful than the poor, and the meaning of choice in the face of starvation or at the edge of a sword; yet soon the discussion makes the political startlingly personal. Reflecting upon how social position can blind the powerful to the quotidian realities of oppression, Jack considers all the things Norrington's life has allowed him to not know, musing, "James had never seen two year olds toddling in the Thames mud, amid the sickening flotsam of the city, searching for odds and ends, anything that could be sold. James was like those boys in poems and stories, filled with ideals and passion." All these daily indignities are precisely what the *Pirates* films allow audiences to not know, and which the day-by-day narrative style of *Pirate Vindaloo* reintroduces. By forcing Norrington, a symbol of romanticized, heroic British Imperialism, to suffer through the daily grind of the poverty that produced colonial wealth, the authors reacquaint readers with the suppressed costs of the lush, romantic colonial landscape the *Pirates* franchise exploited.

Thus, as they love, fight, work, and conspire together, Jack pushes Norrington to see the cost of colonial exploitation and the class system, insistently reframing the British government and navy as perpetrators of brutal domination:

> "'I concede your point that there are different manners of piracy which are not given enough regard in the face of the law.' His [Norrington's] voice was soft. "But there need to be laws. Else it is all just bloodshed."
>
> "And the Navy's never sacked a town or taken a maidenhead, has it?" Jack eyes were dark, the shadow of a smile lingering on his lips. "Tell that t'the local tribes anywhere in the new world, mate."

Yet, while these conversations slowly work upon him, it is only over the matter of slavery and racial oppression, when revelation of Jack's parentage as the son of a native woman inscribes the political directly upon his lover's body, that Norrington begins to lose faith in colonial law entirely. While Johnny Depp's part–Native American ancestry has allowed him to portray ethnicities ranging from white to native to Hispanic, the *Pirates* films never overtly racialize Jack, leaving this yet another context of colonial life that remains largely implicit. By situating Norrington's complete refusal of colonial society as a result of overtly seeing his beloved as a person of color, the authors implicitly question whether the movies could continue to function as an apolitical madcap adventure with Jack as their hero were the implications of his racial status made fully manifest.

In the end, *Pirate Vindaloo* defines freedom as a matter of radical self-determination, which eventually allows Norrington to contemplate not simply becoming the same as all other pirates, but to consider the type of pirate he might want to become, and the type of society that might be built in democratic collaboration on the sovereign decks of a ship. *Pirate Vindaloo* again expresses these political-philosophical maneuvers in physical and sexual form, as only after Norrington accepts that he is not above the life of a pirate, does he allow Jack to sexually penetrate him, stating, "I'm your mate, Jack, your equal.... With all that entails." At the story's close, when Norrington accepts a Letter of Marque he also accepts an ear piercing, branding him publicly as Jack's matelot, not in the style of absolute psychological and sexual surrender or assimilation, as in Sparrington slash that demands Jack cut his locks to live among respectable but oppressive colonial society, but in the spirit of the radical self-fashioning Jack embodied as a supposedly impossible outlaw version of love and justice. Thus by withholding complete romantic resolution until after Norrington completes his journey of education, self-discovery, and renunciation, the authors make social solidarity a condition of Jack and Norrington's sail into the sunset, and write the political back into the colonial romance.

Conclusion: Slash's Hybrid and Multiple Social-Sexual Politics

In sum, ideological analysis of fan fiction requires attention to the many variations between narratives, the numerous interpretive positions of fan readers, and the overlapping social and historical contexts of hierarchy and oppression that make narrative choices politically resonant. This paper only begins to highlight these complexities by showing some possible political frameworks that make *Pirates of the Caribbean* slash meaningful, and the multiple paths through those intersecting frameworks drawn by slash writers as the sexual body and the political polity overlap and entwine. This multiplicity makes straightforward, categorical political valuation of fan fiction nearly impossible; yet it also does not diminish the value of fan fiction circulation as one potential space where progressive politics may arise in individual cases. The political transitions within *Pirates of the Caribbean* fan fiction entirely hinge upon the question of whether those at the top of social hierarchies are capable of recognizing the humanity of those they oppress, and further, under which circumstances change then becomes possible. Certainly love offers no complete assurances, as it might just as easily construct political utopias in which natives swoon at the feet of their captors and Jack Sparrow voluntarily gives up his freedom and braided goatee to become the Commodore's kept man. However, love also inspires other dreams. Through the figures of *Pirates of the Caribbean*, certainly not all, but some slash narratives build a political fantasy of an intimacy that rocks the world view of the powerful. Lauren Berlant wrote of a political desire to push knowledge of oppression's daily torments into the bodies of those in power through an orifice that can't be closed (1997). She had in mind an ear; yet, there is a similar project at work in the way many slash writers use Jack Sparrow to lay siege to Norrington's heart, leading readers through a version of colonial politics that can teach a revolutionary awareness of violence and exploitation through love. Both offer an essentially hopeful vision of politics that runs the risk of disappointment and naiveté. Yet both also offer the vision that once sick with the truth of the human costs of their comfort, people might make other choices, and find themselves in an otherwise politically impossible embrace.

Male Homoerotic Fiction and Women's Sexual Subjectivities

Yaoi and BL Fans in Indonesia and the Philippines

TRICIA ABIGAIL SANTOS FERMIN

Among the various genres that have emerged from Japanese popular culture, perhaps no other has stirred as much curiosity and controversy as Yaoi and Boys' Love (BL). "Yaoi" and "BL" are umbrella terms that refer to romantic genres of manga, anime and text-based fiction (for example, short stories and novels), the storylines of which revolve mainly around love relationships between beautiful young men. While these two terms are often used interchangeably, especially among non–Japanese fans, their main difference is based on the question of original authorship. In Japan, Yaoi usually refers to fan-produced parodies or adaptations of original visual or text-based fiction, many of them taking the form of self-published amateur manga, novels or fan fiction. On the other hand, BL refers to original, commercially-produced narratives in audio-visual or text form. An important point to note about these genres is their predominantly young, female, heterosexual authorship and audience: Yaoi and BL were developed and continue to be produced primarily for and by young heterosexual women, rather than aimed at gay men, as most people readily assume. Moreover, Yaoi and BL's highly erotic, often explicit, yet idealized depictions of male-on-male sexual activity have earned their notorious reputation as an alternative form of pornography for women. Yaoi and BL push the boundaries of what is socially acceptable with respect to women's sexuality and sexual expression in Japanese society.

The social and political significance of male homoerotic fiction for women has been the subject of various scholarly inquiries in recent years. However, the personal and political stances of Yaoi and BL fans concerning homosexuality, and their relationships with gay communities, are perhaps some of the most controversial issues related to the fandom. It is often assumed that by virtue of their enjoyment of male homoeroticism, Yaoi and BL fans are necessarily interested in real-life male homosexuality, and that they are "natural allies" of homosexual men in their fight for social recognition. Yet such is not necessarily the case; in fact, ethnographic research indicates that Japanese fans in general neither equate Yaoi and BL's male homoeroticism with homosexuality in real life, nor show interest in gaining a better understanding of gay men. It has been suggested that Yaoi and BL fans tend to lack political interest and positioning because non-normative sexualities and fantasies are usually "tolerated" in Japan as long as they do not overstep the boundaries set by heteronormative discourses and institutions (McLelland, 2003, p. 53).

For example, based on his ethnographic study of Japanese Yaoi and BL fans, Galbraith (2011) explains that fans draw strict boundaries separating their world of fantasies and fan activities from their normal day-to-day routines. His informants relate that for them their beloved Yaoi and BL characters and their tales of love are extremely idealized and can only exist in the realm of the text. In other words, the homoerotic relationships depicted in Yaoi and BL are merely their fantasies of perfect, egalitarian relationships, and have little to do with real-life homosexual relationships or related social issues. This seemingly detached and disinterested attitude amid enthusiastic consumption of male homoerotic romances has earned severe criticism from several scholars and LGBT activists that Yaoi and BL are essentially "homophobic" genres (see Ishida, 2007) offering a commoditized form of opposition in substitute for a genuine critique of patriarchy (Vincent, 2007, p. 73).

On the other hand, Hori (2013, par. 12) observes that non–Japanese fans tend to connect their interest in Yaoi and BL with sympathy and support for Lesbian, Gay, Bisexual and Transgender (LGBT) causes. However, is this really the case? How exactly do non–Japanese fans read and interpret male homoeroticism in Yaoi and BL? I argue that while non–Japanese fans differ from their Japanese counterparts in that they generally associate Yaoi and BL relationships with real-life homosexuality, their personal moral-ethical and political stances toward homosexuality and LGBT issues are, in reality, quite diverse and more complicated than people normally assume. Moreover, while Yaoi and BL promote open-mindedness toward sexual diversity, and even stimulate involvement in social action when the avenues are available, these are merely incidental effects. Deriving pleasure and entertainment remain the primary reasons for fans' engagement with Yaoi and BL texts and participation in fan activities.

This chapter explores the ways in which the global circulation and consumption of male homoerotic fiction for women influence fans' sexual subjectivities across cultures. In particular, I will show how Yaoi and Boys' Love have spread underground in the religiously conservative societies of the Philippines and Indonesia, and contributed to the formation of fans' attitudes toward their own bodily passions, as well as a reworking of their moral sensitivities concerning non-heteronormative sexualities. Using data gathered from informant interviews of self-identified Yaoi and BL fans in Manila and Jakarta, this chapter ultimately aims to raise the following points. Yaoi and BL are primarily consumed for entertainment and titillation, serving as a non-threatening medium through which readers are able to explore and positively confront their own sexual desires. Informant accounts also show us that fan engagement with Yaoi and BL does not necessarily lead to a full rejection (or critique) of their society's heterosexism and an acceptance of homosexuality as a valid mode of sexual and gender identity. Instead, fans attempt to negotiate their personal stances on homosexuality, which are more often than not still heavily influenced by their religious beliefs and affiliations, in order to accommodate the strong but morally-conflicted interest that they develop in these genres. The discussion will show that while Indonesian and Filipino fans all eventually develop at least an open or permissive attitude toward non-heteronormative sexualities, issues around homosexuality and LGBT rights are merely a secondary concern. The popularity and attraction of Yaoi and BL speak less about fans' interest in homosexuality, and more about women's desire to experience erotic fantasies and pleasures that they are restricted from having within the framework of marital, reproductive sexuality. Nonetheless, I will argue that Yaoi and BL fandom potentially has political significance as a form of subcultural resistance.

Baseline Attitudes: Yaoi and BL Fans' Internalized Heterosexism

In this analysis, it is necessary to first establish the attitudes of Indonesian and Filipino fans toward non-heteronormative sexualities prior to their exposure to Yaoi and BL. When asked to recount their first encounter with Yaoi and BL-themed works, all of my informants elaborated, without having any need to be prompted, on their reactions concerning the male homoerotic content of the genre, pointing to the significance of this issue in their fan experiences. The majority described their experience in a rather negative manner, using words such as "shocking," "disturbing" or "traumatic." Prior to their first encounter with Yaoi and BL, many fans perceived homosexual relationships as a "bad" or "incorrect" form of sexuality. Others more explicitly noted that such relationships are considered "taboo," "dirty" or "forbidden" in their social settings, thus explaining their initial shock and confusion. It is not surprising that most of those who spoke of their shock in such terms were those who identified themselves as actively practicing a certain religious faith, and attributed their reaction to their internalization of their religious upbringing and teachings on sexuality. Hence their original perception that homosexual relationships are morally objectionable.

On the other hand, there was a comparatively small group of readers who did not react negatively, expressing that the homoerotic themes in Yaoi and BL "weren't really such a big deal" for them. In the case of Filipino informants, some identified with the same-sex attraction experienced by Yaoi and BL protagonists, admitting that they are of non-heterosexual orientation, or at least went through a questioning of their (hetero)sexual orientation before their encounter with Yaoi and BL. Moreover, the presence of self-identified gay men and lesbians had been a normal part of their daily lives (such as local celebrities, classmates, friends and co-workers), leading them to perceive homosexuality as a real and common occurrence. For them, male homoerotic fiction merely reflects certain aspects of reality. However, the reasons Indonesian informants gave for their acceptance of male-on-male romantic pairings were more text-centered, compared to Filipinos' context-centered response. They noted how "natural" and "good" the characters just seemed to be together, based on their good chemistry and interactions. For them, if two people are attracted and care for each other so intensely, it only seems proper and logical that they pursue the relationship, regardless of whether it fits with or deviates from the heterosexual norm. Such fans also exhibited open-minded attitudes toward sexual diversity in general, even before they got to know Yaoi and BL.

Here, we can derive three important points from informants' testimonies. First, the majority of fans did not immediately take to Yaoi and BL because of their internalization of overtly heterosexist ideologies promoted in their countries, with many directly attributing their initial discomfort to their personal religious upbringing and faith. Second, it must be noted that there is diversity in fan's baseline attitudes concerning homoeroticism and homosexuality. There are also fans from either country who, from the very beginning, did not think that the homoerotic themes and content in Yaoi and BL were objectionable. Lastly, unlike Japanese Yaoi and BL fans, my Indonesian and Filipino informants immediately connect the fictional male homoerotic relationships with real life homosexuality, rather than simply treating them as mere fantasies not rooted in reality. In the Indonesian and Philippine contexts, two men who are romantically and sexually involved with each other are immediately and categorically defined as "gay" or "homosexual," regardless of whether reference is being made to a relationship that occurs in real life, or a fictional representation. Intolerance toward non-(hetero)normative sexualities in these sociocultural contexts is overtly directed at both real-life homosexuality and fictional representations. Hence, prior to their exposure to Yaoi and BL, most fans were inclined to see fictional representations of homosexuality as socially taboo.

Reconsideration of Moral Convictions Concerning Homosexuality

After the initial shock subsided, most of these women found that they were attracted to male homoerotic narratives. The majority have come to like the genre because of its depiction of romance and, at times, explicit sexual acts. Yaoi and BL provide them with stories that are very "different" and more interesting than conventional heterosexual romances or erotica. Most of all, informants also noted that Yaoi and BL provide them the kind of thrills and excitement that can only come from indulging in the illicit and getting away with it. The following are some representative remarks from my Indonesian and Filipino informants, respectively, when describing the attraction of the homoerotic element in Yaoi and BL.

> "I like the drama. You know, forbidden love? [Gushing, with her hands on her face] Ooooh my God! [Laughs] You know, in every society, gays are very frowned upon, so they struggle to make their love work. And I think that's touching. That and the [unresolved sexual tension]!" [Clara, personal interview, 18 March 2012; explanation mine].

> "I know *shōjo* manga [comics for girls], that it is about boys and girls. Some of them make us cry, but I'm quite bor[ed] with het. So what if you have a third person who stole your boyfriend? Why, why, why, why? You don't even have to worry about your gender! People don't have to judge you by your sexuality at all. When I saw the *Gundam Wing dōjinshi*, 'Wow you have to

struggle this much to even hug!'" [Dewi, personal interview, 4 November 2012; explanation mine].

"I like it when one party initially gets confused with his feelings, especially since it's toward another guy. I like that kind of element. I like that part when, okay, he'll get confused first and then eventually he'll be like, 'Oh, I think I really love him.' Something like that. He loves the guy and he'll make things work, against all odds, especially when society doesn't approve of such relationships. Now isn't that true love?" [Carmela, personal interview, 27 December 2012].

We can see several things at work here. First, male-on-male relationships are used in this genre as a device to trigger conflict and heighten drama in the narratives to make them interesting. For my informants, the mere use of homoeroticism allows Yaoi and BL stories to diverge from established romantic narrative patterns and opens up possibilities for new and fresh storylines. Moreover, these testimonies reveal to us how the deeply ingrained negative biases against homosexuality in their own societies permeate into their reception of male-on-male relationships in Yaoi and BL. In their descriptions of relationship dynamics in Yaoi and BL, the foregoing testimonies all refer to gender identity struggles, coming out and overcoming homophobia in society. This type of reception has not been observed among their Japanese counterparts, whose explanations of their fantasies tend to be notably devoid of any social or political commentary concerning heterosexism. We thus see that fans bring with them their own socio-cultural baggage when they interpret texts; the Indonesian and Filipino fans could not seem to help but associate Yaoi and BL with real-life homosexuality and the problems non-heterosexual people face in terms of social acceptance.

Moreover, as they began to develop a deeper interest in Yaoi and BL and male homoeroticism in general, many began to reflect on, and question, the moral values and beliefs that they held. As homosexuality is greatly stigmatized, even sometimes extra-legally penalized,[1] the majority of informants admit that they could not help but feel guilty or even morally conflicted about being a Yaoi and BL fan. Furthermore, those who are interested in the more sexual aspects said that they felt an additional moral burden for going against religious teachings on sexual innocence. In the process, these fans were moved to reconsider their moral-religious beliefs and to attempt to reconcile the conflict between these beliefs and their fandom.

However, whether this has led them to view homosexuality as morally acceptable is another question altogether. In fact, the attitudes and positions fans eventually take concerning homosexuality are quite varied. On the one hand, there are those who have come to believe in the moral soundness of homosexuality, most of them arguing that love is the foundational value of their respective religions (Catholicism, Protestantism or Islam). Many of them argued that what made Yaoi and BL stories powerful for them was that they showed love that knew no boundaries, even of gender. Another point in their explanations was the emphasis on free will, discernment, and a more personal approach to morality, instead of strict adherence to religious norms, traditions and dogma. Their responses signaled a move toward a more humanist view of relationships:

> "As long as you know what you're doing, it's your life and you should be able to do what you want. I believe in free choice, and I also don't think that homosexuality is bad. I don't think there's anything wrong with homosexuality because it is who you are, and it's about love! How can you condemn love, no matter the race or gender? And I don't think Jesus will condemn you, saying that you are wrong! He never said anything about homosexuals at all" [Arlene, personal interview, 13 March 2009].

> "Now I have a clash in ideology with my family. My parents are strict Muslim. They think that gay thing is forbidden, it's a sin. But I just thought, 'Well, it's love.' Whatever people wish to do is their own responsibility" [Indah, personal interview, 3 November 2012].

On the other hand, there were a few informants who clearly expressed disapproval of homosexuality, and still considered it to be morally unacceptable:

> "Maybe the biggest contribution of BL to my life is that I'm kind of used to seeing homosexuality in the media, and I don't go through my 'conservative shocks' anymore. I think it's like violence [laughs]. It's like, because I've watched so many violent movies, I'm not shocked anymore. It's more like ... how to put it? [Pauses to think] Desensitized! I'm desensitized. And besides, Yaoi is just fiction, and real life homosexual issues are much more serious. Hmmm ... it's like, you know, I respect them. But then again, respect doesn't necessarily mean approval, does it? I just like the stories. That's it" [Miranda, personal interview, 13 December 2012].

> "Before, I think that male homosexual relationships are abnormal and absolutely forbidden, but now I think I am more permissive. It's not about sex or gender anymore, but it is more about the feeling and responsibility. As a Muslim, I have the responsibility to remind others, 'No, [homosexuality] is not good, and this is not allowed in the Muslim community. It has to be men and women.' I still feel obliged to warn others. But if they continue to do whatever it is they do, I just think, 'Okay, it's your sin, it's your responsibility to Allah, not mine.' ... Actually my thesis adviser tells me to go back to

the 'straight path.' I explain to him that it is not about the sex or the homosexuals, but human relationships. I do not see it as pornography, because there is a story and meaning to it. Not like *hentai*" [Dinah, personal interview, 6 November 2012].

There are two common threads observable in these responses: first, the way they categorically distinguish real-life homosexuality, and *fictional stories* of (fictional) homosexuals; and second, is the emphasis placed on their consumption of Yaoi and BL narratives mainly as entertainment and fantasy, which should not necessarily be interpreted as an indicator of their personal beliefs.

As was previously mentioned, Yaoi and BL fan behavior is often criticized because fans derive titillation from depictions of male-on-male love and sexual acts, which are both considered morally unacceptable. I surmise that these fans, as a means of rationalizing to avoid moral culpability, tend to distance themselves from homosexuality as a social "issue." Furthermore, they would emphasize the fictional nature of the stories and argue that the representation of homosexuality is only for entertainment purposes, and nothing to do with faith. The fans avoid moral culpability for indulging in sexually explicit images and narratives by either of two strategies: first, expressing a discerning attitude toward narrative and plot (for example, "it actually has a good story, unlike your typical pornography"), or second, emphasizing that one usually prefers the more romantic stories, and will only allow herself to read "softer" sexual descriptions. It would seem that this strategy has commonalities with the explanations given by Japanese fans who disavow any interest in real-life homosexuality and profess to simply enjoy the stories as pure romance.

The preceding testimonies make it clear that it is incorrect to make causal links between Indonesian and Filipino fans' interest in Yaoi and BL, and moral acceptance of, or overt political support for, homosexuality. Furthermore, it would thus be very unreasonable to expect that Yaoi and BL fans are a homogeneous group, even in one specific socio-cultural context. It would be even more unreasonable to expect Yaoi and BL narratives to express explicitly political views, much less come up with a unified stance on an issue, because of the variety of motivations fans have for consuming these texts as well as the range of different meanings they make from them.

However, the group of fans who maintained conservative attitudes to homosexuality actually share a common attitude with fans who expressed moral acceptance and support for homosexuality: the recognition of individuals' right to exercise free choice to question, reject or rework traditional and religious beliefs. Fans eventually became, at the very least, tolerant and permissive, if not accepting and supportive of non-heterosexuals in their societies. This significant change in mindset can potentially translate to action. These women, faced with intimacies that contested their notions of the "proper" and "correct" ways of experiencing intimacy, were compelled to sincerely reconsider these. In the process of reflection, self-education and interactions with people from the gay community when they had the opportunity, they made the choice to rework and reconcile conflicting parts of their beliefs in order to accommodate their interest in Yaoi and BL. I argue that the realization of this freedom for women to question and choose for themselves their stand on certain issues and how they act is, perhaps, the most critical part of the entire process.

Yaoi and BL as Tools for Opening Minds Toward Sexual Diversity

Apart from a reconsideration of religious and moral beliefs, there were other effects that fans observed in their attitudes and behavior, as they became more involved in Yaoi and BL storytelling practices. For one, informants from both societies, regardless of whether they agreed on the morality of homosexuality or not, credit Yaoi and BL with stirring their curiosity about homosexuality and the experiences of real-life gay people.

Some informants admitted that they started out as homophobic, and would even sometimes laugh at homosexuals. But after being exposed to Yaoi and BL, they realized how little they knew about homosexuality and their curiosity was aroused to learn and understand more. There were several ways in which they went about their learning process. There were informants from the Philippines who took Gender Studies classes offered at their universities. One Filipino informant related that she even seriously pursued this as an intellectual interest, making it the topic of many of her term papers when it was applicable, as well as her graduation thesis. Some other informants took advantage of film screenings and other activities sponsored by LGBT groups.

For instance, two of my Indonesian informants attended the Q! Queer Film Festival when they had the chance. One worked as a volunteer because of her connections in the film industry, while the other was a participant in the festival's market. They both mentioned that they gained insight into the experiences and relationship issues of non-heterosexual people through the movie screenings and talks held in the festival. "It was like sex education class for me and my friends," relates Dinah, who participated in the festival and sold the original BL manga that her *dōjinshi* circle made. She considered her attendance at the film festival as a valuable opportunity to learn about complex issues concerning gender and sexual identity, as well as safe sex, especially since discussion of sexuality and sexual intercourse is noticeably avoided in most schools. "We didn't have sex education in school, except for this one-day AIDS seminar, classes on the reproductive system and what happens to you when you have sex before marriage. It was a very good educational experience."

There were informants who used their interest in Yaoi and BL to initiate friendship and conversations about homosexuality with openly gay members of their peer groups. In fact, all of my Filipino interviewees and most of the Indonesians I interviewed mentioned that there are non-heterosexuals in their circle of friends. A number showed much pride as they mentioned that some of their really close friendships are with gay men. However, based on their stories, I noticed that the reactions and level of intimate disclosure of gay men across these three contexts varied. In the Philippine case, gay men were more inclined to interact and discuss their intimate thoughts and experiences with the fans who showed an open attitude toward them. They also showed curiosity as to what Yaoi and BL was, when some fans attempted to broach the subject with them. Most of the time, it became a common topic of meaningful conversation about gender and sexuality. While most of them did not end up becoming fans themselves because of the highly idealized portrayal of homosexuality, there were no critical, political remarks from gay men about the genre, unlike in the Japanese case. However, some of them ended up liking Yaoi and BL because of its acute depiction of characters' internal lives, thus they eventually enjoyed doing fan activities together with my informants.

On the other hand, the interviewees from Indonesia observed that gay men in their country did not seem to be as open and forthcoming as those in the Philippines, unless they were also fellow Japanese popular culture fans and knew about the genre. They explained that while homosexuality is not legally forbidden, it is not socially accepted, and thus there is great pressure to keep quiet about it, even from their own families. Other informants recounted stories of homosexual friends, both male and female, who felt pressured to get married and settle down, despite their sexual orientation, in order to please their families. My informants expressed disappointment at the concealment of homosexuality in Indonesia as they wanted to gain a fuller and more genuine understanding of homosexual relationships, and learn how they are different from what they imagine.

In addition, some informants related that Yaoi and BL contributed to the development of their political convictions on gender equality and LGBT rights. While Yaoi and BL works and their fan communities are not political in themselves, they still have the power to inspire individual people to participate in activities geared toward political action. My informants' experiences indicated several possible ways in which this happens.

For some informants, Yaoi and BL inspired them to do volunteer work for organizations or participate in activities and events that help raise awareness of LGBT issues within the community or in relation to wider society. For example, in 2009 when I first interviewed Irene, a Filipino fan, she was a university senior. At that time, she related to me that she had been volunteering for a non-government organization in Manila that deals with issues and problems faced by transgender people as part of field work for her graduation thesis. As she progressed in her research, she realized that there is still much to be done to educate people, even those who are part of Filipino LGBT communities, to clarify and understand issues relating to gender and sexual identity. Irene said that she wanted to share what she learned in her research, as she believed that this knowledge could help members of these communities to articulate their ideas more clearly and persuasively in their public campaigns. I meet with her every now and then during my visits to Manila, and when I saw her in December 2012, she told me that she continues to assist people from her network of LGBT organizations whenever they ask for her help. Aditya (Indonesian) volunteers for the Q! Film Festival. Being part of the film production industry, she had the information on how to volunteer and be part of organizing the event. Demi (Filipino) also mentioned having participated in queer film screenings, as she was quite curious to know more about the lives of LGBT people.

I noticed that the accessibility of organizations and events is an essential factor in determining whether Yaoi and BL fans actually participate in LGBT activities. Accessibility may mean that the proximity of organizations' offices, events and activities relative to fans' geographical location encourages participation of more interested people. Accessibility may also mean the approachability or ease of getting into organizations. It may be easy for people like Irene and Aditya to become involved in LGBT organizations and events because they are connected to the field that they work in, or because they already have people in their networks to facilitate their entry. However, an inclusive, friendly and non-threatening approach will definitely be greatly appreciated by an unsure, often heterosexual newcomer. For example, Demi wanted to do more than just attend film screenings, but felt that it was not that easy to go up to an organization and volunteer on her own.

> Interviewer: "You've been going to these events, but since you're already at it, have you considered joining any LGBT-related organization?"
> Demi: "Nope, I haven't done that ... or at least not yet. Maybe it's because it seems that it's not that easy to reach out to, well, say to the *Ladlad* partylist[2] or something. Or maybe the LGBT communities here in the Philippines aren't as mature. I've people I know, classmates from high school who are now living abroad, and ... they somehow participate in the events of the LGBT communities there. They're straight, but it seems to me that it's easy out there for them to reach out. And it doesn't help that I'm also very introverted [laughs]" [personal interview, 28 March 2013].

Nevertheless, Demi mentions that while she is not able to join such communities and organizations, she decided that she could show her support for LGBT issues some other way, for example, by voting for the LGBT political party during the recently-held Congressional by-elections.

Indonesia, however, does not have as many avenues for political action and expression as the Philippines does. While homosexuality may not be legally forbidden in Indonesia, aggressive confrontations from extremist groups greatly limit the public events of LGBT groups. Such an atmosphere makes it more difficult for members of LGBT communities in the country to come out, much less interact with people. Even if they do come out, they don't really discuss their situation with those outside the LGBTQ community, as indicated by several of my interviewees who have gay friends. Thus, it may be that some of them actually want to participate in political organizations and events, but these avenues are just not accessible, available or safe from violent confrontations with opposing groups, or they are downright illegal.

Yet in spite of the difficulties in accessing political organizations and groups, one must not ignore the other things Yaoi and BL fans do in their own little ways to show support for and solidarity with non-heterosexuals. Some may use their own fan works to express their opinions about the problems faced by non-heterosexuals in their societies show support for their causes. An Indonesian informant even mentioned that she was ready to face bashing for the pro-homosexuality works that she self-publishes, as a sign of solidarity. Others would use their position as educators in order to bring gender and sexuality into discussions in their fields of expertise—literature, history, art, English composition—with hopes of being able to open younger people's minds to diversity. I consider such acts to be just as important as participation in organized political activity and they should also be thought of as political acts. Insofar as the constraints of their social location and social institutions allow them, these fans are doing what they can to contribute to social change.

The Primacy of Play and Entertainment

However, overtly politically-engaged Yaoi and BL fans are relatively few. In fact, while almost all of them hold critical views of the current gender and sexual order in their societies, the majority of them choose to adopt a "don't ask, don't tell" attitude concerning their interest in Yaoi and BL. It is interesting to note that while they hold values that are in opposition to dominant society's, the majority choose to keep up appearances of social conformity. Feigning conformity, or at least keeping quiet about their interest in Yaoi and BL and their views on gender and sexuality, serve as survival techniques and tactics to maintain their current standing in society. We must remember that despite the sexual regimentation that they experience as women in patriarchal, heterosexist societies, these leaders still enjoy certain privileges and opportunities as members of the cultural and economic elite in their societies. Many fans are very careful to build a respectable and dignified reputation, for tarnishing it may hurt their career and other life prospects. This cultivation of respectability demonstrates that fans are conscious of their lack of power in certain situations and there is a need to play along with some of the rules of dominant society in order to maintain the advantages that their current social position affords them.

Furthermore, apart from the lack of a unified stance toward issues such as homosexuality, LGBT rights and women's sexual expression, another factor that makes Yaoi and BL difficult to politicize is its primary function as a hobby and playful pastime. This is an attitude my informants shared with Japanese fans (see ethnographic studies by Thorn, 2004; McLelland, 2003 and Galbraith, 2011) and non–Japanese fans in the West (Pagliassotti, 2008). The majority of my interviewees spoke of their fandom mainly as a way of spending their free time. Others also spoke of producing or immersing themselves in Yaoi and BL as a means of relieving the stresses of everyday life. I have noticed that a great bulk of my conversations with my informants concerned personal fantasies, gushing over favorite pairings and the excitement they derive from being involved in an illicit hobby. Talk of real-life issues related to Yaoi and BL, however, are not too common. In fact, some fans express disappointment when a work becomes too political or frustration when fellow fans politicize the genres and fan activities. As the following interview excerpts show us, most of my informants believe that Yaoi and BL exist mainly for entertainment, and overtly injecting politics into it can kill the fun.

> "Sometimes some authors can become a bit political in their works. I dunno.... I mean, being political about homosexuality is good and all, but it kind of takes away the fun out of it. BL is first and foremost about pure romance!" [Mitch, personal interview, 17 August 2011].
>
> "I've got two gay friends whom I fangirl with. They also go giddy and get love tingles with the explicit parts, but they don't inject anything political into it. Honestly, I don't like politics. I don't really like any of those serious and heavy stuff or think about them when I fangirl or write [fan fiction]" [Lea, personal interview, 28 December 2012].
>
> "I don't discriminate, but I'm not political. And it has nothing to do with faith. It's just entertainment" [Theresia, personal interview, 2 November 2012].

Thus, the production and consumption of Yaoi and BL for these fans is, first and foremost, play and fantasy in a space that is clearly delineated from everyday life. It appears that the most prevalent attitude among Yaoi and BL fan communities is that of pleasurable transgression; the most important thing is that everyone has fun in indulging in playful fantasy.

However, while the consumption of Yaoi and BL may seem to non-fans to be nothing but mere play, frivolity or an unusual fetish, I would argue that it is ultimately political in that fan activities, discourses and collective imagination can serve as marginal spaces from which to freely critique and transgress dominant society's norms, as well as propose alternative ways of organizing social life based on the shared values and ideals of the group. The homoerotic fantasies and pleasures Yaoi and BL fans enjoy and produce through their fan activities are, in fact, symbolic inversions (Babcock, 1978) and re-imaginations of the dominant gender order, as well as the nature and conduct of personal, intimate relationships.

Fans' exposure to representations of male homoeroticism, androgyny and coupling were all instrumental in teasing out from fans their dissatisfactions with the dualistic and essentialist constructions of gender and sexuality, as well as intimate relationships in their societies. However, more than that, Yaoi and BL's non-normative representations of masculinity and intimacy also help fans develop a more humanistic and egalitarian vision of men, women and love relationships, rejecting rigid gender norms and oppressive power relationships.

In particular, the majority of informants in all three contexts tended to gravitate toward works in which the main couple are androgynously characterized, not only in terms of their physical attributes but also their personality traits. Yaoi and BL appear to have exposed informants to the charms and possibilities of androgynous gender identities through the genres' attempts at androgynous characterization: mixing and matching traditionally compartmentalized "masculine" and "feminine" traits in a person. Such imaginings suggest to us that a person may be able to conceive him or herself as one satisfactory whole, composed of both masculine and feminine elements with a fluid identity (Jenkins, 1992, p. 193). All of my informants related that they find themselves particularly invested in Yaoi and BL stories that depict relationships between complex and nuanced personalities. In turn, they especially dislike pairings that represent two-dimensional portrayals of gendered binary opposites, such as "masculine and feminine," "dominant and submissive," "cold and emotional," or "strong and weak." This signals a movement away from essentialist notions of gender and sexual identity, which is a condition that is fertile for the growth of more egalitarian relationships.

By showing inversions of normative masculinity and sexual intimacy, the male-on-male couples in Yaoi and BL provoke such commentaries and views, which are in direct opposition to the patriarchal and heterosexist organization of intimate, interpersonal relationships. Thus, we could definitely say that Yaoi and BL fan activities and discourses on gender and sexuality in these countries' contexts constitute discourses of resistance.

Conclusions

In the foregoing discussion, I attempted to tease out Yaoi and BL fan positions concerning homosexuality and LGBT issues in Indonesia and the Philippines. I examined informants' reception of Yaoi and BL's homoerotic themes and assessed whether these resist or conform to dominant gender discourses. I have also assessed Yaoi and BL's potential to encourage political action, and suggested possible reasons as to why it may or may not be successful in doing so.

I have argued that unlike their Japanese counterparts, Indonesian and Filipino Yaoi and BL fans are more inclined to associate their interest in these genres with real-life homosexuality and the socio-political issues related to it. This is because they are situated in contexts where intolerance to non-heteronormative sexualities is more acute and overt, and their marginalization is systematically carried out through a convergence of various social institutions such as the state, the law, family, the education system and organized religion. The confusion, shock and ensuing moral-religious conflict that most fans experienced in their initial encounter with the genre make it apparent that the majority had internalized dominant society's heteronormative mindset.

As such, it is unsurprising that Yaoi and BL do not necessarily lead fans to develop a political mindset about homosexuality and LGBT issues, or to participate in political activism. While it is capable of inspiring people to think about sexuality in more political terms, it seems that until an avenue develops through which one can express these oppositional political discourses without any threats to their personal safety and progress, the average Yaoi and BL fan would remain apolitical in the traditional sense. At most, resistance to heterosexism would still be largely conducted covertly, on a symbolic level. We may be able to better understand the positive political potential of fans' playful engagement with the genre if we think of Yaoi and BL fan activities and textual production as a form of *subcultural resistance*. We can consider these fan activities in light of scholars' diverging interpretations of subculture. According to one influential account (see Lunsing, 2006; Vincent, 2007; Ueno, 2009; Galbraith, 2011; Hori, 2013), leisure-based subcultural practices such as Yaoi and BL fandom are deemed to lack social and political significance. It is argued that resistance at this level is illusory, and the activities escapist, because they do not offer concrete resolution to real-world problems. These subcultures and fan cultures do not have the capacity to overthrow hegemonic social institutions because of their members' relative lack of social power. The expression of their grievances thus stays within the liminal, and possibilities for changing the status quo remain as mere potential.

However, others argue that cultural resistance can be thought of *as* political resistance (see Scott, 1990; Duncombe 2002). Politics is essentially a cultural discourse, a shared set of symbols and meanings that people within a group abide by. If such is the case, it is then reasonable to assert that the rewriting or proposition of alternatives to such discourses, which is essentially what cultural resistance does, is in itself a political act (Duncombe, 2002, p. 7). Abu-Lughod (1989) suggests that we should continue to seek, examine and take seriously all sorts of resistance. However, she argues that the primary purpose of resistance is to help identify the various forms of power, the ways that it operates, and how people are caught up in it (Abu-Lughod, 1989, pp. 41–42). Therefore our primary aim in the examination of subcultural resistance is to uncover the conditions and dynamics of domination and subordination in society, while also highlighting the potential of individuals to engender social change by acting independently.

Viewed this way, I argue that the politics of Yaoi and BL lies in their production of rich counter-hegemonic discourses on the social construction of gender differences and intimate relationships. The explorations of male homoeroticism, androgyny and coupling have helped fans realize and express their dissatisfactions with oppressive constructions of gender, sexuality and intimacy. Yaoi and BL's inversions of normative masculinity and sexual intimacy also led at least some of these fans to reject these and imagine a more egalitarian model of intimate relationships.

NOTES

1. While there are no laws that explicitly criminalize homosexual activity in Indonesia, except for Aceh province to which the Indonesian Government gave permission in 2002 to enforce Sharia law for its Muslim residents, social rules on public decency and sexual morality are extra-judicially enforced by religious fundamentalist groups. The most notorious of such groups is the Front Pembela Islam (Islam Defender's Front) or FPI, which has been criticized by many moderate Muslims for its use of physical violence against anything that it considers an offense against Islamic teachings. Some of the violent incidents instigated by the FPI were the trashing of Playboy's Indonesian headquarters and the international LGBT conference organized in Surabaya by the Asian branch of the International Lesbian and Gay Association (ILG-Asia). Abraham (2010) and my other Indonesian informants confirm that this additional threat of physical violence should they become the target of such fundamentalist fringe groups is one of the main reasons that they keep their fan activities and textual production as discreet as possible.

2. Ang Ladlad is a political party formed in 2007 dedicated to fighting for Filipino sexual minorities' constitutionally-mandated rights and voicing their concerns in the House of Representatives' legislative agenda. While to date Ang Ladlad has yet to obtain a seat in the Philippine congress through the Party List system, it continues to be one of the most vocal and visible political groups in the Philippines.

Selling Authentic Sex

Working Through Identity in Belle de Jour's The Intimate Adventures of a London Call Girl

Victoria Ong

Sex sells ... but what of the women who find both their bodies and their stories so readily marketable? Sex workers in the West have historically struggled to find a space in the media for their issues to be heard and are consistently caricatured in film and literature, but life narrative has persistently been an uninhibited space for sex workers to express themselves freely and at length. While sex worker life narratives are not new, notable examples being *Gypsy: A Memoir* (Lee, 1957) and *The Happy Hooker: My Own Story* (Hollander, 1971), there has been a recent proliferation of elite sex worker narratives in the Anglo-American memoir boom of the twenty-first century that coincides with the increasing incorporation of relatively class privileged women into the global sexual economy. Texts like *Diary of a Manhattan Call Girl* (Quan, 2001), *The Price: My Rise and Fall as Natalia, New York's #1 Escort* (McLennan, 2008) and *Some Girls: My Life in a Harem* (Lauren, 2010) are a far cry from stereotypically negative portrayals of sex workers as victims, drug abusers and criminals. Instead, modern womanhood is foregrounded humorously and light-heartedly as the texts chronicle protagonists' cosmopolitan lifestyles and their efforts to navigate work life and their personal relationships. The enjoyment and pleasure of sex is a major theme of the texts. These texts align with contemporary chick lit, and the heightened rate of publication and increased popularity of such texts signifies the incipience of 'sex worker chick lit' as a subgenre.

This essay is focused on one such text, *The Intimate Adventures of a London Call Girl* (de Jour, 2005), a blog-turned-memoir by Dr. Brooke Magnanti published under the pseudonym Belle de Jour. For clarity's sake, "Belle" will refer to the diary's narrative voice and "Magnanti" to the writer. Magnanti's text describes her experiences as a London call girl. Her text particularly interests me as "Belle de Jour" is associated with a popular franchise of products in different media forms, encompassing an award-winning blog, two best-selling diaries, a fictionalized sequel, a newspaper column and a loosely adapted television programme that ran for four seasons, yet it has drawn little academic attention. Specifically, in this essay I will be looking at the first published work and analyzing how the writing can be seen as a scriptotherapic process that allows Belle to work through her struggles within a hegemonic structure that stigmatizes her labor identity.

Before proceeding, a word on truth-value is relevant here as it is an oft-discussed issue in narrative theory. Speculation over Belle's authenticity as a sex worker was rife at the height of the franchise's popularity, due to two main factors: "the inability to believe that a prostitute could be as articulate, intelligent and well-read as the blog suggested" (Attwood, 2009, p. 8) and partly because Belle's sexual narration "by turns lusty and matter-of-fact, could not be read as authentically female" (2009, p. 8) and must therefore be written by a man. Accusations that the content was fabricated persisted after she came out in 2009, and were exacerbated by a former boyfriend's claim of defamation (Legge, 2013). *The Intimate Adventures of a London Call Girl* (hereafter shortened to *Intimate Adventures*) begins with Belle in a relationship with The Boy that dissolves midway through the text. The Boy, real name Owen Morris, began a defamation suit against Magnanti in 2013. Morris denies Magnanti's career as a sex worker, claimed that her interactions with clients were in actuality based on interactions they had during their relationship, and accused her of ascribing falsified words and conversations to him (Topham, 2013). In reaction to this, N, another character in the memoir, gave a statement to defend Belle's integrity, saying:

> "I know N is an amalgam of characters and that there are things the character said that I never said and events he attended that I was [never] at. There are also things I said and places where I was that are attributed to other people. ... Characters in the book are based on people. There is truth in it, but where the line is of who is real, who is not, I can't tell you. Time, place and context are all mixed up" [Topham, 2013].

Belle reacted to Morris' accusations on her blog and posted solid evidence of her career as a sex worker, though she did not comment on how faithful her writing was to reality (Magnanti, 2013).

This then brings us to the issue of the truth status of autobiographical disclosure. Getting the story straight is a psychological imperative that relates the performance of narrative to the experience of identity (Eakin, 2008, p. 78). However, just as postmodern self-portraits are valued even when the subject is not identifiable, the consensus amongst postmodern theorists is that factual perfection is not mandatory for a life narrative text to embody an authentic portrait of reality. As such, even if life narrators present inconsistent or shifting views of themselves or others, postmodern theorists argue that such accounts nonetheless perform authentic autobiographical work and should still be taken seriously. For example, John Sturrock notes that "it is impossible for an autobiographer not to be autobiographical" (1977, p. 52). Similarly, Stanley Fish observes, "Autobiographers cannot lie because anything they say, however mendacious, is the truth about themselves, whether they know it or not" (cited in Smith and Watson, 2001, p. 12). Sidonie Smith and Julia Watson assert that "autobiographical truth is an intersubjective exchange between narrator and reader aimed at producing a shared understanding of the meaning of a life" (2001, p. 12). As such, even if some of the content of *Intimate Adventures* has been fictionalized to make the rendition of Magnanti's experiences more marketable and pleasurable to read, *Intimate Adventures* is still a site of self-construction that merits analysis.

This essay is structured as follows: I will first identify the raw materials of analyzing self-construction through life narrative and elaborate on the new postindustrial landscape of sex work. I will then look at how Belle's new petite bourgeois sensibility bears upon her sex worker identity, and her usage of life narrative to (1) do identity work and impose narrative coherence upon her marginalized subjectivity, and (2) do emotional labor to deal with the pressures of selling emotionally bounded erotic exchange.

Postmodern Life Narrative and Postindustrial Sex Work

> In order to exist in the social world with a comfortable sense of being a good, socially proper, and stable person, an individual needs to have a coherent, acceptable and constantly revised life story—Charlotte Linde, *Life Stories* [1993, p. 3].

Life narrative refers to diverse self-referential practices, including autobiography, in which people write about their own lives and engage the past in order to reflect on identity in the present. This essay situates itself in third-wave life narrative criticism, drawing upon contemporary theorizing of the life narrative subject as subject-in-process in the analysis of Magnanti's text. In line with the postmodern approach of third-wave life writing criticism, the term "life narrative" is preferred over "autobiography" for two main reasons, and the following explication of these two reasons will also be used to frame this essay's theoretical approach to narrative identity and narrative coherence.

Firstly, traditional theorizing of "autobiography" is informed by Enlightenment conceptions of the sovereign self, wherein identities are thought to be coherent, and individuals are generally conceptualized as autonomous beings with universalizing life stories (Smith and Watson, 2001, pp. 3–4). It thus privileges a particular mode of life narrative as a higher and truer form of life narrative, to the exclusion of other autobiographical modes of everyday and private life, such as letters, diaries, journals or multimedia life narrative. *Intimate Adventures*, with its narrative form of a blog-turned memoir, would not fall under the purview of traditional autobiographical criticism. This essay, however, is informed by postmodernism's deconstruction of any solid ground of selfhood and truth outside of discourse. In particular, it is indebted to Paul John Eakin's analysis of identity formation through narrative in *Living Autobiographically* (2008). Eakin uses interdisciplinary research, including neurology, cognitive science, memory research and developmental psychology to argue that identity work in action is found in narrative, and narrative identity exists "not on the plane of theory but in the lived experience of ordinary individuals telling stories about themselves" (p. xi). He emphasizes life narrative as performance and action, since it is an act of "doing consciousness," and argues

> (1) that "self" content might be distributed throughout an I-narrative and not merely contained in the I-characters and I-narrators where the conventions of autobiographical discourse condition us to look for it; and (2) that "self" is not only reported but performed, certainly by the autobiographer as she writes and perhaps to a surprising degree by the reader as he reads" [p. 84].

Through this lens, non-traditional and fragmentary self-referential modes of life narrative are imbued with act-value,[1] and are thus reclaimed as critically valuable. With this postmodern theoretical alignment, this essay analyzes life narrative as a form of self-invention, a performativity, that constitutes the self.

Secondly, "life narrative" is used instead of "autobiography" in order to dissociate from the notion of representative lives. As Smith and Watson observe, concepts of textual personhood in the first wave of autobiographical criticism are dominated by the notion of a representative life, and the practice of canonizing life narratives as "autobiography" privileges the public sphere of "great" men and designates lesser value to many other kinds of life narratives. This denigration is doubly so for life writing by marginal groups, including the sexually "deviant," who remain as culturally invisible "others" and are unable to access textual histories of their subjectivity (Smith and Watson, 2001). Since sex workers occupy a marginalized and stigmatized position in society, the notion of a representative life in life narrative criticism bears further discussion. In Eakin's exploration of how our participation in a rule-governed discourse "establishes us as normal individuals in the minds of others" (2008, p. x), he invokes Charlotte Linde's views on narrative coherence:

> She claims that an individual's refusal to supply an appropriate answer to the question "what do you do" will appear "anomalous and, eventually, sinister." Our performance of self-narration, then, takes place in an environment of social convention and constraint. Having mastered its rules and developed a repertoire of stories about ourselves, we tend—at least socially—to merge with them: in this sense our stories are our selves [Eakin, 2008, p. 30].

With this notion of narrative coherence, Eakin argues that we are all players in what he terms a narrative identity system, which is "an identity regime that not only sets limits, socially, to what we can say and write about ourselves but determines as well our recognition by others as normally functioning persons" (2008, p. 31). Thus, narrative coherence links person and story in a way that posits that the rules for identity narrative function simultaneously as rules for identity.

As such, narrative coherence refers to how narrative allows the writer's self-presentation to be connected to normality. If so, the regulation of narrative implies the possibility of the regulation of identity and brings to the forefront the questions of what is at stake when a life is described as "representative" and canonized as autobiography, and what is expected of an individual's narrative for her to "get a life" and "count as" a person. The usage of "refusal" in the block quote above is key, then, for if a refusal to supply an appropriate answer is anomalous, what happens when a person not only gives an inappropriate answer but also actively publicizes it unasked? If the rules for identity narrative function simultaneously as the rules for identity, then the autobiographical act in which one fashions one's world as normal is arguably an act that attempts to change the rules for perceiving one's identity, pushing marginality into centre-stage and democratizing the notion of a "representative life." This is increasingly recognized in literary circles, with scholars such as Smith, Watson and Eakin arguing that life narratives by marginalized individuals have the potential for advocacy and empowerment. As such, the usage of "life narrative" over "autobiography" is indicative of this essay's political slant and my decision to analyze self-fashioning in this "unconventional" text.

The personal background, stories of entry, modes of working, types of sex work, and career trajectories of sex workers are diverse. In order to limit the scope of analysis, I have chosen to focus on Belle's life narrative as a sex worker who does out-calls to clients' homes via an agency. Henceforth, unless otherwise stated, the term "sex worker" is used in this essay to refer to sex workers who sell bodily sex for money. As alluded to earlier, the incipience of sex worker chick lit coincides with the increasing incorporation of new social classes into the Anglo-American sex work industry, and an explication of a few of Elizabeth Bernstein's key observations in her analysis of the postindustrial sex industry is worthwhile here.

In *Temporarily Yours* (2007), Bernstein writes that "individuals pertaining to what has been variously termed the 'new' middle class, the 'creative class,' or the 'new petite bourgeoisie'" (pp. 3–4) are increasingly incorporated into the global sexual economy. Bernstein draws upon Pierre Bourdieu's definition of new petite bourgeoisie (hereafter abbreviated to NPG) as comprising individuals of two class trajectories: "those who have not obtained from the educational system the qualifications that would have enabled them to claim the established positions their original social position promised them"; and "those who have not obtained from their qualifications all they felt entitled to" (Bourdieu, 1984 cited in Bernstein, 2007, p. 82). Drawing upon postmodern sociological studies, Bernstein argues that the increased presence of the NPB in the sex industry is facilitated by the emergence of new paradigms of family and community. She writes that this has resulted in isolable individuals with profoundly transformed models of sexuality, new configurations of intimate life and new erotic dispositions: "[b]oth the traditional 'procreative' and the modern 'companionate' models of sexuality are increasingly being supplanted by what sociologist Edward Laumann and his colleagues have referred to as a 'recreational' sexual ethic" (pp. 6–7).

This recreational sexual ethic is premised upon the depth of physical sensation and emotionally bounded erotic exchange, and Bernstein refers to the latter as "bounded authenticity" (2007, p. 7). The authenticity of recreational sex is bounded in the sense that the emotions of erotic exchanges are delimited to their discrete episodes and sex is free of lingering emotional attachments. Unlike domestic-sphere relational sexuality, which "derive[s] its meaning from its ideological opposition to the marketplace, recreational sexuality bears no antagonism to the sphere of public commerce" (pp. 6–7). It is from this clime of normalized recreational sex that the new variety of sexual labor in the sex industry emerges where "middle-class sex workers self-consciously attempted to integrate an ethics of bodily pleasure, appreciation, and authenticity into their occupational practices and their aesthetic ambitions" (p. 101) distinguishing themselves from the "quick, impersonal 'sexual release' associated with the street-level sex trade" (p. 103). Consequently, "bounded authenticity" is available for sale and purchase as readily as any other form of commercially packaged leisure activity; "Girlfriend Experience" is an advertised service in the industry. While postindustrial economic, social and cultural changes have normalized the sex industry and structurally naturalized the NPB's entry into it, arguably it is the conception of a recreational sexual ethic as a part of the postmodern subject's sexual identity that has directly eased individual NPB sex workers' decisions to enter sex work.

Bernstein finds evidence that NPB sex workers make concerted efforts to manufacture authenticity in their simulation of genuine "(if fleeting) libidinal and emotional ties with clients, endowing them with a sense of desirability, esteem, or even love" (2007, pp. 103–4). She writes that this calling forth of genuine feeling is what Arlie Hochschild has termed "deep acting" and Wendy Chapkis has described as the "emotional labor" of sex (pp. 103–4). Arguably, the impulse to develop skill sets for the production of bounded authenticity highlights the NPB impulse to "professionalize" their trade, in contrast with the approach of street-based workers who generally rely upon naturalized heterosexual sexual relations (pp. 94–98). Acquiring skill sets to professionalize their trade is part of a strategy of making work meaningful, since many NPB sex workers "plac[e] a premium on ensuring that the labor fe[el] meaningful to themselves" (pp. 104–5). That work needs to be meaningful aligns with what Bourdieu describes as the NPB's location of its occupational and personal salvation: an ethics of fun (cited in Bernstein, 2007, p. 83). This ethics of fun is where the NPB locates its sense of distinction, and that it "makes it a failure, a threat to self-esteem, not to 'have fun'" (cited in Bernstein, 2007, p. 84). The combination of the mainstreaming of sex as *recreational* and its high income makes it appealing to the NPB who are unable to secure the remunerative jobs they feel entitled to.

Since one's occupation is a fulcrum in one's sense of self as part of a community, the NPB sex worker's success in finding meaning in her work is key to job satisfaction. However, that her work involves intimate sexual relating, something inextricably bound up with identity, complicates the sex worker's meaning-making venture. Pertinent to this discussion is Christine Overall's analysis of identity and sexual relating in "Monogamy, Nonmonogamy and Identity" (1998). Overall argues that "[t]he convention of sexual relating, outside of paid work, is that in that context the woman expresses herself, becomes and is most truly and genuinely herself" (p. 8). As such, a sexual relationship becomes a form of chosen vulnerability. This convention of connecting identity with sexual relating is subverted in the conventions of sex work. Overall writes that sex workers structure sexual relating differently and "define themselves by reference to the paid labour they perform rather than by reference to the men with whom they interact and usually choose not to be vulnerable, self-expressive, or genuinely open" (p. 9).

She attributes this to the "oppressive relationship" between sex worker and client. However, while this may be applicable to street workers who work for survival, this is not the case for NPB sex workers who operate in safe environments, and engage in sex work in order to build a career. Moreover, the idea that sexual relating necessitates opening one's identity and being vulnerable holds less and less true due to the normalization of recreational sex.

Be that as it may, I would argue that NPB sex workers do experience identity ruptures. Not because sexual relating is tied up with their identity, but because they offer bounded authenticity as part of their services. The NPB's differentiation of sexual relating between clients and lovers is intrinsically thorny; sexual interactions with clients outside of monogamous relationships already pressurize their relationships with loved ones and sense of sexual identity, and having to produce and sell bounded authenticity further problematizes the partitioning of feelings.

In the following section, I will analyze how Belle uses self-reflexive writing for identity-work and as a site to construct narrative coherence for her marginalized subjectivity. I am interested in what forms her postindustrial NBP sensibilities manifest, how this bears upon her engagement with work, and how she finds work meaningful through the provision of bounded authenticity.

Belle's Scriptotherapy

> The first thing you should know is that I'm a whore—Belle de Jour, *The Intimate Adventures of a London Call Girl* [2005, p. 1].

Taking the form of a diary, *Intimate Adventures*' "self" content is distributed throughout the narrative. Unlike a traditionally structured life narrative, which is written with hindsight and considerable authority over the presentation of the recorded period of one's life, a diary reveals the everyday subjectivity of a personally experienced self fixed in time—available for the writer's later viewing, comment or emendation. As such, even though they are structurally haphazard in their preoccupations, diaries "gather force by accretion of experience, always chronological ... [a]nd through the force of that accretion, the diarist's voice takes on a recognizable narrative persona" (Smith and Watson, 2001, p. 193). In *Intimate Adventures*, Belle charts her day-to-day experiences from November 2003 to June 2004 as an active call girl in London. Most of the 192 entries in *Intimate Adventures* comprise less than a page and even though experiences with clients at work is the text's selling point, her diary focuses mostly on her personal life. Excluding the introduction, only 29 of her diary entries explicitly describe client interactions, and of these only 9 span longer than a page. This is in contrast to the 58 entries about her past and present partners, particularly A1, A2, A3, A4, and The Boy. The remaining entries, numbering over 100, detail her everyday thoughts and observations that range from her mordantly humorous lists—like her spotter's guides to "Love" (2005, pp. 52–53), "Sex" (pp. 98–99); and "Fuck" (p. 146)—to incidental topics like "Rubbish 'holiday' occurrences" (pp. 31–32) and defrosting freezers (pp. 156–67).

While these entries may seem irrelevant to her identity as a sex worker, there is "self" content in Belle's everyday musings that indicates identity work in action. The morning after her first formal escort booking, Belle tries and fails to register her identity change:

> Held my hand up, stared at it for ages. Was something supposed to be different? Should I have felt victimised, abused? I couldn't say. The finer points of feminist theory didn't seem to apply. Things felt as they always had. Same hand, same girl [p. 38].

In contrast, her cognition of her identity as a sex worker is evident in entries where she writes about quotidian routines such as her interactions with the bank and shopping at the grocery and the chemists. In her entry on 4 November, Belle lists the typical contents of her bag:

> phone (to phone agency on arrival and leaving)
> condoms (polyurethane as well as latex, some people have allergies) ...
> lipgloss (reapplying lipstick after a blowjob is too complicated) ...
> spare knickers and stockings

keys, bankcards, other normal detritus
and sometimes, nipple clamps, ball gag and a multi-tailed rubber whip [p. 14].

Spare knickers and nipple clamps are not unexpected items for a sex worker to carry, and it is the everyday items that are of note. A phone, condoms and lipgloss are conventional items in a woman's bag, but Belle recasts them as sex work apparatus in the elucidatory parentheses. In her entry on 16 December, she describes the concealments she frequently has to fabricate; she lies to the grocer that she works as a nanny in order to explain her mid-afternoon shops; when she runs into neighbours well-dressed and in full make-up, she lies about parties and get-togethers and she gets into taxis "wonder[ing] what story I'm going to tell the taxi driver" (pp. 64–65). The entry on 18 February includes two shopping lists for the different chemists that Belle frequents, as she shops at one for "normal things and another for everything else" (p. 155).

These entries denote Belle's heightened cognizance of what would otherwise be unremarkable encounters. Eakin's observations on "our illusions of autonomy and self-determination" regarding self-construction are pertinent here (2008, p. 22). He writes that while postulations that we "draw on models of identity as we go about the business of making our selves, whether in our lives or in writing about them" (p. 22), are easy to make, they are inadequate in specifying how the process of self-construction works. He thus asserts that "our practice of self-construction is largely unconscious" (p. 22), and claims that "it takes a rupture in the normal unfolding of everyday life to bring it into view and remind us of its value as identity's bedrock" (p. 7). For Belle, her subjectivity as a sex worker frames her everyday encounters such that her perception of regular objects is ruptured. Her phone gains added significance as a security device and her usage of lipgloss over lipstick signifies her experience as a sex worker. Though sex work is normal to her, it is something she has to actively hide every day. The need to be covert with strangers and acquaintances restricts her autonomy to talk truthfully about herself and continually brings her cognizance of her "deviant" identity as a sex worker to the forefront. Belle's tangential entries are anything but trivial and embody her unconscious identity work. Through writing, Belle reconciles the everyday ruptures in the rhythms of her consciousness with her identity as a sex worker. In writing, Belle connects her self-presentation with normality, which embodies a narrative coherence.

Importantly, these ruptures are not framed as difficult experiences as Belle delivers the examples above in a light-hearted and entertaining manner. She frames the list of her bag's contents by remarking on fashion trends, declaring that "a capacious holdall is the order of the day" (2005, p. 14), since "[p]acking all that into a Fendi baguette is a black art not even Houdini could master" (p. 14). Regarding her fabricated job as a nanny, Belle exudes mirthfulness as she describes her excuse as "blatantly unbelievable, as I never have children visibly in tow and ... am only buying for one" (p. 65). In the entry on the chemists, Belle drily intimates an air of confidentiality with the first sentence: "It used to be simple to buy faintly embarrassing items and hide them in the rest of my purchases" (p. 155). Belle lists the purchases at each chemist in contradistinction to each other, with the first list including innocuous products like shampoo and toothpaste, and the second list including sensitive products like "vaginal pessary (for irritation)," "lubricant" and "potassium citrate granules (for cystitis)" (p. 155). Belle ends the entry humorously: "This [list] was met with the vaguely disinterested, 'There are halitosis remedies on the far end of aisle two, if you're interested' / Bitch" (p. 155).

This witty writing style and her focus on lingerie, lipsticks and relationships aligns *Intimate Adventures* with contemporary chick lit. The consumerist attitude coupled with a marked lack of engagement in deep analysis of sex work in spite of her obvious intelligence can be seen as a rather vacuous post-feminist attitude to sex work. Consider, for example, her evasive answer to why she entered the profession:

> Client: "So why do you do this?"
> Me: "I'm not sure I have an answer to that."
> "There must be something that you at least tell yourself."
> "Well, perhaps I'm the sort of person apt to do something for no good reason other than I can't think of a reason not to."
> "So if someone told you to jump off a bridge..."
> "Depends on the bridge. Depends if they were paying. Why?"
> "Oh, no reason. Will you suck me now?" [p. 25].

Her evasiveness can be interpreted as thoughtlessness, which reduces the agency of her decision. This lack of engagement and the text's depiction of mainly positive and luxurious impressions of the sex industry has made the franchise a recipient of public criticism for the glamorization of sex work (Saner et al., 2007) and academic criticism for its contribution to the overall mainstreaming of "ho chic" that "perpetuat[es] a falsely positive perception of global sex industries" and thus "constitutes a form of symbolic violence" (Coy, Wakeling and Garner, 2011).

However, it is important to realize here that the marked distinction between chick lit and sex worker chick lit is authenticity. While chick lit is fictional, this new subgenre fascinates because it contains real life stories of sex workers. As such, the stakes are higher for their authors regarding their political opinions of sex work, and Belle's selective silence on the topic should be seen in the context of media demands on the speech of sex workers. Melissa Gira Grant's point about sex workers as objects of control in *Playing the Whore* (2014) is pertinent here. She writes that demands on sex workers to give testimony on the nature of their work and lives are demands on their speech to "both convey their guilt and prove their innocence" and even as they make efforts toward recognition and popular representations that defy stereotypes, prostitutes, both real and imagined, still remain the object of social control (p. 25). Grant quotes Anne McClintock's 1992 essay "Screwing the System": "The more prostitutes are obliged to speak of their actions in public, the more they incriminate themselves" (p. 24). That the avoidance of debate by Belle in her *diary* is over-determined as disinterest and unethical glamorizing of the industry is already telling of the attitude of control toward sex workers' speech. The charge of media glamorization displaces the debate on the sex industry from material discussions about the labor market, the privatization of education and healthcare, and debt, to discussions about the realm of the representational (pp. 21–22).

Moreover, that the above extract from *Intimate Adventures* constitutes the entirety of a diary entry is significant. Belle subverts the notion that she is unthinking, by actively foregrounding her evasiveness in a way that compels scrutiny. That she "can't think of a reason not to" demands readers' re-evaluation of reasons not to be a sex worker, and shows her complete dismissal of any possible reason. By simultaneously inciting readers to think of these reasons and dismissing all of them, Belle actively constructs sex work as unremarkable. Therein lies the agency of Belle's decision: through the radical subversion of normativity. In this way, Belle reinforces the rationality of choosing sex work, solidifies the normality of her identity as a sex worker through narrative, and bestows it with narrative coherence. As such, while Belle may not overtly analyze sex work, the diary is a personal platform for her to work through a hegemonic structure that stigmatizes her labor identity. This is done on a more personal level in her self-construction as an NPB sex worker, as can be seen in the following analysis.

Belle thinks that temping is beneath her, and this shows her subjectivity as an NPB with a well-educated, white-collar background. On 29 May, Belle writes:

> Somewhere along the way it was implied—not guaranteed, I understand that, but implied—that the reward for working hard at school and completing a degree was a reasonable career. Now here I am wondering whether a six-month appointment colour-correcting magazine illustrations or assistant manager at a high-street retailer would be a better career move. And competing with hundreds of other graduates for the same paltry pickings [p. 268].

In this quote, Belle shows her sense of entitlement to a job and good income with her qualifications, aligning her with the NPB class trajectories of "those who have not obtained from their qualifications all they felt entitled to." Evidently, Belle is aware of the extremity and stigma of sex work and that her choice to take it up in spite of her employability is fairly counterintuitive. But she justifies it by revealing her ethics of fun when it comes to work. She describes working in accountancy as "a fate worse than death," drily stating that "[a]ccountancy trumps even academia in the unsexiness stakes" (p. 1). By describing accountancy as unsexy, she exhibits the importance of excitement in her choice of work, and describes sex work as "better than watching the clock until the next scheduled tea break in a dismal staff room" (p. 1).

Sex work is not merely "better" though, as Belle genuinely enjoys sex. The introduction includes the story of the first time she is paid for sex: Belle has sex with a couple for fun, not money, and is gifted with a sum of money when she leaves. She writes, "I thought I should feel a pang of regret or surprise at being used and paid for. But it was nothing like that. They'd enjoyed themselves and … truth be told, I hadn't exactly found it a chore" (p. 5). Feeling no qualms about this transaction, Belle ventures into sex work. In her entry on orgasms, Belle describes how she "enjoy[s] sex for more than the merely physical tingle" as she thinks that "[b]eing desired is fun," "[d]ressing up is fun," and having "[n]o pressure to either experience physical release for fear of damaging someone's ego, or give someone an orgasm for fear of never hearing from them again, is wicked" (p. 94). Her depiction of her ethics of fun toward work and the multitude of entries depicting her recreational attitude toward sex, both at work and in her private life, show her narrative self-construction as a postindustrial sex worker with NPB sensibilities.

Adhering to the NPB's approach to work with an ethics of fun, Belle finds sex work meaningful due to her recreational attitude toward sex. Sex is fun to Belle, and the fact that she does not have orgasms at work does not affect this, since she sees sex as an end in itself:

> I don't equate number of orgasms with the level of enjoyment of sex, nor good sex with the ability to produce an orgasm. At the age of nineteen, … I

realised that sex was about the quality of your enjoyment and that doesn't always mean coming [p. 94].

With the combined views that sex is intrinsically valuable for its pleasure and that sexual labor "is a customer service position, not a self-fulfilment odyssey" (p. 94), Belle demonstrates a business-like attitude toward sex work. She strives to be professional, understanding that punters are "paying for their orgasm, not [hers]" (p. 94) and "tr[ies] to discern what [their] taste might be and stray not too far off the beaten mainstream" (p. 219). Her perspective on sex work as a professional trade is corroborated by her systematic descriptions of client interactions in a dispassionate voice:

> I crouched between the man's legs. His inner thighs were smooth and I brushed the skin with my fingertips. "How was your holiday?"
> "Good, good. Japan is an interesting place. Have you ever been?" ...
> "No." I took the hardening cock in my hand and pulled on its foreskin gently. It stiffened and lengthened in my palm. "What is your favourite thing to do there?" [p. 28].

That sexual labor can be professionalized is a way of framing sex work as a "proper" job, and Belle brings narrative coherence to her identity in this way. On a larger scale, by writing about her engagement with sex work as *both* fun and professional, Belle frames it in the normative way that the postindustrial NPB structure meaning in their work. This denotes Belle's production of narrative coherence on a deeper, socio-economic level. Altogether, Belle's evasiveness about why she is a sex worker asserts sex work as normal in general, and her writing about her enjoyment of sex and professionalism in the work asserts the normality of sex work as a vocation for someone of her privileged background.

In spite of her matter-of-fact attitude toward sex work as a skilled profession, Belle does indicate that she sees the intrinsic value of sexual labor outside of sexual gratification. This is evident in the serialized glossary that opens every month of her diary, "Belle's A-Z of London Sex Work":

W is for Whore

> Working girl, prostitute, call girl, woman of negotiable affection, ho. I don't think any one term is any more or less degrading than another. ... You sell sex for a living—what did you expect, to be billed as an "erotic entertainments consultant"? "Sex therapist" wouldn't be so bad, though [p. 272].

While she is forthright about the nature of sex work and seems intolerant of euphemisms for it, she makes an exception for the term "sex therapist," viewing it as an acceptable neologism for sex workers. On 6 January, she writes of her interaction with a client who studies psychoanalysis and is interested in working as a psychotherapist, noting that this "makes us comrades, if not exactly colleagues" (pp. 99–100). That she sees the therapeutic value of sex work suggests that she does not view sex work as merely the provision of entertainment. Importantly, her view that sex work is therapeutic does not stem from the sexual release it provides, but from her provision of bounded authenticity.

Bounded authenticity, as mentioned earlier, refers to genuine, yet fleeting, libidinal and emotional ties. In line with her professional attitude, Belle is aware of the demand for bounded authenticity in sex work and strives to excel in providing it. She writes:

> There's a lot of talk in escort circles of Girlfriend Experience (GFE). That's because it is by far the most requested thing we offer. I have been cuddled to within an inch of my life by well-meaning chaps whose only previous acquaintance with me was via a website. I've sipped red wine and watched telly with single gents until the taxi beeped its horn outside [p. 231].

Additionally, Belle observes that bounded authenticity is prioritized over sexual gratification in most of her bookings, since "[p]lenty of the men—more than you might think—never even come at all" and they "never imply it's a failure on [her] part" since they are "just after human contact, a warm body, an erotic embrace" (p. 94). However, the provision of bounded authenticity requires high emotional labor, and it is important at this point to consider the pressures that sex work places on sex workers' personal wellbeing and how writing allows Belle to manage it.

Sex work is considered an extreme profession, as it requires high physical labor (bodily contact is intense, direct and commodified) and high emotional labor (professional distance has to be maintained in spite of sexual relations). The provision of bounded authenticity places added emotional labor on NPB sex workers as it complicates the navigation of professional distance. This is exemplified in the entry where Belle has to be careful with the feelings of the client who loses his virginity with her. She has to maintain an intimate ambience and show that she cares, but at the same time maintain a distance:

> "If you had met me somewhere else, would you fancy me?"
> "How old are you?"
> "Nineteen."
> "Not if I knew your age."
> He frowns. I say he looks older than that but I didn't sleep with nineteen-

year-olds even when I was nineteen. That doesn't seem to have helped; he's looking even more depressed.
"I'd fancy you. I would. You're a dangerous sort."
"How so?" he wonders.
Must be careful here. Say something truthful, but nice, and not obviously flattery. "I wouldn't want to be the first person to break your heart" [p. 185].

Belle has to develop "affective neutrality" and "detached concern" in order to reinforce a professional distance, while at the same time perform deep acting in calling forth genuine feeling for the provision of bounded authenticity.[2] As shown in the above quote, this professional distance has to be negotiated on the spot, highlighting the intensity of the emotional labor during appointments.

While the light-hearted treatment of sex work in her diary seems to show that Belle is unaffected by these pressures, her narrative belies these emotional pressures through the use of humor. In "Controllable Laughter: Managing Sex Work through Humour" (2004), Sanders uses empirical research to show that the usage of humor by female sex workers "contributes to a range of defence mechanisms that are necessary to protect personal and emotional well being" (p. 273). Sanders' research shows that humor was "observed across all markets but usually in collective establishments where several women work together," and is "not as evident amongst women working alone" (p. 275). Since Belle only does out-call assignments through an agency, her experience of sex work is largely solitary. However, through the use of narrative, Belle performs the emotional labor of processing her emotions and asserting her sense of control as a sex worker. Life narrative theorist Suzette Henke coins the term "scriptotherapy" to refer to this process of emotional labor through writing. In *Shattered Subjects* (1998), Henke argues that this process is powerfully therapeutic:

> Because the author can instantiate the alienated or marginal self into the pliable body of a protean text, the newly revised subject, emerging as the semi-fictive protagonist of an enabling counternarrative, is free to rebel against the values and practices of a dominant culture and to assume an empowered position of political agency in the world [p.xv].

As Belle keeps her identity as a sex worker to herself, save a few close friends, she has limited opportunities to talk about her experiences in sex work and process her feelings. Taking scriptotherapy into account, Belle is able to do so in writing as it enables her to imbue her alienated subjectivity with empowered agency and narrative coherence. This sense of empowerment is facilitated through the use of humor in her writing, since humor is a positive strategy that enables professionals in extreme jobs to "reduce tension, reinterpret events and re-frame distressing episodes" (Sanders, 2004, p. 274).

Scriptotherapy in action has already been demonstrated in my earlier analysis of Belle's use of humor to turn routine activities into a site of jest. Through humor, she is able to articulate her subjective experience of everyday ruptures of her consciousness with bravado. This bravado contributes to the presentation of her narrative identity as self-possessed and composed. The presence of humor in her writing can thus be seen as an indicator of Belle's sense of self-composure. In the following section, I will analyze the implications of the absence of humor in some of her descriptions of client interactions with respect to bounded authenticity.

Of the 192 diary entries in *Intimate Adventures*, 29 of them explicitly describe interactions with clients. Out of these, 18 indicate an engagement with the notion of intimacy: 14 entries evince Belle's provision of bounded authenticity; two entries show clients who only want sexual gratification; and two entries indicate unbounded authenticity. These entries are tabulated below, with an asterisk indicating entries that span longer than a page:

Provision of Bounded Authenticity and Sexual Gratification	Provision of Sexual Gratification Only	Unbounded Authenticity
2013	2014	2013
1. November 3	1. February 2	1. December 14*
2. November 6	2. March 9*	2014
3. November 19		2. March 14*
4. December 1		
5. December 8		
6. December 30*		
2014		
7. January 6*		
8. January 7		
9. January 15		
10. January 29		
11. February 21		
12. March 12		
13. April 11		
14. April 15*		

Table: *Provision of Bounded Authenticity in Client Interactions.*

Entries listed in the first column are generally humorous. Belle either frames the entry comically, or it includes banter with her client. However, there is a notable absence of humor in the entries where the provision of bounded authenticity is problematized (columns two and three), and this is worth further analysis.

The entries in column two describe client interactions where they are uninterested in bounded authenticity and seek only sexual gratification. In her 2 February entry, the client is obsessed with photographing or videoing their sexual interaction:

> He just didn't let up. To the point where bucking enthusiastically and making all the right moves was becoming difficult because I couldn't escape the feeling of being watched. At the end of the hour I was so spooked I couldn't help scanning the room for hidden cameras [p. 137].

That he remains unshakeable and disinterested in her efforts to create intimacy or eroticism in the session evidently unnerves Belle. In her 9 March entry, the client is only interested in sexual gratification. It is the most sexually graphic description of a client appointment, and while her dispassionate tone in describing sex with clients is not unorthodox, the unusually curt sentences makes the tone of this entry particularly terse. The client is not interested in kissing—a key component of bounded authenticity—and does not work his way toward anal sex the way her clients usually do, but goes straight into it. It occurs to her that "there was something reckless about the way he handled [her], and all the protection in the world would not stop him if he wanted to harm [her]" (p. 183). After half an hour of anal sex, where she is "literally pinned" to the bed, he comes, and the entry ends as follows:

> He didn't want to be held. I went to the toilet and cleaned myself, came back and dressed. We discussed Iris Murdoch, and I left. There were no taxis outside, so I walked as far as Regent Street, where the lights of the shops and the cars blurred into illusion [p. 183].

In these two entries, Belle's narrative voice is serious and flat, in stark contrast to her usual light-heartedness. Since humor denotes her ability to process her emotions and indicates her self-composure, the grave tone of these entries suggests that she is unable to fully own these experiences in her reframing of them. She is impacted deeply because her provision of bounded authenticity enables her to find her work meaningful, and their disinterest in bounded authenticity means she is unable to find work meaningful in these bookings. In addition, their disinterest in intimacy and blunt usage of her for their sexual needs removes the distinction of her brand of "meaningful" sex work to that of the merely physical service of street-based workers, and destabilizes her narrative coherence as a professional NPB sex worker.

The entries in column three describe client interactions in which authenticity is unbounded, meaning that Belle expresses her inability to maintain a professional distance and has lingering feelings for clients. In the two-hour booking she describes in her 14 December entry, she and the client converse over two bottles of chardonnay before they even kiss: "It felt like a first-date kiss. Tentative" (p. 59). Sex is over quickly, he says romantic things to her, and they "ate crisps and drank wine a full hour past when [she] was supposed to go. It was odd; I felt the cab turned up far too soon" (pp. 59–60). In the entry on 14 March, Belle despondently relates the loss of a regular, melodramatically opening the entry with:

> The end of the affair was written from the beginning. He is a man who hires women for sex, I am the whore, and at some point his taste will move on. I have grown accustomed to him, and while I do not love him I admit to being just as interested in staying up all night talking as in the carnal transaction.... He knows a lot about me, this one [p. 189].

She compares the dissolution of their relationship with that of a real romantic relationship, characterized by "clinginess" and "unfounded suspicion" (p. 190). After quoting his sentimental farewell text, the entry ends with "I'll miss him, too" (p. 190). Again, humor is absent in the narration of these two experiences but this time the serious narrative voice is affectionate. The emotional labor expended on maintaining professional distance from clients is not always effective, and the absence of her usual humor suggests a lack of emotional control.

In the above four examples where clients are not interested in the purchase of bounded authenticity or where she fails to maintain an emotional distance, Belle's narrative self-composure lapses, as indicated by the lack of humor. How this lapse bears upon Belle's narrative coherence can best be contextualized with reference to this quote:

> "You really like what you do, don't you?"
> "I think it would be hard to take if I didn't" [pp. 112–13].

In this telling dialogue with a client, Belle sums up how work relates to her sense of self. She is only able to handle work emotionally if she likes it. As demonstrated above, Belle likes work when she can provide bounded authenticity as it makes the work meaningful to her. When the provision of bounded authenticity is problematized, she is unsettled and unable to like her work. I would argue that it is precisely because of this that Belle performs narrative coherence in her writing. The fact that these four entries are written in a way that evinces her discomposure is consistent with her conceptualization of herself as an NPB sex worker who enjoys her job because she finds the labor fun and who is capable of being professional about it. Her discomposure contributes to the text's construction of her identity as narratively coherent.

This essay has argued that *Intimate Adventures* can be seen as scriptotherapy, in which the writing of Belle's subjectivity enables her to do the emotional labor of working through the pressures of sex work. In so doing, Belle is able to present herself as an active agent, and reconcile her marginalized and stigmatized identity with normality, providing herself with the narrative coherence that society is not ready to concede.

Conclusion

Some people like their jobs. Some people hate theirs. These are acceptable sentiments to have unless the job is selling sex. In choosing to analyze the life narrative of a marginalized subjectivity, this essay aims to look at the ways in which sex workers process their struggles within a hegemonic structure that hinders the acceptance of their labor identity into normality. This struggle is analyzed within the framework of narrative coherence, whereby scriptotherapy is constituted through the successful reconciliation of a ruptured subjectivity. I have looked at how Belle's NPB sensibilities bear upon her sex worker's identity in the way that she structures meaning in her work. I have analyzed how Belle's ruptured subjectivity arises due to her need for meaning in work, which she is able to find as she views sex as an ends in itself. Writing life narrative allows her to do identity work by enabling her to impose narrative coherence upon the everyday ruptured subjectivity. Life narrative also enables her to process the new difficulty of providing the new demand for bounded authenticity in a postindustrial sex work landscape.

In exploring the attitudes and ideas about *work*, I have sidestepped the usual focus on exploitation and empowerment in the sex industry and aim to contribute to the need for creative thinking regarding power relations and worker experiences of sex workers. The occupational arrangements and experiences of sex workers are diverse, and in the light of socio-economic and cultural developments that have given sex workers more platforms to be heard, I urge for more critical analysis of sex worker life narratives.

Notes

1. "Act-value" is one of three defining features of life narrative critic Elizabeth Bruss' theory of autobiographical acts, the other two being truth-value and identity-value (Smith and Watson, 2001, p. 138).

2. Parsons (1951) describes how professionals [in general] are expected to develop "affective neutrality," or what Coombs and Goldman (1973) call "detached concern," in order to reinforce professional power and distance (cited in Sanders, 2004, p. 287).

Sexing Education

Erotica in the Urban Classroom

Alyssa D. Niccolini

While *Fifty Shades of Grey* (James, 2012a) may have shaken up vanilla notions of sex, it has done little to disrupt lily-white conceptions of erotica. Maligned as "mommy porn" and a distraction for bored housewives, erotica has been largely dismissed as the companion of middle-class, heterosexual and presumably white women. While the implicit heteronormativity and misogyny in these constructions merits further analysis, in this essay I want to put pressure on this trope of the white, middle-class erotica reader and turn attention to an altogether different context than the suburban boudoir for erotica enjoyment—the urban secondary classroom.

I have written elsewhere (Niccolini, 2013; 2014) about the alternative curriculum erotica offered the students in my classroom, a small high school in one of the highest poverty sections of New York City. Creating "hot spots" of affective intensity, erotica circulated amongst the Latina and African American girls in the school eliciting arousals of multiple sorts—engrossed attention, fractious power struggles, flashes of shame, stimulated bodies. I argue that students used erotica in ways that mimicked and resignified the "official" English curricula (Niccolini, 2014), opening new spaces for their bodies and desires, and setting off lines of flight that worked to deterritorialize (Deleuze and Guattari, 1980) the curriculum (Niccolini, 2013).

In this essay I draw on data from two focus groups with U.S. high school students aged 14–18 who identify as African American, Black, Afro-Caribbean, and Latina to argue that erotica does more than just offer a means of disrupting identity politics: it teaches. I see erotica as animating different kinds of knowing than those typically recognized in schools. This pedagogy teaches through feeling and sensation and moves pointedly outside of the representational logics that dominate school disciplines. Directly implicating bodies in learning and thinking, erotica dissolves humanist conceptions of the individualized, contained human subject and shares excitement and sensation through a range of bodies. Taking up recent scholarship of "the affective turn" (Clough, 2007; Gregg and Seigworth, 2010), I term this an *affective pedagogy*. I mobilize affect here in a capacious sense that includes both Deleuzian "pre-personal intensities" (Massumi, 1987) as well as a more general interfacing of emotion, feeling, and sensation. In this piece I argue that erotica does interesting things in classrooms—connecting bodies in shared titillation, disrupting the secure paths of telos-driven curricula, and forging readerships or "intimate publics" (Berlant, 2008; 2011) around feeling over identity. I hone in on the work of Zane and her self-termed *erotica noir* in relation to this pedagogy as her books were the most widely circulated and intensely beloved by the students I taught.

Zane's Erotica Noir

While E L James may have become the face of mainstream erotica, Zane commands her own empire. As Andrea Sachs (2012) of *Time* makes clear, "When it comes to bestselling erotica, Zane has been a trailblazer. The 44-year-old, Washington, D.C.–based author had sold more than 5 million copies of her books worldwide before anyone had heard of *Fifty Shades of Grey* ... Zane was indisputably there first" (Sachs). I got to know the covers of Zane's books well during my time as a high school English teacher in New York City. The "Queen of Urban Erotica" (Sachs, 2012) is the most well-known author in the genre that goes by the multiple names black erotica, erotic street lit, urban erotica and Zane's own neologism *erotica noir*. With women of color as the chief protagonists, Zane's books command a large African American and female readership.

Both self-published and increasingly more mainstream (Zane is herself a *New York Times* bestselling author), erotica noir is a fixture in urban landscapes. Donnell Alexander (2005), remarking on Zane's success, declares, "In a brutal market, at least Zane is getting paid." "[H]ood books," as Alexander terms them,

> are not merely surviving—they're outpacing even the mainstream in terms of sales. It's the so-called Urban Lit category, bastard child of the self-publishing boom: freed from the judgments of publishers that once would

have stymied them on the basis of sentence structure alone, these authors, of whom Zane ... is the moment's grand dame, have formed publishing's shadow economy [Alexander, 2005].

From street vendors and bodegas hawking used copies to heavily policed sections of chain bookstores, the sexy covers of Zane and her cohorts' novels can be seen spicing up subways and schoolbags alike. As one of my interviewees marvels, "I mean if you go Downtown Brooklyn, you will find more Zane books than spiritual books."

Nick Chiles (2006) bemoans just this mainstream availability. In the rancorous editorial "Their eyes were reading smut," he decries that there is increasingly "more of this oversexed genre in Barnes & Noble bookstores" (Chiles). Critics seem to think urban lit and urban erotica are anti-intellectual, and at worst, dumbing down and "degrading" African American literature. Jervey Tervalon deems urban erotica "low-rent porn for church-going ladies" (cited in Alexander, 2005). Linton Weeks (2004) champions this anti-pedagogical sentiment claiming that street lit "venerates grams over grammar, sin over syntax, excess over success."

Yet, while some disparage urban lit as degrading the hard-fought space of African American literature on bookshelves, others celebrate it for fostering powerful literacy opportunities for young readers (Hill, Pérez and Irby, 2008) and even potential for critical praxis in schools (Van Ormin and Lyiscott, 2013). Poet Sterling Plumpp declares that urban fiction "is the most inventive thing happening to language in a long time" (cited in Weeks, 2004). Others argue that it offers important cautionary tales for readers navigating the complexities of poverty in America and is helping to foster literacy in groups who may otherwise avoid books. Carol Mackey, senior editor of Black Expressions, makes the rather problematic declaration, "There is a blessing in all of this: African Americans are reading" (cited in Weeks, 2004).

Danyel Smith, editor in chief of *Vibe* and *Vibe Vixen*, admits, "I crave the connection street-lit authors have with their readership" (2006, p. 188). Smith's envy of Zane's "connection" to readers strikes me as particularly telling of the *affective pedagogy* I'm arguing this erotica writer offered students. Zane, unlike most erotica authors, has fostered a passionate community of readers as evidenced by the over one million followers on her Facebook page and her highly-trafficked interactive website (eroticanoir.com). With her active online spaces and Q & A series, Zane herself could be considered a "public pedagogue" (Sandlin, O'Malley and Burdick, 2011). With a degree from Howard University, a family legacy, a mother who was a teacher, and a father who is "a well-known religious scholar"

(Sachs, 2012), Zane is no stranger to education. When asked if her parents' educational background has any influence on her as a writer, she answers:

> Well it has a huge bearing. Yes, both my parents are educators and my father is a theologian. And just like most children, I respect my parents very, very much and I want to make them proud of me. And actually they are. And even though my father is a theologian, he understands that people do have sex in their lifetime, the majority of them. And he also understands that there is a lot of confusion with people when it comes to their sexuality and their spirituality [Jones, 2010].

As CEO of Strebor books, she has in a sense the power to publically address the "confusion" and silence she sees surrounding sex and sexualities and "set the curriculum" for her audience. For Zane, the writing and reading of erotica is an intellectual practice. In the introduction to *Chocolate Flava* she asserts, "To me, erotica is mentally stimulating. It deals with more than just sex but also circumstances, passion, and feelings" (2004, p. xiii).

I want to hone in on Zane's declaration of her work as addressing "circumstances, passion, and feelings." Passion and feelings are often configured as the antithesis to intellectualism; the fact that Zane deems these as the most "mentally-stimulating" aspects of her books gestures toward what I deem an *affective pedagogy*. While Zane does offer a form of identity politics in disrupting the male gaze and delimiting conceptions of black female subjectivities, it seemed to be more the affective work of her texts that appealed to students. Avina, a newly graduated senior in high school, captures this sentiment in her words below:

> [Zane] not only has that "Oh my gosh, wow, my eyes are open while I'm reading it," she also has a storyline. So it's like ok, wow, you get to like these characters because yes these are characters that have feelings and emotions. And she shows that, but then there is also the carnal part of it where it's like, oh, I shouldn't be reading this but I am.

Avina enjoys the riveting plot, which we might mark as part of a representational schema, and she also enjoys the "feelings and emotions" of the characters. While the feelings and emotions of the characters point to an interest in affect, it is her own bodily affective state—what she terms the "carnal part"—that seems to be the real draw for her. When she reads, she feels wide awake—her "eyes are open." This alertness signals an immediacy to the reading experience that is very different than the telos-driven and future-orientedness of school curricula. Erotica's pedagogy is a pedagogy of the present. Its knowledge is about what the body is capable of now. This present-centered feeling of "I shouldn't be reading this but I am" traverses a range of affective intensities that fall somewhere between a guilty pleasure, flouting of discipline, exciting transgression and sense of shame. As standardized tests are more and more the horizon for curricula in U.S. schools, a curriculum centered on immediate intensities may offer a temporal relief from an insistence on knowledge being tied to futurity.

Zane's capacity to affectively captivate some of my more reluctant readers, at least of "official" school texts, was incontrovertible. While Toni Morrison's (1970) *The Bluest Eye*, one of the most frequently challenged texts of U.S. school curricula, is by no means timid about sex, it often was neglected in favor of Zane. Simba Sana observes that urban fiction has the potential to reach "black women who have not been reached by writers such as Toni Morrison, Alice Walker and Terry MacMillan" (cited in Weeks, 2004). When I asked students why they enjoy the books, I was surprised to hear them cite the books' pedagogical capacities:

> Pia: Because some of these book have information. You learn things.
> Alyssa: What do you mean you learn things? Is it a form of sex education?
> All: Yeah!
> Dee: I've seen—you're more questioning and desire for sex, that's when it starts when you're in junior high school. When you're around that age. And you're just like—oh this has sex in it? Let's just flip through the pages and you find a page and you're just like, really, really? Damn, this is—you're just curious about it and here's a book about it so it's like, "Oh, ok."

The students above argue that the books teach, and though they concede to my declaring it a form of sex education, the books' pedagogy is vastly different than official school discussions of sex or even other books marketed toward teen readers. One difference seems to be Zane's speed in transmitting knowledge; she doesn't "beat around the bush" as Jai and Azure discuss:

> Jai: I don't want to sound racist or anything, but when you read books like Gossip Girls or Summer Boys they beat around the bush, but urban fiction get into it –
> All: [Yes!]
> Azure: They've got detail. That's the difference between urban fiction and—cause I used to read those romance books. [They] are so boring! Like I don't know how people read those. Urban fiction is riveting, entertaining. It's almost like a shocker. Oh my god, I can't wait to get to that page—what number? She got pregnant!

While Azure characterizes urban fiction as having more "detail" than other books, it seems to be more the affective intensities—the shock and eager anticipation ("I can't wait")—the books elicit that keep her coming back. Her call out to an imaginary co-reader—"What number?"—suggests that her reading experience is shared. I find the addressing of this phantom reader as evocative of the communal reading I observed Zane fostering in our classroom. When a Zane book came out, a group of erotica enthusiasts and curious onlookers was never far behind. Azure intuitively extends her reading experience beyond her body, hailing, even in her hypothetical example, a collectivity of readers.

Body Knowledge

Galvanized by a shared constellation of affective intensities, this community of readers that enjoyed Zane opened the frequent drudgery of the school-day to an array of instant feeling: excitement, shame, secrecy, boldness, intimacy and, of course, sexual arousal. In her study of female romance readers in *Reading the Romance: Women, Patriarchy, and Popular Literature,* Janice Radway (1984) found that for her largely white and middle-class "Smithton readers" the body was preferred to be ensconced in euphemism and allusion. As she learns from her interviewees, "explicit description of bodily reaction is offensive" (p. 105). In contrast to these romance-readers, the students I interviewed cite Zane's self-described "straight-talk" as part of what drew them in as readers. Zane's stories are purposely explicit, devoid of euphemism, and intend to invoke the body of the reader in the reading experience. Zane's characters are also knowledgeable about their bodies and happy to share their wisdom. Below a female character provides an example:

> I don't give a damn what anyone said. I could cum the hardest when I was on top. A man hitting it from the back could give it a lot of depth, but unless his dick was shaped like a candy cane, he was *not* hitting the G-spot. Sometimes I could get close to the G-spot in the reverse cowgirl position, but I recognized what it felt like when that part of me was touched, and it wasn't happening with a dick [Zane, 2010, p. 7].

In an intimate fusing of body and text, Zane is currently working on starting her own line of sex toys (Williams, 2010).

For students, Zane may have provided a means of experiencing their bodies differently within school. Aside from a few affective states—mild interest, calm attentiveness, or respectful boredom—there is not a wide range of accepted feeling states in schools. There are even fewer available options for bodily sensation and movement. Urban schools, in particular, have been critiqued for their strict surveillance mechanisms, punitive discipline, and the perpetuation of what's been deemed the "school-to-prison pipeline" for youth of color (Hirschfield, 2008; Kim, Losen and Hewitt, 2010; Nolan, 2011; Wald and Losen, 2003). Classroom management in urban contexts is focused on tamping down and carefully controlling bodily arousals and unwieldy affects. While measures to control affect often involve disaggregating, individualizing and hierarchizing students, Zane's shared reading space offered students a chance to form a collective body. These collective forms of belonging may have offered students a means of getting outside of disciplinary forms of control. They also move outside of the humanist container model that such practices rely on.

Though emotional and affective states tend to get constructed as individualized and interior, Teresa Brennan explores how affect is shared between bodies: "By the transmission of affect, I mean simply that the emotions or affects of one person, and the enhancing or depressing energies these affects entail, can enter into another" (2004, p. 3). Indeed, Zane had the power to electrify groups of readers and sometimes an entire classroom. There was a "buzz" around Zane's books that I want to take seriously as a form of pedagogy. While teachers often craft their pedagogies around the performance of the individual, Zane's readerships may have been modeling collective forms of knowledge production.

In many ways the collective Zane cohered was a joint-body that moved through affective contagion. As Anna Gibbs explores, "[a]ffect contagion produces a mimetic relation between bodies" (2008, p. 133). I can vividly recall moments indicative of such contagion. In one, a group of girls surrounded a friend as she read a Zane novel before class. "No! No she didn't!" she'd yell at a character. Her audience squirmed in chairs as she let out gasps and squeals while reading. The group read her face, anticipated her excitement at certain scenes, and shared in her visceral stimulation. This sharing of affect was pedagogical. It fostered non-competitive forms of female belonging where sexuality, bodily arousal, and excitement were celebrated rather than pathologized. It also reconfigured the classroom space around the affective intensities literature generates. This was very different from the meaning-based praxes I emphasized in my own pedagogy which were largely based on New Critical practices of close reading, interpretation, analysis of literary technique and structure, and discussions of authorial intent. Rather than the text as the sole container of meaning, these students were mobilizing their bodies as vital producers of knowledge.

Intimate Publics

In many ways these communities are what Lauren Berlant (2008; 2011) deems "intimate publics." Intimate publics are enclaves of social belonging forged through shared "structures of feeling" (Williams, 1977). For Raymond Williams (1977) structures of feeling are affective spaces of relational knowledge production:

> We are talking about characteristic elements of impulse, restraint, and tone: specifically affective elements of consciousness and relationships: not feeling against thought, but thought as felt and feeling as thought: practical consciousness of a present kind, in a living and interrelating continuity [p. 132].

The readers in my study seemed to be mapping out such an affective space, a new school geography marked by corporeal, affective and emotional intensities rather than grades, abilities and subjects. This pedagogy taught about bodies, feelings and desires in a very different way than did official curricula. It also positioned affect as an important form of knowledge—*feeling as thought, thought as feeling*. Intimate publics take these other forms of knowledge and galvanize alternative forms of belonging around them.

In the following exchange, as students debate whether Zane is a space for women they seem to be gesturing toward an articulation of an intimate public:

> Avina: It's for women.
> Alyssa: So it's kind of like a female space for women?
> Avina: Yes. Yes. I feel like it is.
> Kay: I don't know.
> Sila: I don't know if it's a female space, but it's a girl thing.
> Alyssa: [laughs] What's "a girl thing"?
> Kay: Exclusive?
> Alyssa: It's gendered? It's female? ...
> Sila: I think so.

The women reveal an ambivalence about labeling Zane an exclusive "female space," but as Avina declares, she "feel[s] like it is." While the language of "female space," a representational schema, is resisted, an affective one is not. Zane's books offer an affective or felt space of belonging and legitimacy engendering something akin to *feeling feminine* or what Berlant (2008) terms "women's culture."

Indeed, many of Zane's books explicitly depict enclaves of female community. *Purple Panties* (Zane, 2008), an edited collection of lesbian erotica (which was a favorite amongst both my straight- and LGBTQ-identified students), is a prime example. There is Tammy in "Woman of the Year" who is a member of The National Association of Female Small Business Owners and is "always game for a weekend hailing the successes of my overachieving, go-getter colleagues" (Copeland, 2008, p. 180). Juanita, Monica, and Chenoa are an intimate group of activists in "Bread and Roses" (Black, 2008). In "My Side of Things," Sabela, on exchange from Tanzania, reveals her cliterectomy to Marsalis, a university researcher. She calls it "[a] gift from the women of the village" (Moore, 2008, p. 32) and the two work through "embodied" knowledges in a scene that follows:

> I retrieved *Woman, Thou Art Loosed* from the shelf. My clit throbbed as I watched the book's rounded edges glide through her pussy lips. Against her un-clit. Back and forth. She glossed it with her juices.
> "Are you ready for real knowledge?" she asked, tossing the book aside [Moore, 2008, p. 37].

Avina, one of my interviewees, echoes the sentiment that Zane focuses on women's "issue[s]":

> Avina: I don't think I have ever seen or heard of a Zane book in which men are the ones who are going through some sort of emotional issue wh[ere] they turn to sex. I haven't heard of one in which men are the focus of the novel. It's always women.

While we might read the linking of women to "some sort of emotional issue" as reinvoking historical couplings of women to emotionality and irrationality, Zane may also be providing a space where both women and affect have authority. Zane's books both legitimize and actively cultivate affective intensities, something, as I've argued, schools largely do not. "In an intimate public emotional contact, of a sort, is made," Berlant (2008, p.viii) argues, and Zane, indeed, opened up precisely such a point of contact, a place to explore and experience "emotional issue[s]" as well as the capacities of the body.

For these young women of color, this intimate public may have been far more valuable for enduring daily life at an urban public school than my own self-declared "social justice" and "culturally sensitive" curriculum. Berlant explains:

> Public spheres are always affect worlds, worlds to which people are bound, when they are, by affective projections of a constantly negotiated common interestedness. But an intimate public is more specific. In an intimate public one senses that matters of survival are at stake and that collective mediation through narration and audition might provide some routes out of the impasse and the struggle of the present, or at least some sense that there would be recognition were the participants in the room together [2011, p. 226].

Certainly attending school in a high-poverty section of NYC demands unique strategies for survival in terms of recognition, social belonging and weathering the "visceral impact" (p. 226) of urban life. While mainstream media has recently opened discussion about the daily wear of city-life such as the catcalling at women with the viral video "10 Hours of Walking in NYC as a Woman" (Bliss, 2014), as a white middle-class woman, in spite of all my progressively-minded pedagogy, I could not begin to account for the affective costs of navigating a world of gender, racial and economic disprivilege. An intimate public, however, may offer a form of such accounting as it offers a structure of social belonging that provides legitimacy, reciprocity and affective communication. Participants may not even be aware or only vaguely cognizant of belonging to such a public, yet that does not mitigate it as a powerful affective space.

Yet while this social belonging may have provided a shared affective space, intimate publics are not sites of celebratory empowerment and, as Berlant (2011) explores, can stubbornly attach us to impossible promises of "the good life." In *The Female Complaint*, Berlant (2008) follows how intimate publics center on commodity cultures. In the case of the students here, Zane' books engendered their own gray economy in the school—they were shared, exchanged, poached from parents and older relatives, confiscated by teachers, fought over and at times stolen. That this economy operated outside of dominant economic flows is telling as it mimicked the marginal place women of color endure in dominant economies of power and capital. This shared commodity culture both coalesces and shapes the intimate public as Berlant explains:

> What makes a public sphere intimate is an expectation that the consumers of its particular stuff *already* share a worldview and emotional knowledge that they have derived from a broadly common historical experience. A certain circularity structures an intimate public therefore: its consumer participants are perceived to be marked by a commonly lived history; shaping its conventions of belonging; and, expressing the sensational, embodied experience of living as a certain kind of being in the world, it promises also to provide a better experience of social belonging—partly through participation in the relevant commodity culture, and partly because of its revelations about how people can live [2008, p. viii].

Zane surely offers an alternative pedagogy about "how people can live," particularly in regards to their sexual lives. This alternative pedagogy may have been their most valuable commodity to students. Official school discussions of sex often rely on scare tactics and discussions of risk. Michelle

Fine (1988) has famously called out these curricula for the "missing discourse of desire."

Indeed, pleasure, desire and female agency are conspicuously missing from most school curricula. My own class text, *The Bluest Eye* (Morrison, 1970), did little to remedy this lack. In Morrison's complex tale of racial self-loathing, sex is repeatedly linked to trauma. Cholly and Pauline are forced to have sex in front of a group of jeering racists while the young female characters are almost all victims of pedophiles, culminating in Pecola's violent rape by her father. It's no wonder Zane's tales of consensual sexual relations and female desirability, agency and pleasure were more appealing.

Yet, while Zane may fill in Fine's (1988) "missing discourse of desire," her depictions of unhindered female pleasure and agency may also be "cruelly optimistic," to borrow Berlant's (2011) phrase. The women in Zane's books frequently occupy high-powered careers, with Ivy-league educations and middle-class comforts. In *The Sisters of APF: The Indoctrination of Soror Ride Dick* (Zane, 2003), for example, a sorority founded on sexually liberating women is comprised of "well-educated women from all walks of life: bankers, lawyers, accountants, doctors, teachers" (p. 4). Zane conjures a triumphalist progress narrative of female sexual liberation and economic mobility at the opening of the novel:

> The change began to take place; right around the time women gained the right to vote. Women's sexual inhibitions began to vanish. Sistahs began to realize that if they can work hard every day, bring home the bacon and raise a family, then they deserved a little hellified sex in their lives. No, make that a lot of hellified sex. They started telling men what they liked and disliked in the bedroom. They started teaching men how to please women. Most importantly, women learned how to please themselves. Now is the time for the revolution! The female sexual revolution! [2003, n.p.].

Zane offers a progress narrative that is oddly anachronistic. The "sexual revolution," usually associated with the 1960s and '70s, get transplanted to the present of the book, presumably the early 2000s. Zane may, however, be heralding a separate revolution enacted by women of color as signaled by her use of "sistahs." Such an invocation may be a commentary on the oft-cited white-dominance in first- and second-wave feminism. When I asked the students about Zane's portrayals of women, many of them revealed a weariness with her depictions of empowered women:

> Alyssa: So what about Zane? How does she portray women?
> Azure: They always strong black women.
> All: Yes!

Pia: They remind me a lot of *For Colored Girls*.[1]
Dee: I've never heard of Zane talk about a homeless girl who gets into prostitution.
Alyssa: So they're always—it's a class issue? They're never poor?
Dee: They're not poor. They're not rich definitely. They're just pretty much like anybody. You don't read about a homeless woman in Zane's book.

While Zane's stories sometimes portray women with low economic status, they more frequently present relatively successful women of color. When characters do come from low-income backgrounds, they have often leveraged their street smarts to navigate social hierarchies. The students quoted above describe an everydayness to Zane's characters and Dee goes so far as to declare them "definitely not rich." Yet, frequently they are just that. A thirty-year old protagonist in *Gettin' Buck Wild: Sex Chronicles II* (Zane, 2002), for example, describes her privileged upbringing, Yale education, and current role as "vice president of corporate development, pulling down 250K a year plus bonuses" (p. 4). Describing these often extraordinary women as "like anybody" naturalizes their economic and social success-stories.

We could see these stories tapping into what Berlant (2011) deems "aspirational normalcy,"

> a collective will to imagine oneself as a solitary agent who can and must live the good life promised by capitalist culture. It tells a story from the perspective of the economic bottom's thick space of contingency. It is about the fantasy of meritocracy, a fantasy of being deserving, and its relation to practices of intimacy, at home, at work, and in consumer worlds [p. 167].

By conjoining twin narratives of sexual and economic progress, Zane seems to be offering a utopian narrative of female agency and social power. Some may argue that this perpetuation of the myth of a meritocratic good life may do more emotional damage than good for young people navigating conditions that largely stymie economic and social privilege for people of color, particularly women. Or, perhaps, more generously, this affective world-building may itself offer a form of pleasure and agency. Avina tellingly uses the language of "worlding" in our discussion:

> Avina: Wow, you're in this whole new world for a minute where literally anything goes. I don't think there is anything that hasn't been talked about in a Zane book. So anything goes. So you can enter this world and do anything you want and you're not going to be judged. And you don't feel like you're being judged because all your friends are reading Zane, too.

Avina describes Zane as offering up a type of mobility, a "world" in school where there is a certain level of freedom denied in reality. This world offers both a space of affective relief from shaming ("you're not going to be judged") and a site of community ("all your friends are reading Zane, too"). As an affective pedagogy, Zane's books cohere sites of belonging animated around feeling over identity. They also offer, as I explore below, opportunities to go *public* with these feelings.

Brazen Publics

I want to end by thinking a bit more about the "public" in Berlant's notion of intimate public. Erotica reading tends to be thought of as belonging in the intimacy of the home or private sphere. The students I interviewed explore this association with privateness, describing how erotic literature often gets hidden from others:

> Sila: I remember one time a friend came over and she like left her book. She didn't give it to me to read she just left it. And my mom was like cleaning my drawers I think and she flipped out! Not even because of the cover of the book –
> Alyssa: She knew who Zane was?
> Sila: No, the cover of the book was explicit. And I was just—I tried to hide it. And I think it was under my drawers. I didn't even read it! I was just waiting for her to come and pick up her book and leave and I got in trouble! My mom was like, is that what you're interested in? You want to read these books? And I was like, oh my god. It looks bad.
> Avina: But that's horrible because in a way, I don't want to say it's too critical, but honestly if my aunt saw I was reading a Zane book, she'd be, Oh my gosh! Why are you reading that? Yet her herself I know she would read something like that.
> [laughter]
> Sila: Yeah!
> Avina: I'm not joking! And I think women, so many women do that. Something that they hide under their bed.
> Kay: Maybe they're just being discrete. They don't want everyone to know that.
> Avina: But why? When sex is so flamboyant anyways these days.... But people hide it! They hide it!

The exchange above highlights erotica being constructed as belonging in the home as a solitary and private activity. An older generation of women (a mother and aunt) are invoked as shaming the discovered erotica-reader. Yet Avina pushes back on this necessary privateness. She is aghast at the hypocrisy in shaming and hiding erotica. As opposed to the older vanguard conjured above, the erotica readers I observed openly read Zane in school and even defied teachers' commands to put the books away. This flouting of social decorum, resisting of authority, and performative display of female desires and sexualities could be considered a political act.

Berlant's (2008; 2011) work on intimate publics is in dialogue with Michael Warner's (2005) *Publics and Counterpublics*. I find Warner's conceptualization of *counterpublic* to be helpful in thinking through the politics of publically reading erotica. Warner puts pressure on Jürgen Habermas' (1989) theorizations of the "bourgeois public sphere," particularly his model of this realm being mobilized through "rational-critical debate" (Warner, 2005, p. 51). As Warner argues, "The bourgeois public sphere consists of private persons whose identity is formed in the privacy of the conjugal domestic family and who enter into rational-critical debate around matters common to all by bracketing their embodiment and status" (p. 57). Zane's intimate publics seem to be doing precisely the opposite—students' identities as "Zane readers" in school were publically enacted and their embodied and affective experience as readers became a means of debating the very devaluing of those forms of embodiment. As such we might think of these forms of belonging as being both an intimate public as well as a counterpublic. Counterpublics, as Warner describes, "are defined by their tension with a larger public" (2005, p. 56) and "[t]heir protocols of discourse and debate remain open to affective and expressive dimensions of languages. And their members make their embodiment and status at least partly relevant in a public way by their very participation" (p. 58). There are multiple publics that are put in tension by the public enjoyment of erotica—the public of student bodies that gets addressed by official curricula in schools, the larger normative social public that largely excludes the voices, agency and bodies of women of color, as well as the more sentimentalized publics coalesced around other forms of women's culture.

A public is a soliciting of attention. It demands reception. By openly reading erotica, students were in a sense demanding reception of their affective experiences. In this final exchange, the interviewees describe this bold publicness they observed in school:

> Alyssa: What about, what did you see in school going on? Like people sneaking the books—
> Kay:—No!
> Sila: No!
> Kay: It was brazen.
> Sila: I mean if girls weren't doing gym, they were on the floor half-way done with the book already.

Gym class demands a docility of the body that the girls depicted refuse to acquiesce to. They address this public's call with their own counterpublic. Splayed out on the gymnasium floor and literally over-laying the official curriculum with their bodies, enjoyment, and desires, these students were scaffolding an affective pedagogy. This pedagogy countered the affective norms of schooling where intense feeling and bodily sensation is generally eschewed. As Warner argues, a counterpublic, "[c]an work to elaborate new worlds of culture and social relations in which gender and sexuality can be lived, including forms of intimate association, vocabularies of affect, styles of embodiment, erotic practices, and relations of care and pedagogy" (2005, p. 57).

Conclusion

Erotica is generally thought of as antithetical to the sanctity of places of learning; like bodies and intense feeling, it doesn't belong. And yet, my own experience as a teacher and discussions with students revealed that erotica was very much present and visible. Rather than a dangerous distraction from academic work or the corruption of young readers, erotica offered important forms of knowledge. The women I talked to describe erotica as bringing their bodies and desires robustly into school space. This affective pedagogy allowed for a wider range of affect than typically cultivated in schools and gave the body an important place in knowledge production. Coalescing intimate and counterpublics, erotica also taught about new forms of alliance and politics. These alliances and political potentialities may be especially important to historically devalued bodies in mainstream public spheres, such as young women of color. While Zane may not be as much of a household name as E L James, she's cultivating important pedagogies beyond the bedskirts of the middle-class bedroom; this may explain why "in a brutal market at least Zane is getting paid."

NOTE

1. *For Colored Girls* is a 2010 film starring Janet Jackson and Whoopi Goldberg, based on the novel *for colored girls who have committed suicide/when the rainbow is enuf* by Ntozake Shange (1997).

Bibliography

ABC Radio National. 2012. *Panel: Erotic Fiction*, Sunday Extra. Interviewer: Jonathon Green. Guests: Linda Jaivin, Michelle Griffin and Kate McCombs. [radio broadcast: Australia] 8 July. Available at http://www.abc.net.au/radionational/programs/sunday extra/panel3a-erotic-fiction/4116830 [accessed 19 October 2013].

About Ellora's Cave. n.d. *Ellora's Cave*. [online] Available at http://www.ellorascave.com/about-ellora-s-cave/ [accessed 24 July 2013].

About Red Sage. n.d. *Red Sage Publishing, Inc.* [online] Available at http://redsage.securesites.net/store/ABOUT_RED_SAGE.HTML [accessed 9 December 2013].

Abraham, Y. 2010. Boys' Love thrives in conservative Indonesia. In A. Levi, M. McHarry and D. Pagliassotti, eds., *Boys' Love manga: Essays on the sexual ambiguity and cross-cultural fandom of the genre*. Jefferson, NC: McFarland, pp. 44–55.

Abu-Lughod, L. 1989. The romance of resistance: Tracing transformations of power through Bedouin women. *American Ethnologist*, 17, pp. 41–55.

Aditya, 2012. Interview on Yaoi and BL fan activities in Indonesia. Interviewed by Tricia Fermin. [audio recording] Jakarta, 19 March.

Adorno, T. 1970. *Aesthetic theory*. Translated and edited by R. Hullot-Kentor. Minneapolis: University of Minnesota Press, 1997.

Adorno, T. 2005. *Minima moralia: Reflections on a damaged life*. London: Verso.

Adorno, T., and Horkheimer, M. 1972. *Dialectic of enlightenment*. New York: Herder and Herder.

Al-Mahadin, S. 2013. Is Christian a sadist? *Fifty Shades of Grey* in popular imagination. *Feminist Media Studies*, 13(3), pp. 566–70.

Albrechtsen, J. 2012. Fifty shades of feminist sneering at mummy porn. *The Australian*, 18 July, p. 12.

Alexander, D. 2005. In a brutal market at least Zane is getting paid. *San Francisco Gate*. [online] Available at http://articles.sfgate.com/2005-02-13/books/17361200_1_random-house-cd-review-anthem [accessed 3 December 2009].

Alibhai-Brown, Y. 2012. Do women really want to be submissive? *The Independent*, 2 July, p. 16.

Alibhai-Brown, Y. 2013. Women are complicit in misogyny. *The Independent*, 14 October, p. 17.

Allen, K. 2008. *One-two punch*. [Kindle version] Akron: Ellora's Cave. Available at: http://www.amazon.com [accessed 28 October 2013].

Althusser, L. 1971. Ideology and ideological state apparatuses. In L. Althusser, *Lenin and philosophy and other essays*. London: Unwin, pp. 127–86.

Amazon Results Page. 2015. Search query: erotic lesbian fiction. *Amazon*. [online] Available at http://www.amazon.com.au/s/ref=nb_sb_noss?url=search-alias %t3Daps&field-keywords=erotic%20lesbian%20fiction [accessed 22 March 2015].

Andrews, D. 2006. *Soft in the middle: The contemporary softcore feature in its contexts*. Columbus: Ohio State University Press.

Ang, I. 1985. *Watching Dallas: Soap opera and the melodramatic imagination*. London: Methuen.
Ang, I. 1987. Popular fiction and feminist cultural politics. *Theory, Culture and Society*, 4, pp. 651–58.
Arlene, 2009. Interview on Yaoi and BL fan activities in the Philippines. Interviewed by Tricia Fermin. [audio recording] Manila, 13 March.
Arnold, S. 2012. Audio: Sue Arnold's choice: *Fifty Shades of Grey* by EL James, read by Becca Battoe. *The Guardian*, 4 August, p. 6.
Assister, A., and Carol, A., eds. 1993. *Bad girls & dirty pictures: The challenge to reclaim feminism*. London: Pluto Press.
Associated Press. 2006. Erotica finds home in mainstream publishing. *AP News Archive*. [online] Available at http://www.apnewsarchive.com/2006/Erotica-Finds-Home-in-MainstreamPublishing/idf38e6ea3ac9d6fd697cc56763d8a771d?SearchText=erotica%20finds%20home%20in;Display_ [accessed 2 November 2013].
At the back fence issue #10. 1996. *All about romance novels*. [online] Available at http://www.likesbooks.com/10.html [accessed 14 August 2013].
At the back fence issue #16. 1996. *All about romance novels*. [online] Available at http://www.likesbooks.com/16.html [accessed 14 August 2013].
Attwood, F. 2005. Fashion and passion: Marketing sex to women. *Sexualities*, 8, pp. 392–406.
Attwood, F. 2006. Sexed up: Theorizing the sexualization of culture. *Sexualities*, 9(1), pp. 77–94.
Attwood, F. 2009. Intimate adventures: Sex blogs, sex "blooks" and women's sexual narration. *European Journal of Cultural Studies*, 12(1), pp. 5–20.
Attwood, F. ed., 2009. *Mainstreaming sex: The sexualization of western culture*. London: I.B. Taurus.
Austen, J. 1815. *Emma*. In *The novels of Jane Austen*, 3d ed. Edited by R.W. Chapman. Oxford: Oxford University Press, 1969.
Babcock, B.A. 1978. Introduction. In B.A. Babcock and V. Turner, eds., *The reversible world: Symbolic inversion in art and society*. Ithaca: Cornell University Press, pp. 13–36.
Backstein, K. 2001. Soft love: The romantic vision of sex on the Showtime Network. *Television & New Media*, 2, p. 303.
Barlow, T.E. 1994. Theorizing woman: Funü, guojia, jiating. In A. Zito and T.E. Barlow, eds., *Body, subject and power in China*. Chicago: University of Chicago Press, pp. 253–90.
Barlow, T.E. 2004. *The question of women in Chinese feminism*. Durham: Duke University Press.
Barnett, R. 2010. Soul full of heat: Zane and the trajectory of black women's literature. *Racialicious*, [online] Available at http://www.racialicious.com/2010/06/10/soul-full-of-heat-zane-and-the-trajectory-of-black-womens-literature/ [accessed 7 June 2011].
Barthes, R. 1964. The metaphor of the eye. In *Critical essays*. Evanston: Northwestern University Press, pp. 239–48.
Barthes, R. 1975. *The pleasure of the text*. Translated by R. Miller. New York: Hill and Wang.
Bast, A. 2006. *Seduced in twilight*. [e-book] Akron: Ellora's Cave. Available at http://ellorascave.com [accessed 18 August 2011].
Bataille, G. 1986. *Erotism: Death and sensuality*. Translated by M. Dalwood. San Francisco: City Lights Books.
Bauman, Z. 1999. On postmodern uses of sex. In M. Featherstone, ed., *Love and eroticism*. Special Issue of *Theory, Culture and Society*, 15(3–4). London: Sage, pp. 19–33.
Bend over boyfriend 2. 2003. [video] San Francisco: S.I.R. Productions.
Bennett, A., and Royle, N. 2009. *An introduction to literature, criticism and theory*, 4th ed. London: Pearson.
Bennett, J. 2010. *Vibrant matter: A political ecology of things*. Durham: Duke University Press.
Berlant, L. 1997. *The queen of America goes to Washington City*. Durham: Duke University Press.

Berlant, L. 2008. *The female complaint: The unfinished business of sentimentality in American culture*. Durham: Duke University Press.
Berlant, L. 2011. *Cruel optimism*. Durham: Duke University Press.
Bernstein, E. 2007. *Temporarily yours: Intimacy, authenticity, and the commerce of sex*. Chicago: University of Chicago Press.
Bersani, L. 1986. *The Freudian body*. New York: Columbia University Press.
Bersani, L. 1987. Is the rectum a grave? *October*, 43, pp. 197–222.
Bersani, L. 1987. Is the rectum a grave? In *Is the rectum a grave? And other essays*. Chicago: University of Chicago Press, 2010, pp. 3–30.
Bersani, L. 2000. Sociality and sexuality. In *Is the rectum a grave? And other essays*. Chicago: University of Chicago Press, 2010, pp. 102–119.
Bersani, L. 2002. Sociability and cruising. In *Is the rectum a grave? And other essays*. Chicago: University of Chicago Press, 2010, pp. 45–62.
Bersani, L., and Phillips, A. 2010. *Intimacies*. Chicago: University of Chicago Press.
Birmingham, J. 2012. Everyone has a book in them: That's the best place for it. *Sydney Morning Herald*, 15 March, p. 11.
Black, A. 2008. Bread and roses. In Zane, ed., *Purple panties*. New York: Strebor Books, pp. 13–26.
Bliss, R. 2014. 10 hours of walking in NYC as a woman. [online] Available at http://www.robblisscreative.com/#/10-hours-of-walking-in-nyc-as-a-woman-1/ [accessed 28 Jan 2015].
Bo, R. 2004. *Double jeopardy*. [e-book] Akron: Ellora's Cave. Available at http://elloras cave.com [accessed 10 August 2011].
Bosman, J. 2012. Discreetly digital, erotic novel sets American women abuzz. *New York Times*. [online] 9 March. Available at http://www.nytimes.com/2012/03/10/business/media/an-erotic-novel-50-shades-of-grey-goes-viral-with-women.html?pagewanted=all&_r=0 [accessed 9 September 2013].
Boswell, J. 1989. Revolutions, universals, and sexual categories. In M. Duberman, M. Vicinus, and G. Chauncey, Jr., eds., *Hidden from history: Reclaiming the gay and lesbian past*. New York: NAL, pp. 17–36.
Brennan, T. 2004. *The transmission of affect*. Ithaca: Cornell University Press.
Briggs, R. 2003. Don't fence me in: reading beyond genre. *Senses of Cinema*, 27 (July). Available at http://sensesofcinema.com/2003/feature-articles/beyond_genre/ [accessed 20 October 2013].
Briggs, R. 2007. Culture and pedagogy: On the popular art of reviewing popular art. *Cultural Studies Review*, 13(2), pp. 115–33.
Bright, S. 1991. Introduction. In S. Bright and J. Blank, eds., *Herotica 2*. New York: Plume, pp. ix–xvii.
Bristow, J. 2011. *Sexuality*. 2d ed., Abingdon: Routledge.
Broverman, N. 2013. Patti Davis, Reagan's daughter, publishes lesbian novel. *Advocate*. [online] 23 March. Available at http://www.advocate.com/arts-entertainment/books/2013/03/23/patti-davis-reagans-daughter-publishes-lesbian-novel [accessed 22 March 2015].
Brown, D. 2003. *The Da Vinci Code*. New York: Doubleday.
Brown, W. 1995. *States of injury: Power and freedom in late modernity*. Princeton: Princeton University Press.
Brown, W. 2001. *Politics out of history*. Princeton: Princeton University Press.
Burg, B. 1983. *Sodomy and the pirate tradition*. New York: New York University Press.
But what she really wants to do is write. 1999. *Subversion Romance*. [online] Available at http://subversionromance.com/but-what-she-really-wants-to-do-is-write/#more-30 [accessed 2 August 2013].
Butler, C. 2012. Sex therapists see silver lining in wild and wildly popular novel. *Washington Post*, 22 May, p. E04.
Butler, J. 2004. *Undoing gender*. New York: Routledge.
Califia, P. 1996. Feminism and sadomasochism. In S. Jackson and S. Scott, eds., *Feminism and sexuality: A reader*. New York: Columbia University Press, pp. 230–37.

Candelaria, C. 1980. La Malinche, feminist prototype. *Frontiers: A Journal of Women Studies*, 5(2), pp. 1–6.
Caplan, P.J. 1985. *The myth of women's masochism*. Toronto: University of Toronto Press.
Carmela. 2012. Interview on Yaoi and BL fan activities in the Philippines. Interviewed by Tricia Fermin. [audio recording] Manila, 27 December.
Carter, A. 1979. *The Sadeian woman and the ideology of pornography*. London: Penguin.
Chancer, L.S. 2000. From pornography to sadomasochism: Reconciling feminist differences. *Annals of the American Academy of Political and Social Science*, 571 (September), pp. 77–88.
Chen, E. 2012. Shanghai(ed) babies: Geopolitics, biopolitics and the global chick lit. *Feminist Media Studies*, 12(2), pp. 195–213.
Chen, J. 2004. The Muzimei phenomenon and the blogs' possible expansion of female discourse (Cong muzimei xianxiang kan bokewang dui nvxing huayu kongjian de tuozhan). [online] 15 August. Available at http://club.history.sina.com.cn/thread-908293-1-1.html [accessed 2 May 2012].
Chen, R. 1998. *Private life (siren shenghuo)*. Taipei: Maitian.
Chien, E. 2005. Chinese women sex bloggers explore uncharted territories. *New American Media*. [online] 29 October. Available at http://news.newamericamedia.org/news/view_article.html?article_id=30576ff1dd2beb5da172e6a41ffe5f33 [accessed 3 April 2013].
Child, B. 2013. Fifty shades of angry. *The Guardian*, 5 September.
Chiles, N. 2006. Their eyes were reading smut. *New York Times*. [online] 4 January 2006. Available at http://www.nytimes.com/2006/01/04/opinion/04chiles.html [accessed 21 December 2009].
China Internet Network Information Center. 2013. *Statistical report on Internet development in China*. Beijing: CINIC.
Christie, O. 1996. *Dance of obsession*. London: Black Lace.
Claire, A. 2013. *Male bonding*. [Kindle version]. Akron: Ellora's Cave. Available at http://ellorascave.com [accessed 3 December 2013].
Clara. 2012. Interview on Yaoi and BL fan activities in Indonesia. Interviewed by Tricia Fermin [audio recording] Jakarta, 18 March.
Clark-Flory, T. 2012. *Before "Fifty shades of grey."* [online] Available at http://www.salon.com/2012/07/14/before_fifty_shades_of_grey/ [accessed 15 November 2013].
Cleland, J. 1985. *Memoirs of a woman of pleasure*. Oxford: Oxford University Press.
Clough, P., ed. 2007. *The affective turn: theorizing the social*. Durham: Duke University Press.
Copeland, J. 2008. Woman of the year. In Zane, ed., *Purple panties*. New York: Strebor Books, pp. 179–89.
Coppa, F. 2008. Women, Star Trek, and the early development of fannish vidding. *Transformative Works and Cultures*, 1. [online] Available at http://journal.transformativeworks.org/index.php/twc/article/view/44 [accessed 1 April 2015].
Coren, V. 2012. Finally, I get the sex in *Fifty Shades of Grey*. *The Observer*. [online] 29 July. Available at http://www.theguardian.com/commentisfree/2012/jul/29/victoria-coren-fifty-shades-of-grey [accessed 15 April 2014].
Cornell, D. 1991. Feminism always modified: The affirmation of feminine difference rethought. In *Beyond accommodation*. New York: Routledge, pp. 119–64.
Corsianos, M. 2007. Mainstream pornography and "women": Questioning sexual agency. *Critical Sociology*, 33, pp. 863–85.
Costanza, J.A. 2012. Why do modern women love romance novels? Call it the *"Fifty Shades of Grey"* syndrome. *International Business Times*. [online] 30 June. Available at http://www.ibtimes.com/why-do-modern-women-love-romance-novels-call-it-fifty-shades-grey-syndrome-720842 [accessed 29 August 2013].
Cowie, E. 1997. *Representing the woman: cinema and psychoanalysis*. Basingstoke: Macmillan.
Coy, M., Wakeling, J., and Garner, M. 2011. Selling sex sells: Representations of prostitution and the sex industry in sexualised popular culture as symbolic violence. *Women's Studies International Forum*, 34, pp. 441–48.

Crampton, R. 2012. "Twice in half an hour?" My worst fears are on these pages. *The Times*, 7 July, p. 4.
Creed, B. 1995. Lesbian bodies: tribades, tomboys and tarts. In E. Grosz and E. Probyn, eds., *Sexy bodies: The strange carnalities of feminism*. London: Routledge, pp. 86–103.
Cremen, C. 2012. Steamy resolve dissolves in a proverbial fumbling of the literary bra straps. *Sydney Morning Herald*, 23 June, p. 30.
Crystal. 2011. The best lesbian romance novels. *Jezebel*. [online] 24 June. Available at http://jezebel.com/5815289/the-top-10-lesbian-romance-novels [accessed 22 March 2015].
Cupiscent. 2004. *Caribbean cartography*. [online] Livejournal.
Cvetkovich, A. 1995. Recasting receptivity: femme sexualities. In K. Jay, ed., *Lesbian erotics*. New York: New York University Press, pp. 125–46.
Davis, E. 2007. Romance as political aesthetic in Ahdaf Soueif's *The map of love*. *Genders*, 45.
Davis, P. 2013. *Till human voices wake us*. Self-published.
Day, S. 2012. *Bared to you*. London: Penguin.
Dean, M. 2013. Ronald Reagan's daughter, Patti Davis, self-publishes lesbian book on Amazon. *GlobalNewsDesk*. [online] 22 March. Available at http://www.globalnewsdesk.co.uk/north-america/ronald-reagan-daughter-lesbian-book-amazon/03743/ [accessed 22 March 2015].
Deane, B. 2011. Imperial boyhood: Piracy and the play ethic. *Victorian Studies*, 53(4), pp. 689–714.
De Berg, J. 1956. *The image*. London: Nexus, 1992.
Deleuze, G., and Guattari, F. 1980. *A thousand plateaus: Capitalism and schizophrenia*. Translated by B. Massumi. Minneapolis: University of Minnesota Press, 1987.
Deller, R.A., Harman, S., and Jones, B. 2013. Introduction to the special issue: Reading the *Fifty Shades* "phenomenon." *Sexualities*, 16(8), pp. 859–63.
Demi. 2013. Interview on Yaoi and BL fan activities in the Philippines. Interviewed by Tricia Fermin. [audio recording] Manila, 28 March.
Dewi. 2012. Interview on Yaoi and BL fan activities in Indonesia. Interviewed by Tricia Fermin. [audio recording] Depok, 4 November.
Dinah. 2012. Interview on Yaoi and BL fan activities in Indonesia. Interviewed by Tricia Fermin. [audio recording] Jakarta, 6 November.
Dines, G. 2012. Why are women devouring *Fifty shades of Grey*? *Counter-Punch*. [online] 27 July. Available at http://www.counterpunch.org/2012/07/27/why-are-women-devouring-fifty-shades-of-grey/ [accessed 31 January 2013].
Dixon, j. 1999. *The romance fiction of Mills & Boon, 1909–1990s*. London: Philadelphia.
Dowd, M. 2012. She's fit to be tied. *New York Times*, 1 April, p. 1.
Downing, L. 2013. Safewording! Kinkphobia and gender normativity in *Fifty Shades of Grey*. *Psychology & Sexuality*, 4(1), pp. 92–102.
Duggan, L., and Hunter, N., eds. 1995. *Sex wars: Sexual dissent and political culture*. New York: Routledge.
Duncombe, S. 2002. Introduction. In S. Duncombe, ed., *Cultural resistance reader*. London: Verso, pp. 1–15.
Dworkin, A. 1981. *Pornography: Men possessing women*. London: The Women's Press.
Dworkin, A. 1987. *Intercourse*. New York: The Free Press.
Dworkin, A. 1990. *Mercy*. London: Secker & Warburg.
Dymock, A. 2013. Flogging sexual transgression: interrogating the costs of the "*Fifty Shades* effect." *Sexualities*, 16(8), pp. 880–95.
Eakin, P.J. 2008. *Living autobiographically: How we create identity in narrative*. Ithaca: Cornell University Press.
Elessil and Hippediva. 2005. *Pirate vindaloo*. [online] Livejournal.
Ellora's Cave, 2013. *About our imprints*. [online] Available at http://www.ellorascave.com/ [accessed 5 November 2013].
Ellora's Cave. 2014. *Exotica®*. [online] Available at http://www.ellorascave.com/imprints/exotika.html [accessed 10 May 2014].

Ellora's Cave. 2015. *Ellora's Cave: The world's first and foremost publisher of erotic romance.* [online] Available at http://www.ellorascave.com/about-ellora-s-cave/ [accessed 16 January 2015].

English, K. 2012. It's not the size of the book, it's the motion in the ocean: Filthy novels, rated. *Jezebel.* [online] 17 August. Available at http://jezebel.com/5935454/its-not-the-size-of-the-book-its-the-motion-in-the-ocean-filthy-novels-rated [accessed 9 September 2013]. Reproduced from English, K. 2012. The penis poll: How the best selling erotic books measure up. *Indie Reader.* Available at http://indiereader.com/2012/08/the-penis-pollhow-the-best-selling-erotic-books-measure-up/.

Evans, A., Riley, S., and Shankar, A. 2010. Technologies of sexiness: Theorizing women's engagement in the sexualization of culture. *Feminism and Psychology*, 20, pp. 114–31.

Evans, H. 1997. *Women and sexuality in China: Dominant discourses of female sexuality and gender since 1949.* Cambridge: Polity Press.

Fahs, B. 2009. Compulsory bisexuality? The challenges of modern sexual fluidity. *Journal of Bisexuality*, 9, pp. 431–49.

Farrer, J. 2007. China's women sex bloggers and dialogic sexual politics on the Chinese Internet. *China Aktueli: A Journal of Contemporary China*, 36(4), pp. 1–35.

Faust, B. 1980. *Women, sex and pornography.* London: Pelican.

Feehan, C. 2000. *Dark magic.* New York: Dorchester.

Felschow, L. 2010. "Hey, check it out, there's actually fans": (Dis)empowerment and (mis)representation of cult fandom in *Supernatural. Transformative Works and Cultures*, 4. [online] Available at http://dx.doi.org/10.3983/twc.2010.0134.

Fiedler, L. 1948. Come back to the raft ag'in, Huck honey! *Partisan Review*, pp. 664–71.

Fine, M. 1988. Sexuality, schooling, and adolescent females: The missing discourse of desire. *Harvard Education Review*, 58(1), pp. 29–53.

firesignwriter. 2003–2004. *Moonverse.* [online] Livejournal.

Flood, A. 2012a. *Fifty shades* condemned as manual for "sex torture." *The Guardian.* [online] 25 August. Available at http://www.theguardian.com/books/2012/aug/24/fifty-shades-grey-domestic-violence-campaigners [accessed 31 January 2013].

Flood, A. 2012b. *Fifty shades of Grey* thrusts erotica into the mainstream. *The Guardian.* [online] 26 April. Available at http://www.theguardian.com/books/2012/apr/25/fifty-shades-grey-erotica-mainstream [accessed 31 January 2013].

For Colored Girls. 2010. Directed by Tyler Perry. Lionsgate.

Foxon, D. 1965. *Libertine literature in England 1660–1745.* New York: University Books.

Frank, T. 1997. *The conquest of cool.* Chicago: University of Chicago Press.

Frantz, S.S.G. 2012. "How we love is our soul": Joey W. Hill's BDSM romance *Holding the Cards.* In S.S.G. Frantz and E.M. Selinger, eds., *New approaches to popular romance fiction: Critical essays.* Jefferson, NC: McFarland, pp. 47–59.

Fromm, E. 1941. *Escape from freedom.* New York: Henry Holt, 1994.

Galanes, P. 2012. Fifty shades of red. *New York Times*, 13 May, p. 8.

Galbraith, P.W. 2011. *Fujoshi:* fantasy play and transgressive intimacy among "rotten girls" in contemporary Japan. *Signs*, 37(1), pp. 211–32.

Gemmell, N. (as Anonymous). 2003. *The bride stripped bare.* London: Fourth Estate.

Gibbs, A. 2008. Panic! Affect contagion, mimesis and suggestion in the social field. *Cultural Studies Review*, 14(2), pp. 130–45.

Gibson, P.C., and Gibson, R., eds. 1994. *Dirty looks: Women, pornography, power.* London: B.F.I.

Gibson, P.C., ed. 2004. *More dirty looks: Gender, pornography and power.* London: British Film Institute.

Gill, R., and Harvey, L. 2011. Spicing it up: Sexual entrepreneurs and the sex inspectors. In R. Gill and C. Scharff, eds., *New femininities: Postfeminism, neoliberalism and subjectivity.* New York: Palgrave Macmillan, pp. 52–67.

Gill, R., and Herdieckerhoff, E. 2007. Rewriting the romance: New femininities in chick-lit. *Feminist Media Studies*, 6, pp. 487–504.

Gilligan, C. 1982. *In a different voice.* Cambridge: Harvard University Press.

Global Times. 2012. Muzimei returns. *Global Times.* [online] 16 July. Available at http://www.globaltimes.cn/content/721339.shtml [accessed 5 May 2013].
Godson, S. 2012. Midlife sex: The twenty questions you should ask. *The Times,* 11 August, pp. 4–5.
Gracen, J. 1999. Too darn hot. *Salon.* [online] Available at http://www.salon.com/1999/10/05/romance_2/ [accessed 13 August 2013].
Grant, M.G. 2014. *Playing the whore.* London: Verso.
Green, S., Jenkins, C., and Jenkins, H. 1998. "Normal female interest in men bonking": selections from the Terra Nostra Underground and Strange Bedfellows. In H. Jenkins, 2006. *Fans, bloggers, and gamers: exploring participatory culture.* New York: New York University Press. Ch.3.
Greenfield, J. 2011. *DBW profiles: Raelene Gorlinsky, publisher, Ellora's Cave Pub-lishing Inc.* [online] Available at http://www.digitalbookworld.com/2011/dbw-pro files-raelene-gorlinsky-publisher-elloras-cave-publishing-inc/ [accessed 3 November 2013].
Gregg, M., and Seigworth, G.J., eds. 2010. *The affect theory reader.* Durham: Duke University Press.
Griffin, S. 1981. *Pornography and silence: Culture's revenge against nature.* London: The Women's Press.
Grose, J. 2012. A million shades of smut: A field guide for the erotic-lit virgin. *New York Books.* [online] 8 April. Available at http://nymag.com/arts/books/features/romance-novels-2012-4/# [accessed 9 September 2013].
Groskop, V. 2012. *Fifty shades of Grey* has done wonders for book selling, but nothing for literature. *The Independent,* 5 July, p. 18.
Guillone, S. 2007. *Barely undercover.* [e-book] Akron: Ellora's Cave. Available at http://ellorascave.com [accessed 23 September 2013].
Habermas, J. 1989. *The structural transformation of the public sphere: An inquiry into a category of bourgeois society.* Translated by T. Burger. Cambridge: MIT Press.
Halberstam, J. 1998. *Female masculinity.* Durham: Duke University Press.
Hall, L. 2003. ROMStat report: Romance publishing sales statistics for 2002. *Romance Writers' Report,* pp. 17–20.
Hall, L. 1999. ROMstat 1998. *Romance Writers' Report,* pp. 19–23 (approx.).
Hall, S. 1981. Notes on deconstructing the popular. In R. Samuel, ed., *People's history and socialist theory.* London: Routledge, pp. 227–39.
Halperin, D. 1990. *One hundred years of homosexuality.* New York: Routledge.
Hanmer, R. 2013. Xenasubtexttalk. *Feminist Media Studies,* 14, pp. 608–622.
Happe, F. 2012. Discrete ebooks have unlocked a huge erotic fiction market. *Business Insider Australia.* [online] 14 October. Available at http://www.businessinsider.com.au/discrete-ebooks-have-unlocked-a-huge-erotic-fiction-market-2012-10 [accessed 29 August 2013].
Hardy, S. 2001. More Black Lace: Women, eroticism and subjecthood. *Sexualities,* 4(4), pp. 435–53.
Hardy, S. 2009. The new pornographies: representation or reality? In F. Attwood, ed., *Mainstreaming sex: The sexualization of western culture.* London: I.B. Tauris.
Hardy, T. 1891. *Tess of the d'Urbervilles; A pure woman.* Hertfordshire: Wordsworth Editions, 1992.
Harlequin Temptation. n.d. *RomanceWiki.* [online] Available at http://www.romancewiki.com/Harlequin_Temptation [accessed 29 April 2014].
Harlequin Temptation Blaze. n.d. *RomanceWiki.* [online] Available at http://www.romancewiki.com/Harlequin_Temptation_Blaze [accessed 29 April 2014].
Harrison, K., and Holm, M.-L. 2013. Exploring grey zones and blind spots in the binaries and boundaries of E.L. James' fifty shades trilogy. *Feminist Media Studies,* 13(3), pp. 558–62.
Henke, S.A. 1998. *Shattered subjects: Trauma and testimony in women's life-writing.* New York: St. Martin's Press.
Herdt, G. 1981. *Guardians of the flutes: Idioms of masculinity.* New York: Columbia University Press.

Hernandez, G. 2013. Ronald Reagan's daughter doesn't think her dad would've stood in way of gay marriage. *Gay Star News*. [online] 4 April. Available at http://www.gaystarnews.com/article/ronald-reagans-daughter-doesnt-think-her-conservative-icon-dad-wouldve-stood-way-gay-marriag [accessed 22 March 2015].

Hill, J. 2004. *Natural law*. Hudson, OH: Ellora's Cave.

Hill, M.L., Pérez, B., and Irby, D.J. 2008. Street fiction: What is it and what does it mean for English teachers? *English Journal*, 97(3), pp. 76–81.

Hilton, P. 2013. Ronald Reagan's daughter wrote the NEW 50 shades of grey??? www.Perezhilton.com. [online] 24 March. Available at http://perezhilton.com/perezitos/2013-03-24-ronald-reagans-daughter-patti-davis-writes-a-lesbian-novel-till-human-voices-wake-us/ [accessed 22 March 2015].

Hirschfield, P. 2008. Preparing for prison? The criminalization of school discipline in the USA. *Theoretical Criminology*, 12(1), pp. 79–101.

Hollander, X. 1971. *The happy hooker: My own story*. Translated by R. Moore and Y. Dunleavy. London: Sphere Books.

Hori, A. 2013. On the response (or lack thereof) of Japanese fans to criticism that *yaoi* is antigay discrimination. *Transformative Works and Cultures*, 12. [online] Available at http://journal.transformativeworks.org/index.php/twc/article/view/463/388 [accessed 2 May 2013].

Hunting, K. 2012. Queer as folk and the trouble with slash. *Transformative Works and Cultures*, 11. [online] Available at http://journal.transformativeworks.org/index.php/twc/article/view/415/315 [accessed 1 April 2015].

Indah. 2012. Interview on Yaoi and BL fan activities in Indonesia. Interviewed by Tricia Fermin. [audio recording] Jakarta, 3 November.

Irene. 2009. Interview on Yaoi and BL fan activities in the Philippines. Interviewed by Tricia Fermin. [audio recording] Manila, 16 March.

Ishida, H. 2007. "Hottoite kudasai" to iu hyōmei wo megutte: yaoi / BL no jiritsusei to hyōshō no ōdatsu [About the expression "leave us alone": the misappropriation of yaoi / BL autonomy and symbols]. *Eureka*, 36(16), pp. 114–223.

Jacobs, K. 2012. *People's pornography: Sex and surveillance on the Chinese Internet*. Chicago: Intellect.

Jagose, A. 2013. *Orgasmology*. Durham: Duke University Press.

James, E L 2011. *Fifty shades of Grey*. New South Wales: The Writer's Coffee Shop Publishing House.

James, E L 2012a. *Fifty shades of Grey*. London: Arrow Books.

James, E L 2012b. *Fifty shades darker*. London: Arrow Books.

James, E L 2012c. *Fifty shades freed*. London: Arrow Books.

James, E L 2013. *E L James—provocative romance*. [online] Available at www.eljamesauthor.com [accessed 31 December 2013].

Jenkins, H. 1992. *Textual poachers: Television and participatory culture*. New York: Routledge.

Jenkins, H. 2006. *Convergence culture*. New York: New York University Press.

Jewel, C. 2013. Post RWA post—the state of publishing. *Writer's Diary*. [online] Available at http://carolynjewel.com/wordpress/2013/07/22/post-rwa-post-the-state-of-publishing/ [accessed 5 August 2013].

Johnson, S. 1995. *Brazen*. New York: Bantam.

Johnson, S. 2013. Phone interview with Susan Johnson. Interviewed by Katherine Morrissey. [telephone] Milwaukee, WI. 13 August.

Johnson, S., Devine, T., and Schone, R. 1999. *Captivated*. New York: Kensington.

Jones, A. 2010. Zane interview with April Jones. *The April Jones Show*. [online] Available at http://www.youtube.com/watch?v=MZsSu-NOnW0 [accessed 2 February 2015].

Jones, S. 2002. The sex lives of cult television characters. *Screen*, 43(1), pp. 79–90.

de Jour, B. 2005. *The intimate adventures of a London call girl*. London: Phoenix.

Juffer, J. 1998. *At home with pornography: Women, sexuality, and everyday life*. New York: New York University Press.

Juno, A., and Vale, V., eds., 1991. *Angry women*. San Francisco: Re/Search.

Kane, S. 2006. *The courage to love.* [Kindle version] Akron: Ellora's Cave. Available at http://ellorascave.com [accessed 11 November 2013].
Kane, S. 2007. *At love's command.* [e-book] Akron: Ellora's Cave. Available at http://ellorascave.com [accessed 20 July 2011].
Kappler, S. 1986. *The pornography of representation.* Cambridge: Polity.
Kaufman, R. 2002. Aura, still. *October,* 99, Winter, pp. 45–80.
Kelly, S. 2012. Fifty shades nod to Tess is a mark of guilt. *The Guardian.* [online] 25 July. Available at http://www.theguardian.com/books/booksblog/2012/jul/24/fifty-shades-grey-tess-guilt [accessed 31 January 2013].
Kendrick, W. 1987. *The secret museum: Pornography in modern culture.* Berkeley: University of California Press.
Kersten, S. 2008. *Past lies.* [Kindle version] Akron: Ellora's Cave. Available at http://ellorascave.com [accessed 20 August 2013].
Kim, C.Y., Losen, D.J., and Hewitt, D.T. 2010. *The school-to-prison pipeline: Structuring legal reform.* New York: New York University Press.
Klein, N. 2000. *No logo: Taking aim at the brand bullies.* Toronto: Knopf.
Ko, D. 2005. *Cinderella's sisters: A revisionist history of footbinding.* Berkeley: University of California Press.
Krupka, Z. 2012. Sir Lancelot meets Mr Sheen. *New Matilda.* [online] 31 July. Available at https://newmatilda.com/2012/07/31/sir-lancelot-meets-mr-sheen [accessed 31 January 2013].
Lamb, P., and Veith, D. 1986. Romantic myth, transcendence, and Star trek zines. In D. Palumbo, ed., *Erotic universe.* Westport, CT: Greenwood Press, pp. 236–55.
Lannutti, P., and Denes, A. 2012. A kiss is just a kiss? Comparing perceptions related to female–female and female–male kissing in a college social situation. *Journal of Bisexuality,* 12, pp. 49–62.
Laqueur, T. 1992. *Making Sex: The body and gender from the Greeks to Freud.* Cambridge: Harvard University Press.
Lauren, J. 2010. *Some girls: My life in a harem.* New York: Plume.
Lea. 2012. Interview on Yaoi and BL fan activities in the Philippines. Interviewed by Tricia Fermin. [audio recording] Manila, 28 December.
Lee, A. 2006. *Girl with a one track mind.* London: Random House.
Lee, G.R. 1957. *Gypsy: A memoir.* New York: Harper & Bros.
Legge, J. 2013. Belle de Jour author sued by ex-boyfriend. *The Independent.* [online] 12 August. Available at http://www.independent.co.uk/arts-entertainment/books/news/belle-de-jour-author-sued-by-exboyfriend-8757584.html [accessed 1 September 2014].
Leibold, J. 2011. Blogging alone: China, the Internet, and the democratic illusion? *The Journal of Asian Studies,* 70(4), pp. 1023–41.
Leigh, M. 1997. *Career girls.* October Films.
Leo, J. 2005. Behavior: Battling over masochism. *Time.* [online] 21 June. Available at http://content.time.com/time/magazine/article/0,9171,1074806,00.html [accessed 15 April 2014].
Levy, A. 2005. *Female chauvinist pigs: Women and the rise of raunch culture.* London: Pocket Books.
Lewis, L., ed. 1992. *The adoring audience.* London: Routledge.
Li, Z. 2003. Why we cannot be over tolerant about the Muzimei phenonmen (Weishemo buneng dui Muzimei guodu kuanrong). *New Express* (*Xin kuai bao*). [online] 17 October. Available at http://news.sina.com.cn/cl/2003-11-17/20012153321.shtml [accessed 4 November 2013].
Linde, C. 1993. *Life stories: The creation of coherence.* New York: Oxford University Press.
Lorde, A. 1984. Uses of the erotic: The erotic as power. In *Sister Outsider.* Freedom, CA: Crossing Press.
Lothian, A., Busse, K., and Reid, R.A. 2007. "Yearning void and infinite potential": Online slash fandom as queer female space. *English Language Notes,* 45(2) Fall/Winter, pp. 103–111.
Lulgjuraj, S. 2013. *Ellora's Cave, a digital publishing pioneer, still going strong in erotic*

romance. [online] Available at http://www.teleread.com/publishing/elloras-cave-a-digital-publishing-pioneer-still-going-strong-in-erotic-romance/ [accessed 3 November 2013].

Lunsing, W. 2006. Yaoi ronsō: Discussing depictions of male homosexuality in Japanese girls' comics, gay comics and gay pornography. *Intersections: Gender, history and culture in the Asian context*, 12. [online] Available at http://intersections.anu.edu.au/issue12/lunsing.html [accessed 2 July 2008].

The Lustful Turk (1828). Hertfordshire: Wordsworth, 1997.

Lynne, C. 2008. *Necklace of shame*. [Kindle version] Akron: Ellora's Cave. Available at http://ellorascave.com [accessed 15 October 2013].

Mackie, E. 2005. Welcome the outlaw: Pirates, maroons, and Caribbean countercultures. *Cultural Critique*, 59, pp. 24–62.

MacKinnon, C.A. 1989. Sexuality, pornography, and method: "Pleasure under patriarchy." *Ethics*, 99(2), pp. 314–46.

MacKinnon, R. 2008. Flatter world and thicker walls? *Public Choice*, 134(1–2), pp. 31–46.

Magnanti, B. 2013. BREAKING NEWS: I was a sex worker. *Belle de Jour*. [online] 11 August. Available at http://belledejour-uk.blogspot.co.uk/2013_08_01_archive.html [accessed 12 February 2015].

Mantell, S. 1996. Love on the rocks? *Publishers Weekly*, 243, p. 40.

Mantell, S. 2002. Reinventing the wheel? *Publishers Weekly*, 249, p. 38.

Marrin, M. 2013. Beyond the swish of Grey's cane is the soothing sound of male defeat. *The Sunday Times*, 6 January, p. 22.

Marshall, G. 1990. *Pretty woman*. Silver Screen Partners IV.

Martin, N.K. 2007. *Sexy thrills: Undressing the erotic thriller*. Urbana: University of Illinois Press.

Mason, G., and Lo, G. 2009. Sexual tourism and the excitement of the strange: Heterosexuality and the Sydney Mardi Gras parade. *Sexualities*, 12, pp. 97–121.

Massumi, B. 1987. Translator's foreword: Pleasures of philosophy and notes on the translation and acknowledgements. In G. Deleuze and F. Guattari, *A thousand plateaus: Capitalism and schizophrenia*. Minneapolis: University of Minnesota Press, pp.ix-xix.

McAlister, J. 2013. Breaking the hard limits: Romance, pornography and genre in the *Fifty Shades* trilogy. Unpublished paper. Available at https://www.inter-disciplinary.net/critical-issues/wp-content/uploads/2013/07/mcalistereropaper.pdf [accessed 28 March 2015].

McClintock, A. 1995. *Imperial leather*. New York: Routledge.

McLelland, M. 2000. No climax, no point, no meaning? Japanese women's boy love sites on the Internet. *Journal of Communication Inquiry*, 24(3), pp. 274–91.

McLelland, M., 2003. Japanese queerscapes: Global/local intersections on the Internet. In C. Berry, F. Martin and A. Yue, eds., *Mobile cultures: new media in queer Asia*. Durham: Duke University Press, pp. 52–69.

McLennan, N. 2008. *The price: My rise and fall as Natalia, New York's #1 escort*. Beverly Hills: Phoenix Books.

McNair, B. 1996. *Mediated sex: Pornography and postmodern culture*. London: Arnold.

McNair, B. 2002. *Striptease culture: Sex, media and the democratization of desire*. London: Routledge.

McNair, B. 2013. *Porno? Chic!* Hoboken: Taylor and Francis.

McRobbie, A. 2004. Post-feminism and popular culture. *Feminist Media Studies*, 4(3), pp. 255–64.

McRobbie, A. 2009. *The aftermath of feminism: Gender, culture and social change*. Los Angeles: Sage.

Melissa P. 2004. *One hundred strokes of the brush before bed*. London: Serpent's Tail.

Michaels, M. 1991. Taking him on a Sunday afternoon. In S. Bright and J. Blank, eds., *Herotica 2*. New York: Plume, pp. 18–19.

Millet, C. 2002. *The sexual life of Catherine M.* London: Serpent's Tail.

Miranda. 2012. Interview on Yaoi and BL fan activities in the Philippines. Interviewed by Tricia Fermin. [audio recording] Manila, 13 December.

Mitch. 2011. Interview on Yaoi and BL fan activities in the Philippines. Interviewed by Tricia Fermin. [audio recording] Manila, 17 August.

Modleski, T. 2008. *Loving with a vengeance: Mass-produced fantasies for women.* New York: Routledge.

Monaco, R. 2013. Patti Davis says lesbian love story is not an autobiography: "This is not me." *Examiner.* [online] 22 March. Available at http://www.examiner.com/article/patti-davis-says-lesbian-love-story-is-not-an-autobiography-this-is-not-me [accessed 22 March 2015].

Moon, K. 2010. *Beyond Eden.* [Kindle version] Akron: Ellora's Cave. Available at http://ellorascave.com [accessed 15 October 2013].

Moore, R. 2008. My side of things. In Zane, ed., *Purple panties.* New York: Strebor Books, pp. 27–38.

Moore, S. 2012. What's dangerous about *Fifty shades of Grey* isn't the kinky sex but the tired old fantasy of romance that keeps women in their place. *The Guardian*, 5 July, p. 5.

Morrison, T. 1970. *The bluest eye.* New York: Plume, 1994.

Morton, T. 2007. *Ecology without nature: Rethinking environmental aesthetics.* Cambridge: Harvard University Press.

Morton, T. 2010. Ecology as text, text as ecology. *The Oxford Literary Review*, 32(1), pp. 1–17.

Mowery, L. 1999. Captivated by Bertrice Small, Susan Johnson, Thea Devine & Robin Schone. *The romance reader.* [online] Available at http://www.theromancereader.com/small-captivated.html [accessed 14 August 2013].

Mulvey, L. 1989. *Visual and other pleasures.* London: Macmillan.

Murongliansheng. 2013. "I am not as promiscuous as they thought" ("wo mei tamen xiang de namo luan"). [online blog] Available at http://murongliansheng.blog.163.com/blog/static/167871345201327039138191/ [accessed 5 May 2013].

Mussell, K. 1984. *Fantasy and reconciliation: Contemporary formulas of women's romance fiction.* Westport: Greenwood Press.

Muzimei. 2003. Muzimei diaries: Left-over love letters (Muzimei riji: yiqingshu). [online] Available at http://tieba.baidu.com/p/820096047 [accessed 5 January 2014].

Muzimei. 2005. *Left-over love letters (yiqingshu).* Taipei: Dongwenlintang.

Nayar, S.J. 2011. A good man is impossible to find: *Brokeback Mountain* as heteronormative tragedy. *Sexualities*, 14, pp. 235–55.

Newton, E. 1984. The mythic mannish lesbian: Radclyffe Hall and the New Woman. *Signs*, 9, pp. 557–75.

Niccolini, A. 2013. Straight talk and thick desire with *erotica noir*: Reworking the textures of sex education in and out of the classroom. In M.L. Rasmussen and D. Carlson, eds., *Sex Education: Sexuality, Society and Learning*, 13(1), pp. S7-S19.

Niccolini, A. 2014. Spicing up the curriculum: The uses and pleasures of *erotica noir* in the urban classroom. In D. Carlson and E. Meyer, eds., *Gender and sexuality in education: a reader.* New York: Peter Lang, pp. 159–74.

Nick, P. 2012. Guilty pleasure of prosaic porn. *The Sunday Times*, 24 June, p. 5.

Nilson, M. 2013. From *The Flame and the Flower* to *Fifty Shades of Grey. Akademisk Kvarter*, 7, Fall, pp. 119–31.

Nin, A. 1978. *Delta of Venus.* London: Nexus.

Nolan, K. 2011. *Police in the hallways: Discipline in an urban high school.* Minneapolis: University of Minnesota Press.

Now News. 2011. Muzimei shows off her thighs and resurfaces to talk about sex (Muzimei luolu datui chongchu jianghu, tanchuang tanxing). *Now News.* [online] 1 March. Available at http://www.nownews.com/2011/03/01/11490-2692683.htm [accessed 2 June 2013].

O'Connor, A. 2012. I'll take a spanking good read over online porn any day. *The Sunday Times*, 8 July, p. 11.

O'Hagan, A. 2012. Travelling southwards. *London Review of Books*, 34(19), 19 July, p. 29.

Ortner, S. 1972. Is female to male as nature is to culture? *Feminist Studies*, 1(2), pp. 5–31.

Ortner, S. 1996. So, is female to male as nature is to culture? In *Making Gender*. Boston: Beacon Press, pp. 173–80.
Overall, C. 1998. Monogamy, nonmonogamy, and identity. *Hypatia*, 13(4), pp. 1–17.
Paasonen, S., Nikunen, K., and Saarenmaa, L., eds., 2007. *Pornification: Sex and sexuality in media culture*. Oxford: Berg.
Pack, T. 1997. All about books—online. *Database*, 20(1), pp. 12–21.
Pagliassotti, D. 2008. Reading Boys' Love in the west. *Particip@tions*, 5(2). [online] Available at http://www.participations.org/Volume%205/Issue%202/5_02_pagliassotti.htm [accessed 28 May 2012].
Patrick, B.K. 2006. It's not just you—it really is hot in here. *Publishers Weekly*. [online] 24 July 2006. Available at http://www.publishersweekly.com/article/CA6355135.html [accessed 12 March 2008].
Paul, P. 2005. *Pornified: How pornography is damaging our lives, our relationships, and our families*. New York: Times Books.
The Pearl (1879–80). New York: The Grove Press, 1968.
Penley, C. 1991. Brownian motion: Women, tactics, and technology. In *Technoculture*. Minneapolis: University of Minnesota Press, pp. 135–61.
Penley, C., Shimizu, C., Miller-Young, M., and Taormino, T. 2013. The politics of producing pleasure. Introduction. In T. Taormino et al., eds., *The feminist porn book: The politics of producing pleasure*. New York: The Feminist Press, pp. 9–20.
People.com. n.d. Interpreting the Muzimei phenomenon (Jiedu Muzimei xianxiang). [online] Available at http://www1.people.com.cn/BIG5/paper81/11029/999184.html [accessed 12 November 2012].
Peterson, R.A. 1978. The production of cultural change: The case of contemporary country music. *Social Research*, 45, pp. 292–314.
Petri, A. 2012. Fifty shades of what? E-readers and the end of shame. *The Washington Post*. [online] 12 April. Available at http://www.washingtonpost.com/blogs/compost/post/fifty-shades-of-what-e-readers-and-the-end-of-shame/2012/04/12/gIQACSCbDT_blog.html [accessed 31 January 2013].
Petridis, A. 2012. Men, the book you've all been waiting for: Fifty shades of Andre. *The Guardian*, 12 July, p. 3.
Poladian, C. 2013. Reagan's daughter, Patti Davis, pens lesbian love story novel, "Till human voices wake us." *International Business Times*. [online] 22 March. Available at http://www.ibtimes.com/reagans-daughter-patti-davis-pens-lesbian-love-story-novel-till-human-voices-wake-us-1145199 [accessed 22 March 2015].
Pomfret, J. 2003. A new gloss on freedom: Sexual revolution sweeps China's urban youth. *Washington Post*. [online] 12 June. Available at http://www.highbeam.com/doc/1P2-305068.html [accessed 2 May 2012].
Powell, J. 2013. Till human voices wake us. *People Magazine*, 24 June. Reproduced at http://booksbypattidavis.com/people-magazine-review/#more-279 [accessed 22 March 2015].
Pratt, M. 1993. "Yo soy La Malinche": Chicana writers and the poetics of ethnonationalism. *Callaloo*, 16(4), pp. 859–73.
Pullen, C. 2010. "Love the coat": Bisexuality, the female gaze and the romance of sexual politics. In A. Ireland, D.E. Palumbo, and C.W. Sullivan, eds., *Illuminating Torchwood: Essays on narrative, character and sexuality in the BBC Series*. Jefferson, NC: McFarland, pp. 135–52.
Quan, T. 2001. *Diary of a Manhattan call girl*. New York: Three Rivers Press.
Queen, C. 1994. Sweating profusely in Mérida: A memoir. In S. Bright, ed., *Herotica 3*. New York: Plume, pp. 190–95.
Radford, J. 1986. *The progress of romance: The politics of popular fiction*. London: Routledge and Kegan Paul.
Radway, J. 1984. *Reading the romance: Women, patriarchy, and popular literature*. London: Verso.
Radway, J. 1986. Reading is not eating: Mass-produced literature and the theoretical, methodological, and political consequences of a metaphor. *Book Research Quarterly*, 2(3), pp. 7–29.

Ramsdell, K. 2001. Sexy, steamy reads. *Library Journal*, 126, p. 153.
Ray, A. 2007. *Naked on the Internet: Hookups, downloads and cashing in on Internet sexploration*. Emeryville: Seal Press.
Read, J. 2009. A genealogy of homo-economicus: Neoliberalism and the production of subjectivity. *Foucault Studies*, 6, pp. 25–36.
Réage, P. 1954. *Story of O*. London: Corgi Press, 1972.
Red Sage moves to ebook publishing. n.d. *Dear author*. [online] Available at http://dear author.com/ebooks/red-sage-moves-to-ebook-publishing/ [accessed 15 August 2013].
The Red Shoe Diaries. 1992. [TV program] Showtime. 1992–1999.
Regis, P. 2007. *A natural history of the romance novel*. Philadelphia: University of Pennsylvania Press.
Richardson, S. 1740. *Pamela; Or, virtue rewarded*. London: Penguin Books, 1980.
Robbins, S.J. 2008. The new E- in erotica: Digital delivery helps boost the readership and sales. *Publishers Weekly*. [online] Available at http://www.publishersweekly.com/pw/print/20080623/9437-the-new-e-in-erotica.html [accessed 13 July 2013].
Robbins, S.J. 2010. Erotica fanning the flames. *Publishers Weekly*. [online] Available at http://www.publishersweekly.com/pw/by-topic/new-titles/adult-announcements/article/44013-erotica-fanning-the-flames.html [accessed 14 June 2013].
Robin Schone: A writer rants about sexuality. n.d. *All about romance novels*. [online] Available at http://www.likesbooks.com/wb16.html [accessed 9 December 2013].
Rofel, L. 2007. *Desiring China: Experiments in neoliberalism, sexuality and public culture*. Durham: Duke University Press.
Roiphe, K. 2012. Working women's fantasies. *Newsweek*. [online] 16 April. Available at http://www.newsweek.com/working-womens-fantasies-63915 [accessed 15 April 2014].
Romance Writers of America. 2007. ROMStat Report 2006. *Romance Writers Report*, pp. 34–36.
Rose, J. 1998. *States of fantasy*. London: Clarendon Press.
Rosen, J. 1999. Love is all around you. *Publishers Weekly*, 246, p. 37.
Rosen, J. 2000. And the sales keep climbing. *Publishers Weekly*, 247, p. 42.
Rosman, K. 2012. Books women read when no one can see the cover. *Wall Street Journal*. [online] 14 March. Available at http://online.wsj.com/news/articles/SB10001424052702304450004577279622389208292 [accessed 8 May 2014].
Ross, M.B. 2013. "What's love but a second hand emotion?" Man-on-man passion in the contemporary black gay romance novel. *Callaloo*, 36(3), pp. 669–87.
Rubin, G. 1975. The traffic in women: notes on the "political economy" of sex. In R.R. Reiter, ed., *Toward an anthropology of women*. New York: Monthly Review Press, pp. 157–210.
Rubin, G. 1984. Thinking sex: Notes for a radical theory of the politics of sexuality. In H. Abelove, M.A. Barale, and D. Halperin, eds., *The lesbian and gay studies reader*. New York: Routledge, 1993, pp. 3–44.
Russ, J. 1985. Pornography by women for women, with love. In *Magic mommas, trembling sisters, puritans and perverts*. New York: Crossing Press.
Sachs, A. 2012. "Queen of Erotica" Zane on how *Fifty Shades* affects the sexy book scene. *Time*. [online] Available at http://entertainment.time.com/2012/08/01/queen-of-erotica-zane-on-how-fifty-shades-affects-the-sexy-book-scene/ [accessed 2 February 2015].
Sade, Marquis de. 2012. *Justine, or the misfortunes of virtue*. Oxford: Oxford University Press.
Sanders, T. 2004. Controllable laughter: Managing sex work through humour. *Sociology*, 38(2), pp. 273–91.
Sandlin, J., O'Malley, M.P., and Burdick, J. 2011. Mapping the complexity of public pedagogy scholarship: 1894–2010. *Review of Educational Research*, 81, pp. 338–75.
Saner, E., Hedley, S., Matthews, R., Daubney, M., Kelly, L., Mitchell, C., and Pelling, R. 2007. Politics: Wrong call. *The Guardian*. [online] 20 September. Available at http://www.theguardian.com/politics/2007/sep/20/ukcrime.immigrationpolicy [accessed 1 February 2015].

Schulhafer, J. 1994. Wooing the buyers. *Publishers Weekly*, 241, p. 29.
Scodari, C. 2003. Resistance re-examined: Gender, fan practices, and science fiction television. *Popular Communication*, 1(2), pp. 111–30.
Scott, J. 1990. *Domination and the arts of resistance: Hidden transcripts.* New Haven: Yale University Press.
Sedgwick, E. 1985. *Between men.* New York: Columbia University Press.
Segal, L., and McIntosh, M., eds. 1992. *Sex exposed: Sexuality and the pornography debate.* London: Virago Press.
Selinger, E.M., and Frantz, S.S.G. 2012. Introduction: New approaches to popular romance fiction. In S.S.G. Frantz and E.M. Selinger, eds., *New approaches to popular romance fiction: Critical essays.* Jefferson, NC: McFarland, pp. 1–19.
Shainess, N. 1984. *Sweet suffering: Woman as victim.* Bobbs-Merrill.
Shalit, W., ed. 2006. *Becoming myself: Reflections on growing up female.* New York: Hyperion.
Shange, N. 1997. *for colored girls who have committed suicide/when the rainbow is enuf.* New York: Scribner.
Shao, Y. 2005. *Study on the phenomenon of "beautiful women literature"—from '70s and after to '80s and after ("Meinu wenxue" xianxiang yanjiu—cong '70hou dao '80hou).* Guilin: Guangxi Normal College Press.
Sharp, K., ed. 1999. *The Black Lace book of women's sexual fantasies.* London: Black Lace.
Sigel, L.Z. 2002. *Governing pleasures: Pornography and social change in England, 1815–1914.* London: Rutgers University Press.
Simmonds, A. 2012. 50 shades of WRONG. *Daily Life.* [online] March 16. Available at http://www.dailylife.com.au/news-and-views/dl-opinion/50-shades-of-wrong-20120316-1v8z7.html [accessed 31 January 2013].
Sina News. 2005. Muzimei: Sister Furong is more daring than me (Muzimei: haishi Furong jiejie shengfeng). *Sina News.* [online] 6 July. Available at http://news.sina.com.cn/c/2005-07-06/12317148272.shtml [accessed 1 May 2013].
Sinclair, C. 2009. *Master of the mountain.* San Francisco: Loose Id, LLC.
Sinclair, C. 2011. *Masters of the Shadowlands 5: Make me, sir.* San Francisco: Loose Id LLC.
Singbao. 2013. "I am still exploring the road of sex" ("Wo haizai xingai de lushang"). *Singbao.* [online] 28 July. Available at http://www.singpao.com/xw/ht/201307/t20130728_448882.html [accessed 23 October 2013].
Smith, C. 2007. *One for the girls! The pleasures and practices of reading women's porn.* Bristol, UK: Intellect Books.
Smith, C. 2009. Pleasing intensities: Masochism and affective pleasures in porn short fictions. In F. Attwood, ed., *Mainstreaming sex: The sexualization of western culture.* London: I.B. Taurus, pp. 17–35.
Smith, C.G. 2000. Sex, lust, drugs: Her novel's too much for China. *New York Times*, 11 May, p. A4.
Smith, D. 2006. Black talk and hot sex: Why "street lit" is literature. In J. Chang, ed., *Total chaos: The art and aesthetics of hip-hop.* New York: Basic Civitas, pp. 188–97.
Smith, S., and Watson, J. 2001. *Reading autobiography: A guide for interpreting life narratives.* Minneapolis: University of Minnesota Press.
Snitow, A.B. 1979. Mass market romance: Pornography for women is different. *Radical History Review*, 20, pp. 141–61.
Sonnet, E. 1999. "Erotic fiction by women for women": The pleasures of post-feminist heterosexuality. *Sexualities*, 2(2), pp. 167–87.
Sontag, S. 1967. The pornographic imagination. In *Styles of radical will.* New York: Farrar, Straus and Giroux.
Stanley, M. 2008. 101 Uses for boys: Communing with the reader in Yaoi and Slash. In A. Levi, M. McHarry, and D. Pagliassotti, eds., *Boys' Love manga: Essays on the sexual ambiguity and cross-cultural fandom of the genre.* Jefferson, NC: McFarland, pp. 99–109.

Star, D. 1998–2004. *Sex and the city*. Darren Star Productions; HBO Original Programming; Warner Bros. Television.
Stoddart, J. 2000. She's gotta have it. *The Observer Magazine*, 10 September.
Stoker, B. 1897. *Dracula*. London: Penguin Classics, 2011.
Stoler, A. 2002. *Carnal knowledge and imperial power*. Berkeley: University of California Press.
Stowaway, 2003–2006. *Sparrington arc*. [online] Livejournal.
Sturrock, J. 1977. The new model autobiographer. *New Literary History*, 9(1), pp. 51–63.
Tan, W. 2000. *Shanghai Baby* confiscated in Spring Book Festival (Chunji shushi zhankou Shanghai Baobei). *Beijing Youth Daily*, 4 May, p. 1.
Tarn. 2004. *Things nautical*. [online] Livejournal.
Tavel, C. 1991. Claudia's cheeks. In S. Bright and J. Blank, eds., *Herotica 2*. New York: Plume, pp. 171–81.
Tavel, C. 1994. About penetration. In S. Bright, ed., *Herotica 3*. New York: Plume, pp. 56–69.
Teo, H.-M. 2012. *Desert passions: Orientalism and romance novels*. Austin: University of Texas Press.
Theresia. 2012. Interview on Yaoi and BL fan activities in Indonesia. Interviewed by Tricia Fermin. [audio recording] Jakarta, 2 November.
Thorn, M. 2004. Girls and women getting out of hand: The pleasure and politics of Japan's amateur comics community. In W.W. Kelley, ed., *Fanning the flames: Fan and consumer culture in contemporary Japan*. Albany: State University of New York Press, pp. 169–87.
Thurston, C. 1987. *The romance revolution: Erotic novels for women and the quest for a new sexual identity*. Urbana: University of Illinois Press.
Topham, L. 2013. Belle de Jour was my lover ... and I don't believe she was a prostitute: Boyfriend of seven years claims author invented her notorious best-selling sexploits. *Daily Mail*. [online] 10 August. Available at http://www.dailymail.co.uk/news/article-2388986/Belle-Jour-lover-I-dont-believe-prostitute-Boyfriend-seven-years-claims-author-invented-notorious-best-selling-sexploits.html [accessed 12 February 2015].
Tsaros, A. 2013. Consensual non-consent: Comparing E.L. James's *Fifty Shades of Grey* and Pauline Réage's *Story of O*. *Sexualities*, 16(8), pp. 864–79.
Ueno, C. 2009. Sakai-shi shiritsu toshokan, BL hon: Haijō sōdō tenmatsu [An account of the public outrage and call for the exclusion of BL books from the Sakai city public library's collection]. *Tsukuru*, 15(5), pp. 106–113.
van Dijck, J. 2009. Users like you? Theorizing agency in user-generated content. *Media, Culture and Society*, 31(1), pp. 41–58.
van Gulik, R.H. 1974. *Sexual life in ancient China: A preliminary survey of Chinese sex and society from ca. 1500 B.C. till 1644 A.D.* Leiden: Brill.
Van Orman, K., and Lyiscott, J. 2013. Politely disregarded: Street fiction, mass incarceration, and critical praxis. *English Journal*, 102(4), pp. 59–66.
Veldman-Genz, C. 2012. The more the merrier? Transformations of the love triangle across the romance. In S.S.G. Frantz and E. Selinger, eds., *New approaches to popular romance fiction*. Jefferson, NC: McFarland, ch.8.
Verbinski, G. 2003. DVD Commentary: *Pirates of the Caribbean: The curse of the Black Pearl*. Walt Disney Studios Home Entertainment.
le Verdier, Z. 1999. A dangerous addiction. In K. Sharp, ed., *The best of Black Lace*. London: Black Lace.
Vicinus, M. 1992. "They wonder to which sex I belong": The historical roots of the modern lesbian identity. *Feminist Studies*, 18, pp. 467–97.
Vincent, K. 2007. A Japanese electra and her queer progeny. *Mechademia*, 2, pp. 64–79.
Vivanco, L., and Kramer, K. 2010. There are six bodies in this relationship: An anthropological approach to the romance genre. *Journal of Popular Romance Studies*, 1(1). [online] Available at http://jprstudies.org/2010/08/there-are-six-bodies-in-this-relationship-an-anthropological-approach-to-the-romance-genre-by-laura-vivanco-and-kyra-kramer/ [accessed 25 November 2013].

Wald, J., and Losen, D. 2003. *Deconstructing the school-to-prison pipeline: New directions for youth development.* San Francisco: Wiley Periodicals.
Ward, S. 2009. Hoodlum and interactive television. *Communication, Politics, and Culture,* 42(2), pp. 136–58.
Wardrop, S. 1995. The heroine is being beaten: Freud, sadomasochism, and reading the romance. *Style,* 29(3), pp. 459–512.
Warner, M. 2005. *Publics and counterpublics.* New York: Zone Books.
Washington Post. 2012. Fifty shades of popular demand. *Washington Post,* 11 June, p. A12.
Waters, M. 2007. Sexing it up? Women, pornography and third wave feminism. In S. Gillis, G. Howie, and R. Munford, eds., *Third wave feminism: A critical exploration.* 2d ed. Basingstoke: Palgrave MacMillan, pp. 250–65.
Waugh, T. 1995. Men's pornography: Gay vs. straight. In C.K. Creekmur and A. Doty, eds., *Gay, lesbian and queer: Essays on popular culture.* Durham: Duke University Press, pp. 307–327.
Weeks, L. 2004. New books in the hood: Street lit makes inroads with readers and publishers. *Washington Post,* 31 July, p. C01.
Weihui. 2000. *Shanghai baby (Shanghai baobei).* Taipei: Shengzhi.
Weiss, M.D. 2012. BDSM and feminism: Notes on an impasse. *Tenured Radical.* [online] 23 May. Available at http://chronicle.com/blognetwork/tenuredradical/2012/05/bdsm-and-feminism-notes-on-an-impasse/ [accessed 29 August 2014].
Weiss, M.D. 2006. Mainstreaming kink. *Journal of Homosexuality,* 50(2–3), pp. 103–32.
Wendell, S., and Tan, C. 2009. *Beyond heaving bosoms: The smart bitches' guide to romance novels.* New York: Simon & Schuster.
Williams, L. 1999. *Hardcore: Power, pleasure and the frenzy of the visible.* Berkley: University of California Press.
Williams, R. 1977. *Marxism and literature.* Oxford: Oxford University Press.
Williams, Z. 2012. The reason I won't be buying fifty shades loungewear. *The Guardian,* 16 August, p. 32.
Wolfe, T. 1987. *The bonfire of the vanities.* London: Cape.
Women: Stories of passion. 1996–1999. [TV program] Showtime. 1996–1999.
Wood, A. 2006. "Straight" women, queer texts: Boy-Love manga and the rise of a global counterpublic. *Women's Studies Quarterly,* 34(112), pp. 394–414.
Woolf, V. 2012. *Mrs. Dalloway.* London: Urban Romantics.
Writing guidelines: Harlequin Blaze. 2012. *Harlequin.* [online] Available at http://web.archive.org/web/20120813095246/http://www.harlequin.com/articlepage.html?articleId=544&chapter=0 [accessed 28 December 2014].
Yang, X. 2011. *From beauty fear to beauty fever: Critical study of contemporary Chinese female writers.* New York: Peter Lang.
Yost, M., and McCarthy, L. 2012. Girls gone wild? Heterosexual women's same-sex encounters at college parties. *Psychology of Women Quarterly,* 36, pp. 7–24.
Yu, Z. 2002. From Tie Ning, Chen Ran to Weihui—A study of female consciousness in contemporary literature (Cong Tie Ning, Chen Ran dao Weihui—jian tan dangdai xiaoshuo nvxing yishi). Culture.eNorth.com.cn (Beifang Wang). [online] Available at http://culture.enorth.com.cn/system/2002/06/21/000356711.shtml [accessed 20 January 2015].
Zane. 2002. *Gettin' buck wild: Sex chronicles II.* New York: Atria Books.
Zane. 2003. *The sisters of APF: The indoctrination of soror ride dick.* New York: Atria Books.
Zane. 2008. *Zane's sex chronicles.* New York: Atria Books/Simon & Schuster.
Zane. 2010. *The hot box: A novel.* New York: Atria Books.
Zane, ed. 2004. *Chocolate flava.* New York: Atria Books.
Zane, ed. 2008. *Purple panties.* New York: Strebor Books.
Zhao, S. 2001. *Searching for Eve: Analysis of contemporary Chinese women's literature (Zhaoxun xiawa: zhongguo dangdai nvxing wenxue toushi).* Changsha: Hunan Normal College Press.
Zhao, Y. 2003. Also commenting on the Muzimei phenomenon: Opinions of the experts

(Yeshuo Muzimei xianxiang: Laizi zhuanjiamen de yijian). *Eastday News* (*Dongfang xinwen*). [online] 17 October. Available at http://news.eastday.com/epublish/gb/paper248/12/class024800002/hwz1044252.htm [accessed 2 November 2013].

Ziv, A. 2015. *Explicit utopias: Re-writing the sexual in women's pornography*. Albany: State University of New York Press.

About the Contributors

Naomi **Booth** is a lecturer in literature and creative writing at York St John University. She has recently published work on femininity and swooning in eighteenth-century fiction; queer ecologies and vampire narratives; and point of view in the work of Ian McEwan.

Eva **Chen** teaches in the Department of English at National Cheng-Chi University in Taipei, Taiwan. She is the author of two books and more than twenty refereed journal articles on women and urban modernity.

Jude **Elund** is a lecturer at Edith Cowan University, Perth, Western Australia. She lectures in public relations, cultural studies, communication and new media, specializing in the social uses of technology as well as its political, philosophical and cultural implications. Her research interests include the investigation of social and subversive spaces on the Internet.

Tricia Abigail Santos **Fermin**'s main research interests include the globalization of Japanese popular culture and fan practices, sexuality and sexual politics in Japan and Southeast Asia, and the sociological analysis of story-telling practices. Her work has been published in the *Electronic Journal of Contemporary Japanese Studies* and the *Indonesian Journal of Japanese Studies*.

Simon **Hardy** is a senior lecturer in sociology, media and culture and head of English, journalism and cultural studies at the University of Worcester, England. His research has been concerned with various aspects of pornography, including qualitative work on young men's use and experience of it and a series of textual analyses.

Anne **Kustritz** is a visiting scholar in the Television and Cross Media Culture program and the Amsterdam School for Cultural Analysis at the University of Amsterdam. Her teaching focuses on queer theory and new media convergence. Her work deals with creative fan communities, new media economies and the public sphere.

Katherine E. **Morrissey** is a visiting assistant professor of English at the Rochester Institute of Technology and a PhD candidate in media, cinema and digital studies at the University of Wisconsin–Milwaukee. Her research interests include the representation of female desire in popular culture, production environments for romantic storytelling, popular romance studies and participatory culture.

Alyssa D. **Niccolini** teaches English Language Arts to public high school students in New York City and is a doctoral candidate at Columbia University's Teachers College. Her research has focused on affect, sexuality, gender and secondary education. She has taught in Brooklyn, New York, the Khayletisha Township in Cape Town, South Africa and in Germany.

Victoria **Ong**'s research areas include moral theory, queer theory and feminist theory, with a particular interest in representations of the sex industry. She also has a penchant for science fiction.

Kristen **Phillips** is a lecturer in the School of Media, Culture, and Creative Arts at Curtin University, Perth, Western Australia. Her research interests include law, gender, sexuality, the politics of borders and migration, critical race and whiteness theory, kinship, post-feminism and erotic writing.

Tanya **Serisier** is a lecturer in criminology at Queens University Belfast and vice-president of the Australian Women's and Gender Studies Association. She has published widely on the cultural politics of sexuality and sexual violence in journals such as *Women: A Culture Review*, *Diegesis*, and *Australian Feminist Law Journal*.

Carole **Veldman-Genz** worked as a content editor for e-publisher Ellora's Cave and is a contributor to the online Popular Romance Project. She is head of the scientific English department at RWTH Aachen University, Germany. She specializes in contemporary gender and cultural theory, popular culture and genre theory.

Amalia **Ziv** is a senior lecturer in gender studies at Ben-Gurion University of the Negev. Her research areas are pornography and sexual representations, queer culture, queer activism, and queer kinship. She is the author of *Explicit Utopias: Rewriting the Sexual in Women's Pornography* (State University of New York Press, 2015), and *Sexual Thoughts: Queer Theory, Pornography, and the Politics of Sexuality* (Resling Press, 2013, in Hebrew).

Index

Adorno, Theodor 102, 119, 170
affect 110, 129–30, 219, 225–39
"affective pedagogy" 226–28, 237, 239
Annie Sprinkle 76n5
authenticity 28, 32, 61, 81, 84–85, 87, 152, 155, 204–24
authorial intent 154, 231
autobiography and memoir 9, 25, 32, 81, 204–11

Barthes, Roland 11, 101–102, 121
Bataille, Georges 11–14, 59, 76n3
BDSM (fiction) 4, 7, 10, 11, 13, 31, 37–38, 40, 48, 54, 109–10, 127, 134, 136–37, 144–45, 148n2
BDSM (sexual practice/identity) 10, 32–33, 110–11, 155–56
Belle de Jour 204–24
Bennett, Jane 103–104
Bersani, Leo 59, 76, 100–101, 105, 110, 112, 114, 115n1–2
Black Lace (Virgin Books imprint) 4–5, 8, 26, 29–32, 49, 54, 60–61, 139, 149n4, 154, 166
bliss 101–2
blogs (sex blogs) 82, 87–94, 205
"bounded authenticity" 209–11, 218, 220–23
Boys' Love (manga) 187–203
Brown, Wendy 127, 131

capitalism 14, 61, 95n1, 99, 107–10, 112, 133, 139, 155, 158–59
"charmed circle" 32, 40
China—Erotica 79–95
class 39, 89, 114, 123–24, 130, 150–51, 154, 156–58, 176, 182, 184, 204, 209–10, 216, 225, 230, 234–36
Cleland, John 15, 26–27
colonial narratives 169–86

Deleuze, Gilles 102, 225
digital publishing 2, 3, 42–43, 48, 53–58, 134–36, 149n7
Dworkin, Andrea 29, 59, 62–66, 76n3, 131, 165

Ellora's Cave 54, 134–49
"erotica noir" *see* "urban erotica"

fan fiction 169–86
Fanny Hill see Cleland, John
fans and fandom 151, 170–71, 187–203
fantasy 20, 31, 35–36, 45, 51–52, 67–69, 74, 76n6, 107–8, 113–14, 117–32, 135–38, 149n12
"female body writing" 79–83, 88–89, 94
female sexuality 15, 18, 27–28, 31, 41, 61, 78n22, 79–94, 106, 109, 114, 119, 133, 138–39, 150, 155, 159, 162, 166, 169; subjectivity 32, 59, 62, 65, 75–76, 76n3, 78n22
feminism 6, 29, 34, 82, 85, 90, 120, 122, 124, 127, 129–30, 132, 139, 156, 165–66
Fifty Shades of Grey 3, 5, 8, 11, 15, 17, 26, 33–41, 99–100, 104–15, 117–32, 226
Foucault, Michel 5, 2, 86, 102

gay male sexuality 18, 73–76, 143, 145, 160, 187–88, 190, 196
genre 1–13, 16, 27–28, 31–34, 37–39, 42–43, 44, 47–48, 51, 56–58, 60, 109, 114, 120, 126, 134, 137, 147–48
"genre fiction" 100, 106–7
Guattari, Félix 102, 225

Herotica series 16, 60, 67–75
heteronormativity 18–20, 110–11, 153, 159, 163, 166, 169, 177, 188–89, 201–202

homoeroticism 19–20, 135, 140–43, 145, 160, 173–75, 187–203
Horkheimer, Max 102, 119, 170

ideology 13, 65, 158
The Intimate Adventures of a London Call Girl see Belle de Jour

James, E L *see Fifty Shades of Grey*
jouissance 11, 101, 104

lesbian romance/erotica 18, 20, 60, 76n4, 77n10, 134, 150–66, 232–33
lesbian sexuality 65, 67, 158–59, 162–66
liberation 2, 5, 11, 18, 29–31, 80–85, 92, 110–11, 140, 235
literature 11, 80, 83, 87, 92, 99–100, 122–23, 227, 231
Lorde, Audre 14

MacKinnon, Catherine 65, 85, 131, 165
markets and marketing 5, 16, 12, 32, 42–58, 83, 120, 133–40, 150–59, 226–27
masochism 101, 109–15, 118–19, 123
Memoirs of a Woman of Pleasure see Cleland, John
ménage 9, 11, 133, 137, 146
"m/m" and "m/m/f" 133–149
Muzimei 16, 82, 87–94

neoliberalism 14, 17, 80–87, 100
Nin, Anaïs 5, 11, 28

orgasm 13, 27, 35, 67, 69, 71, 84–85, 102, 105, 114, 143, 216–17, 230

penetration 16, 59–78, 145
postcolonialism 78n19
post-feminism 154, 159

"pro-sex feminism" 16, 59, 62, 66–67, 77n7
pseudonym 28, 32, 205
publishing industry 42–58, 133–49, 226–27

queerness and erotic fiction 60, 68–69, 72–74, 100–104, 140–43, 150–53, 157, 169, 171–72

Radway, Janice 12–13, 106, 108, 121, 126, 230
Red Sage 49–50
reviews and reviewers 51, 58, 117–132, 153, 159
Rubin, Gayle 32–33, 40, 77n17, 149n11

sex workers 104–224
"sexual tourism" 156–67, 166
Shanghai Baby see Weihui
short stories 2, 11, 16, 20
slash fiction 19, 140–41, 169–86
submissive sexuality 10, 15, 27–33, 35–39, 69

threesomes *see* ménage
Thurston, Carol 5, 13, 16, 44–48, 56, 148n1
transgression 10–15, 18, 150, 157, 200, 229

"urban erotica" 226–27

vibration 99–116

Weihui 16, 83–91

Yaoi 19, 140–41, 149n8, 187–203

Zane 9, 20, 225–39